Feminist Perspectives on the Body

FEMINIST PERSPECTIVES SERIES

Series Editors:

Professor Pamela Abbott, University of Teesside
Professor Claire Wallace, Institute for Advanced Studies, Austria
and University of Derby, UK.

Forthcoming Titles:

Feminist perspectives on language
Margaret Gibbon

Feminist perspectives on politics
Chris Corrin

Feminist perspectives on postcolonialism
Maryanne Dever and Denise Cuthbert

Feminist perspectives on disability
Barbara Fawcett

Feminist perspectives on domestic violence
Laura Goldsack and Jill Radford

Feminist perspectives on environment and society
Beate Littig and Barbara Hegenbart

Feminist perspectives on ethics
Elizabeth Porter

FEMINIST PERSPECTIVES SERIES

Feminist Perspectives on the Body

Barbara Brook

LONGMAN
London and New York

Pearson Education Limited
Edinburgh Gate
Harlow
Essex CM20 2JE
England
and Associated Companies throughout the world

Published in the United States of America
by Pearson Education Inc., New York

Visit us on the world wide web at:
http://www.awl-he.com

© Pearson Education Limited 1999

The right of Barbara Brook to be identified as author of this Work has been asserted by her in accordance with the Copyright, Designs and Patents Act 1988.

First published 1999

ISBN 0 582 35639 3

British Library Cataloguing-in-Publication Data
A catalogue record for this book is available from the British Library

Library of Congress Cataloging-in-Publication Data
Brook, Barbara, 1949–
    Feminist perspective on the body / Barbara Brook.
      p.   cm. — (Feminist perspectives series)
    Includes bibliographical references and index.
    ISBN 0–582–35639–3
    1. Body, Human—Social aspects. 2. Body, Human—Political aspects. 3. Women—Physiology. 4. Human reproduction.
5. Body image in women. 6. Surgery, Plastic—Psychological aspects. 7. Feminist theory. I. Title. II. Series.
GT495.B76 1999
391.6'082—dc21   98–52841
                                                          CIP

Typeset by 35 in 10/12pt New Baskerville
Printed in Malaysia, PP

Contents

Series Editors' Preface   vii
Preface   ix

1   Bodies of feminist knowledge   1

2   Reproducing bodies   22

3   Bodies on the threshold   44

4   Cutting bodies to size   65

5   Public bodies   89

6   Performance and spectacle   111

7   Virtual bodies   136

Glossary   158
Bibliography   162
Index   178

Series Editors' Preface

The aim of the Feminist Perspectives series is to provide a concise introduction to different topics from a feminist perspective. The topics were chosen as being of interest for students on a range of different degree courses and in a range of different disciplines. They reflect the current interest in feminist issues and in women's studies in a wide range of fields. The series aims to provide a guide through the burgeoning and sometimes rather arcane literatures which have grown around various feminist topics. The texts are written by experienced teachers and academics providing lively and interesting accounts of topics of current interest. They include examples and case studies or statistical information where relevant in order to make the material more accessible and stimulating.

The texts contain chapter outlines and summaries for convenient, quick access. There are also suggestions for further reading.

By focusing on feminist perspectives on the body, this text by Barbara Brook cuts across a range of issues and a range of theories to provide new insights. Many people have written either explicitly or implicitly about the body and the literature cited here includes many of the major social theorists of our times. The author begins by considering feminist theories and accounts of the body but then moves onto issues which affect women's bodies in particular, including pregnancy, childbirth, menstruation, menopause and debates about reproductive technology. She then considers the discipline and shaping of female bodies through the examples of eating disorders, cosmetic surgery and body building, offering a feminist understanding of these issues as well as a revue of the debates. The accounts seeking to recognise the 'swampy' messy feminine body are contrasted with ideas about the performance of femininity using contrasting examples such as transvestism, athleticism and circus artists, as well as the usual activity of teaching. A further area covered by the book is that of the body as it is situated in law, human rights and public discourse. In her final chapter, Barbara Brook looks at virtual bodies. Does cyberspace represent disembodiment? She considers to what extent cyberspace offers a liberation from gender identities and how feminists can offer alternative visions of cyberspace, an arena dominated by masculine fantasies and male-dominated technologies. The book is, therefore, a useful guide through many much contested areas of research as well as offering an interesting – feminist – perspective on the subject of the body.

Claire Wallace and Pamela Abbott

Preface

While I was working on this book I was also visiting the University of Manchester and had been asked to give a paper: I had decided to rework one that I had originally given in Australia, and had started almost a year previously, on some issues of teaching/learning women's studies within the Australian university system. I was concerned, in the paper, with the contradictory ways in which, as women's studies and feminist thought start to become more 'legitimate' within the university, they acquire the tools and trappings (in every sense) of the institution, including its inertia. I was looking at the (modest) proliferation of feminist 'texts' that are starting to acquire the status of 'required reading' and what this means for women's studies. As I reworked the paper for a different, English, audience, it dawned on me that I was currently engaged in producing something that aspired to be just such another 'text': this book.

It was a salutary moment that jolted me out of the enjoyable but essentially solitary research and re-reading I was immersed in and reminded me of the people for whom I had originally wanted to write this book: different bodies who are students – whether in an institutional setting or, more broadly, in their engagement with ideas. I called that earlier paper 'Dirty Little Secrets' borrowing a phrase used by the North American feminist, Jane Tompkins (1990) in her questioning of why so many academics are reluctant to identify themselves as teachers. I was concerned with the ways that many feminist writers, when writing 'text(book)s', seem to adopt unreflectively many of the most distancing and, one might say, masculinist, writing habits of the academy: and this includes those writers centrally engaged with how meanings develop and are circulated! It seemed important to keep all this in mind while writing this book.

Now, this question of language and accessibility is a very tricky one. Let me be clear that I don't think there is any point in calling on researchers who are engaging with new and complex theories to try, *as they are developing them*, to 'translate' them immediately for a broad readership. To suggest this is possible, let alone desirable, is a simplifying notion that can be traced to a **commonsense** idea that language is a transparent transmitter of a pre-existing reality. A different view, and one with considerable influence in contemporary western cultural and communication theories, is that there is a much more fluid interchange of words, ideas and what we think of as the material world. When we engage with new ways of thinking, we are often (some would say, always) confronted with the inaccuracy and inadequacy of the terms already available: there may be no 'clear' and 'transparent' (commonsense) way of writing/ talking through these thoughts. However, it is also important, since as feminists we are committed to ideas of transformation of women's lives, to ensure that those theories and the new terms in which they develop themselves do not remain in isolation as an exclusive and hierarchical 'body of knowledge' constituting what Meaghan Morris has called (speaking of the 'idol-worship' of a whole stable of mainly French, mainly male, theorists) 'a peculiar *doxa*' that constitutes a very single-minded, ponderous and **phallocentric** conversation (cited in Kwok 1995: 50).

So it is a feminist task to offer an engagement with these theories that avoids fixing them – avoids taking them artificially out of the continuing stream of thinking, arguing and adjustment that goes on through time – and also avoids some of the worst aspects of conventional teaching roles. By the latter, I do not mean only the robot-positioning that places 'the teacher' as the impersonal conduit through which information flows, supposedly untouched by any personal context. There are also the insidious dangers of the more seductive, charismatic approach, as explored in the central character of Muriel Spark's novel *The Prime of Miss Jean Brodie* (1961) and less critically represented in the stock Hollywood rendering of the rugged individualist teacher, whereby everything is cannibalised by the personal presence and desires of the teacher.

One of the most useful ways, I have found, for talking about the process I have tried to engage in here, is that of translation. In translation something is always lost, but something else is created. This is what Hélène Cixous says:

> When I write, I read-write; I know that the works of others are
> being resurrected in translation. When I write, I rewrite; of course
> I write my own work, but my own work is already a gathering of
> other works. An answer; if I write, it's because I have received a
> letter. My writing is the letter that answers the letter I've received,
> and the correspondence goes on.
>
> (In Wilcox *et al.* 1990: 26)

This book, then, is offered as a sort of translation of some feminist thinking around bodies. It is part of a continuing correspondence conducted in classrooms and outside them with students and
colleagues from many subject areas and interests. It is not offered
as part of the sacred texts, as a contribution to the *doxa*, but as part
of a correspondence which may draw in some new re-writers.

In writing an overview of a field of writing as an introduction
for others, I am concerned to address two issues: first, the ways in
which the writer's (my) own beliefs, biases, perspectives and range
of reading necessarily organise and create a boundary around the
material; secondly, the question of where to start – or, to think of
it another way, where and how, within the field of writing, to meet
up with you, the intended readers.

To address the first: my reading is in English, with some French,
and is organised by my own position within an anglophone country, Australia. In feminism as elsewhere, Australia has been permeated by influences from the United States and France. So, when
I write 'feminist perspectives', I am writing within that particular
configuration. It is a configuration which is also having to acknowledge, in the face of increasing challenges, its/our own implicit
'whiteness' and the ways in which the unthinking use of terms
such as 'western', 'anglo', 'First World' and their counterpoints –
'eastern', 'non-anglo', 'Third World' – indicates an assumption
of a privileged and central position against a world of 'others'. I,
because of my embodied, enculturated position, cannot escape
from complicity with that privileging but I can be vigilant in examining the assumptions, practices and incipient desires to colonise,
in the texts I draw on, and in my own, not only in terms of 'racial'
or 'ethnic' differences, but also in terms of sexuality, of 'able'-
bodiedness, of economic privilege, of age.

The second issue in writing a book of this kind is where to start!
Whatever the approach taken there will always be many readers
who are not suited by it. This presents the writer with a choice:
ranging between the extremes of speaking out/down from a kind
of impersonal seat of judgement with no acknowledgement of

any readers and, from the other end of the spectrum, trying to be totally inclusive. For a number of feminist-political reasons, the first is untenable, though frequently practised unquestioningly by non-feminists. The second is impossible because it assumes that there can be a universally understood language independent of the readers. Donna Haraway suggests that the desire for such a language is not politically innocent: 'The feminist dream of a common language, like all dreams for a perfectly true language, of perfectly faithful naming of experience, is a totalizing and imperialist one' (1991: 215). This book tries to explain the terms it is written in and which form the nexus of the developing theories and engagements with 'the body' made by some feminists within contemporary western feminist thought. These terms are in the process of (re)writing the body and are not always translatable. This book is a starting point with some 'tasters' of that writing. The real meals are out there: see the short list of recommended further reading at the end of each chapter, and the bibliography.

The book is organised with the recognition that readers will use it in multiple ways: some reading through it as a whole and editing out for yourselves things you already know or don't want to know right now, in order to get a broad idea of how some thinkers in the 'western' feminist tradition are writing about the body and applying it across particular fields of inquiry; others, homing in on a particular chapter or topic. The fields with which I primarily engage here could be broadly termed 'social' rather than in the cultural areas of literary and media production: however, as we shall see, it is neither very useful nor even feasible to police these disciplinary boundaries too closely. And by Chapters 6 and 7 these boundaries are well and truly dissolving. A very readable brief introduction to the cultural studies arena is Anne Cranny-Francis's *The Body in the Text* (1995).

My first chapter is introductory and gives a brief account of some developments of concepts in thirty years of feminist theory around the body: it is, inevitably, a partial account that offers a kind of intellectual map, showing where the rest of the book comes from in terms of my thinking and reading. It is hard to come across feminist writing that *is not* at some point connected to issues of the body, so my focus is mainly on the question of what conditions in the late twentieth century have occasioned the current proliferation of feminist books with 'body' in the title.

The chapters are organised around themes that may be of interest to students in particular courses which do not necessarily focus on feminist theory: for example, those associated with the different areas of health care and human development. The book as a whole will, hopefully, be useful for students in women's studies, gender studies, or related areas that take interdisciplinary or transdisciplinary approaches, and will be of interest to more general readers.

Chapters 2 and 3 address aspects of women's bodies that have been held to ground us so absolutely in biology and nature: reproduction, menstruation and menopause. In examining feminist theorising of these aspects, the framing disciplines of science and medicine are critiqued along with key concepts such as 'abjection': more colloquially expressible as 'women's leaky bodies'. Chapter 4 looks at ways in which women's bodies are 'cut down to size', with specific reference to eating disorders and cosmetic surgery. In Chapter 5, a central feminist concern with the 'public/private divide' is examined and the idea of the 'body politic' addressed, with particular attention to issues of women and the law. Chapter 6 looks at ways in which ideas of healthy bodies and their movement demonstrate contradictory cultural ideas about women's bodies as objects of 'the male gaze', with examples from bodybuilding, Japanese music theatre, circus, and performance art. Finally, Chapter 7 ventures briefly into cyberspace to indicate some of the implications for feminist understanding of 'the body' when women engage with new communication technologies.

The appearance of readers (Welton 1998; Conboy *et al.* 1997) and textbooks on a particular theme, like 'The Body', contradictorily signal both the theme's arrival and its demise as a 'hot' research topic! 1998 saw the staging of a conference, '*After* the Body'. However, the real bodies remain with us – or rather, we remain real bodies – and, as a review of Vicki Kirby's *Telling Flesh* reminds us, even though the academy may think that all 'the bodies have been accounted for and tagged', the flesh in its substance still matters, and still has something to say (Grinham 1998: 18–19).

Some of the central terms that are used repeatedly by the writers discussed in the book are briefly described in the glossary. Terms included in the glossary are printed in **bold** on their first use. The glossary is not a dictionary but tries to place each term as it is used in the context of writing on the body with which this book is concerned.

This book was enabled by study leave granted by Victoria University, Melbourne and undertaken at the University of Manchester. It grows out of my teaching at Victoria University and has been moulded by many of my students. I am grateful for the support, in body and mind, of colleagues at both universities: in particular, Judith Gleeson, Katie Hughes, Jane Landman, Jeannie Rea, and Liz Stanley. Finally, I owe much to the volatile bodies and minds of my three daughters: Kate, Alice and Bronwen Brook.

Chapter 1

Bodies of feminist knowledge

Chapter outline

An overview of some changes in feminist thinking about 'the body' from early second-wave feminism to the present:

- What about the body?   corporeality; subjectivity.
- 'Woman' and women   epistemology; ontology.
- Essential bodies   binarism; essentialism.
- Identity politics   identity politics; subjectivity.
- Sex and gender   sex; gender; social
                               constructionism.
- Performing gender   performativity; the abject.
- Multiplying beyond twos   dualism; feminist revisions.

What about the body?

Try reading that heading with different emphases! *What* about the body? What *about* the body? What about the *body*? Think too about that strange collective single entity that is thus named (and which, incidentally, in capitals, has become the media's name for the super-model Elle MacPherson). Unless you, as you read, *are* Elle MacPherson – and this is unlikely, since she once said she would never read a book she had not written herself – 'the body' is not the way you would immediately designate yourself, nor is it possible to come up with a picture of what 'the body' is, since that single term strives to encompass all the multiple ways human material is formed and arranged not only within space but also through time. As Moira Gatens says, 'I have never encountered an image of a *human* body. Images of human bodies are images of either men's bodies or women's bodies' (Gatens 1990: 82). Note, too, that 'human' is the qualifier unspoken but implicit, defining the boundary between 'the body' and the rest of the material world: a boundary which, as we shall see, is not as clear cut as it might seem. (When a researcher in the physical sciences asked me what I was working on and I replied 'the body', she asked, 'but *what* body?')

(Non-feminist) sociology sometimes seems to be surprised by its relatively recent discovery that bodies are present within the social formations that sociology is concerned with.[1] Feminist thinkers, however, have always been interested in the ways female bodies are talked about, classified, disciplined, invaded, destroyed, altered, decorated, pleasured (this last is a more recent interest, at least in the public domain) and more. Moreover, feminists have been, and still are, engaged not only in thinking through what happens to bodies that are 'female' but also in what ways our bodies actively construct and 'write' our selves. (What this rather odd idea of writing, or **inscription**, might mean will be taken up later.) In a way, all feminist thinking might be described as an engagement of one sort or another, with what it means to be, and to be perceived to be, a female body.

Needless to say, feminist thinkers through time and in different contexts have had very different responses to female bodies, and these differences continue in the present. While issues of 'the body' have in one way or another been central to all feminist thinking, it is also evident that there has been a proliferation of feminist publications with the word 'body' in the title, over the last decade or so. Scott and Morgan, the editors of *Body Matters: Essays on the Sociology of the Body*, refer to the development, as they write in 1993, of 'a veritable explosion of feminist work on "the body"' (1993: 13). The majority of these books and articles, published by large international publishers, have not been **empirical**, in a traditional social-science sense, but comprise more philosophical or **textual** studies concerned with developing the concept of **corporeality**. This raises the question of why there has been this explicit turn of attention, together with the accompanying question of what is happening to embodied living women within feminist inquiry – and beyond.

'Corporeal feminism' is a shorthand for some of these new developments. Perhaps to date the best-known anglophone writer in this field is Elizabeth Grosz. Grosz's exploration is firmly and explicitly located within a nexus of European philosophical inquiries that includes the work of Nietzsche, and more contemporary thinkers such as Merleau-Ponty, Deleuze, Guattari and Foucault. Her concentration on the work of male philosophers has been criticised as excessive by some feminists who share Audre Lorde's much-quoted position that 'the master's tools will never dismantle the master's house' (Lorde 1981). However, arguably, Grosz herself endorses this position when she insists on the need for moving away from traditional questions and recasting them. Grosz asks questions about what constitutes a body and, in particular, about where, if at all, there can be located a specifically sexed body that is somehow before or beyond culture. This is something like the 'which came first, the chicken or the egg?' question. Rather than attempting to answer it, Grosz suggests that it is more useful to develop a different explanation of the body that, in a way, renders the question redundant. Precisely because her theory is new, and pushes at the boundaries of existing terms, it is difficult to describe simply. Integral to this theorising is a movement away from definitions that describe the body as a fixed 'thing' (in grammar terms, a noun) towards descriptions that focus on movement through time (in grammar terms, a verb). Grosz suggests **subjectivity** is bound up with the specificities of sexed bodies but is indeterminable. For Grosz, therefore, the answer to 'Who do you think you are?' – or, 'where/what is your individual subjectivity?' – seems to be, at any given moment, the unique meeting place of the corporeal (the body) and the circulating **discourses** (the network of ideas, practices, art, beliefs and so on that constitute culture), which will change from moment to moment. A central figure for Grosz in rethinking the self as bodyandmind rather than body separated from mind is the Möbius strip:

> Bodies and minds are not two distinct substances or two kinds of attributes of a single substance but somewhere in between . . . The Möbius strip has the advantage of showing the inflection of mind into body and body into mind, the ways in which, through a kind of twisting or inversion, one side becomes another. This model also provides a way of problematizing and rethinking the relations between the inside and outside of a subject.
>
> (Grosz 1994: xii)

A point of contestation between 'corporeal' feminists and radical feminists is in the latter's concern that the former, while taking 'the body' as their focal point, abstract it away from the 'lived' bodies of women. Renate Klein, for example, asks: 'How is it possible to theorise "bodies" in thousands of pages, yet invisibilise women? . . . The bodies I have been reading about in post-modern feminism writings do not breathe, do not laugh, and have no heart' (Klein 1996: 349). Similar questions are raised by other contributors to the collection *Radically Speaking* in which Klein's article appears.

'Woman' and women

Feminist interest in the **epistemology** and the **ontology** of female bodies is closely tied to questions about what is 'a woman' and to issues of 'female subjectivity'. While, from a **commonsense** position, 'what is a woman?' would seem to be a silly question, it is one which has some important, even crucial, implications for feminist politics. At a basic level, the idea of a recognisable female subject is the cornerstone of any feminist inquiry, the subject of early second-wave women's liberation politics, embedded in slogans like 'Sisterhood is powerful', and integral to any social formation that identifies as a 'women's' area or issue – women's health centres, votes for women and, of course, women's studies.

But to move from the commonsense acceptance that it is obvious what we mean by 'woman' is to start to acknowledge that it is not always clear whose specific bodies are being talked about or envisioned in these formations, nor whose bodies are excluded. To identify with someone only or predominantly in terms of their perceived sex and presume that as the ground for common interests and experience is to risk denying the relevance of other aspects of both our lives. This has been powerfully argued, for example, by some indigenous writers in Australia who resist identification with the women's movement on the grounds that the movement is itself racist, since it insufficiently acknowledges its own (white) privilege and that, therefore, the 'Australian women's movement' has a hidden (white) in front of 'women' (see, e.g., Huggins 1994; Lucashenko 1994). Donna Haraway has also pointed to the dangers of an exclusive focus on **gender**, and to the ways in which the establishment of a 'gender-identity' can obscure how bodies 'including sexualized and racialized bodies appear as objects of knowledge and sites of intervention' (Haraway 1991: 135). In a different context, Judith Butler argues that the concept of gender, based on the opposition of male or female, is inherently heterosexist and allows no other sexualities: 'The internal coherence or unity of either gender, man or woman . . . requires both a stable and oppositional heterosexuality' (Butler 1990: 22).

Many feminist writers have been engaged in the last ten years or so in wrestling with different ways of answering the question 'what is a woman?' or of critiquing the question. This has many crucial links to ideas about bodies, and specifically female bodies. One useful collection is Kathleen Lennon and Margaret Whitford's edited collection, *Knowing the Difference* (1994). Looking through the 'Name Index' of a collection gives a quick map of who are the writers recognised as most significant by the book. In *Knowing the Difference*'s index (pp. 289–92), the names who get significantly more than one line and are referred to across different articles are Seyla Benhabib, Michel Foucault, Donna Haraway, Sandra Harding, Luce Irigaray, Jacques Lacan, Helen Longino and Jean-François Lyotard. Each of these is in one way or another heavily implicated in debates about questions of ethics and subjectivity within/around **postmodernist** theories. It is a mark of the influence of postmodernist thinking that 'the body', which was once the ultimate material presence we could hang on to and be certain about, has become increasingly less certain: 'The body emerges at the centre of the theoretical and political debate at exactly the time in history when there is no more unitary certainty or uncontested consensus about what the body actually is . . . The body has turned into many, multiple bodies' (Braidotti 1994: 19).

Much current feminist thinking about the body can be traced to the work of Mary Douglas in the late 1960s and 1970s. Douglas discusses ways in which bodies, particularly female bodies, occupy an ambivalent place in space and are socially 'policed' for leakages and crossings between outside and inside spaces. In addressing this she also implicates the body in the more complex and pervasive ideas about communication that inform contemporary theory, challenging the notion of communication as a straightforward transmission of a message to a receiver: 'The body, as a vehicle of communication, is misunderstood if it is treated as a signal box, a static framework emitting and receiving strictly coded messages . . . It is itself the field in which a feedback interaction takes place. It is itself available to be given as the proper tender for some of the exchanges which constitute the social situation' (Douglas 1975: 83).

Essential bodies

For most of history, the female social situation has been dominated or even prescribed by the identification of women's bodies with child-bearing and, frequently, those bodies have been the objects of exchange between men. In the late twentieth century a range of safe and reliable contraceptive measures is still not universally available nor do cultural beliefs and institutions endorse uniformly all women's rights to choose whether or not, when, or how, to bear children. Conversely, not all female bodies are able to conceive or bear children. However, for many women there is more choice than would have been the case in the past.

'Commonsense' beliefs about the need to accommodate the changes placed on women's bodies by pregnancy were – still are – used to justify many if not all the social inequalities constructed around women. It is, therefore, understandable that a great deal of feminist energy has gone into trying to minimise or even erase this particular marker of women's bodily difference. Some of the issues around this will be discussed in Chapter 2. In summary, it seemed necessary to many, though by no means all, the feminist writers in the 1970s to follow the lead of Simone de Beauvoir's *The Second Sex* (1953) in concentrating on the cultural formations of femininity and either ignoring their own potential to be pregnant bodies, or minimising, as far as possible, the impact of pregnancy. One of the first major feminist writers to move away from this was Adrienne Rich, in *Of Woman Born*. While she is concerned to reclaim the body of mother for women in positive ways, she is also passionate in her recognition of the ways in which '(w)omen are controlled by lashing us to our bodies' and 'how, under patriarchy, female possibility has been massacred on the site of motherhood' (1976: 13).

Shulamith Firestone (1970), in contrast, represents an extreme version of the view that child-bearing is a sort of dirty trick played by nature on women when she, memorably, compares giving birth to 'shitting a giant pumpkin' and enthusiastically heralds the development of artificial wombs as a way of rescuing women from nature and 'the temporary deformation of the body of the individual for the sake of the species' (1970: 226). It is important to remember that, at the time of Firestone's writing, artificial means of reproduction were still in the realms of science fiction. Firestone, while hopeful in 1970 about severing the connection between women and pregnancy, also forecast the dangers of medical scientific intervention in female reproductive bodies: dangers which have, of course, become a major arena of feminist debate as 1970s science fiction becomes the banal everyday reality of the 1990s. Firestone emphasises the 'natural female body' as necessarily lim- iting women's opportunities, in contrast to Rich's careful distinction that the limits are the product of cultural forces: 'If rape has been terrorism, motherhood has been penal servitude. *It need not be*' (Rich 1976: 14). The reverse side of Firestone's hostility to nature is the celebration of woman as close to/equivalent to Nature, a view which, like Firestone's, is based on the notion of an essential female biology.

Susan Griffin (1978) is one exponent of this, and into the 1990s this view is endorsed within certain areas of eco-feminism (see also Daly 1984). At its most extreme, this is connected to a belief that women, through our 'natural bodies' and reproductive pos- sibilities, have a privileged, superior ethical position. Carol A. Stabile (1994), and others, have critiqued the ways in which this kind of privileging, in addition to endorsing the ways in which societies have justified women's exclusion from public/cultural life, can also cloak other forms of privilege: economic and/or racialist. This equation of woman = life = nature can also be used by anti- feminist, anti-choice proponents in debates about abortion. Carol McMillan, for example, contends that feminist pro-choice advocates are evidence that a women's liberation politics must be grounded in a death-wish:

> Feminists are trying to escape from the fact that woman will always be related to animal life because she is indissolubly linked with the life process . . . Caught in the falsehoods of the rationalist net, they are therefore compelled to deny, and even to destroy, life – the demand for abortion is the most articualte expression of this – in order to feel both equal with men and distinct from animals.
> (McMillan 1982: 153–4)

These very different perspectives (which, however, share the assumption of a 'natural female body') provoke criticism from those who are concerned that any attempt to define such an essence supports rather than contradicts oppressive cultural beliefs. Some critics are also concerned that essentialising definitions are in fact exclusive rather than inclusive. Put baldly, if the essence of being a woman depends on the possession of a womb and giving birth, does that mean that someone without a womb or someone who is unable or who chooses not to bear children is less a woman? This argument about what constitutes a woman becomes particularly fraught in disputes about the claims of individuals who have undertaken genital reconstruction (male to female transsexuals) to be defined as 'women'.

So, while some feminists were reclaiming the 'essential' female body, others were down-playing it, sometimes to the point of invisibility, and emphasising the social construction of gender. As Anne Balsamo (1996) has recently described, in terms of the contemporary situation, there are many dangers in this move. In a discussion which reiterates some of the concerns about the move away from identity politics voiced by writers such as Nancy Hartsock and bell hooks (discussed below), Balsamo suggests that feminists need to be careful that moves to de-essentialise 'woman' are not co-opted: 'Diverse feminist action directs its attention to de-essentializing the biological identity of woman, thus working to deconstruct the organic foundation of feminist thought . . . In the process, feminists encounter unsolicited assistance in doing away with "the body", which served – at one point, if not now – as the necessary foundation of women's empowerment' (1996: 31). Balsamo goes on to advise feminists about the need to avoid alliance with what she describes as 'panic postmodernist theorists' and to engage in 'constructing and critiquing theories of the body within postmodernism . . . it is time for feminism to crash the postmodern party' (1996: 31).

The 'essential' definition of women's bodies in many areas of early second-wave feminist writing, and in some of its later developments, has been frequently described in the contemporary writing identified with 'corporeal feminism' as symptomatic of the stranglehold of **binarism**, and particularly, of the **mind/body split**, in western thought. That is, while feminist critiques were being made of binarism, the general direction of much feminist theorising has itself been divided between the binaries of privileging either the mind and its transcendence, or the body and its immanence. One interesting effect of this can be seen in the way feminist writers position themselves/ourselves in writing. There is a tendency for many of us to write 'they' when talking in general terms about women or feminists, as in 'when women talk about themselves, they often speak at a distance'. This has a different impact, in terms of how we perceive the writer, from 'when women talk about ourselves, we often speak at a distance'.

Identity politics

A problem generated by a politics organised around a universal and essential woman's body is that it can be seen as an imperialist politics that ignores self-defined differences. Through the 1980s there was an increasing development of identity-based politics that raised this issue.

The usefulness or otherwise of identity politics is currently under debate, with different situations and perspectives offering widely different positions. Heidi Safia Mirza, in her introduction to a recent edited collection (Mirza 1997: 6–19), provides a **genealogy** of 'Black British Feminism' which includes a consideration of identity politics in the British context. Mirza suggests that an over-emphasis on identity in the 1980s led to concentration on examination of the self, at the expense of political engagement with 'how we come to be located in the racialized and sexualized space where we reside. Whiteness, that silent pervasive patriarchal discourse, the father of identity politics, with its complementary discourse on anti-racism and new-right anti-anti-racism, was never named' (p. 9).

On the other hand, for some feminists, it seems ironic that just at the point when some women are gaining a recognition in the public arena and feeling able to 'write ourselves' as subjects, the idea of identity is being contested: this is an issue with racial and class inflections. Nancy Hartsock asks: 'Why is it that just at the moment when so many of us who have been silenced begin to demand the right to name ourselves, to act as subjects rather than objects of history, that just then the concept of subjecthood becomes problematic?' (1990: 163). And bell hooks takes up a similar point: '[It's not surprising] when black folks respond to the critique of essentialism, especially when it denies the validity of identity politics, by saying, "Yeah, it's easy to give up identity, when you got one"' (1990: 28).

The arguments around identity politics are part of a larger problem posed for any movement that uses a human rights appeal for justice at a time when the **Enlightenment project** in which 'human rights' arguments are situated is being challenged and the concept of 'the human' is itself being debated.

Although issues of skin colours and their social–cultural interpretations by self and others clearly indicate the interconnectedness of self and body, 'the subject' and 'the body' are not identical. As subjects we are constantly attempting to adapt our bodies in more or less extreme ways to fit or adjust ideas of self, and our bodies frequently resist. Probably the most dramatic example of this in western society is the phenomenon of dieting and eating disorders. Many of the feminists engaged with thinking about 'the body' are interested in just how the body interacts with subjectivity and consciousness but is neither totally separate nor totally contained by those concepts. Much feminist theory rejects traditional empiricist knowledge in favour of a more subjective knowing that includes the perspectives and 'embodied' origins of the knower: in a sense moving from traditional ideas of epistemology to ontology.

However, there is a logical problem with this which can be related back to second-wave feminism's enthusiastic acceptance of a **sex–gender division**. In the early 1970s there was a concerted feminist move to detach female subjects ('women') from their ahistoric grounding in the sexed-female body and to argue that what is considered to be naturally female, and therefore unalterable, is socially constructed – 'gendered' – and therefore open to change. If this is joined with the 'human rights' argument, a political campaign can be waged around the issue of women's oppression. If the rationale for inequalities is based implicitly or explicitly on a difference in the sexed bodies of men and women, then a demonstration that those differences are socially constructed rather than natural should defeat the rationale. But . . . if the idea of what constitutes a woman is a social construct, constructed by a society that is organised by male values and concepts, then how can 'she' think about herself in different ways, and why would these ways be necessarily better or somehow more authentic than the other ones?

Contemporary feminist inquiry into subjectivity is often engaged with coming to terms with this problem. And at the centre of it is the question of what do we do with bodies – or what do our bodies do with us. If we try to filter out our bodies they have a habit of coming back at/to us. When we read or write, for example, there is an illusion that we are pure thought and words, but our bodies are engaged too – sometimes making clear that they do not want to be reading or writing by drawing attention to the discomfort of the seat, the view out of the window, the desirability of a cup of coffee and so on.

So, what is the feminist history (or as a follower of Foucault may term it, the genealogy) of the sex–gender division?

Sex and gender

In the early years of the second-wave western feminist movement it was considered to be important, if not crucial, to establish the capacity for women to occupy positions within society traditionally occupied by men. A key text in this project was the work, translated into English in the early 1950s, of the French philosopher, Simone de Beauvoir, and published as *The Second Sex*. A sentence from de Beauvoir reverberated through the feminist thinking that was developing through the 1960s and 70s: 'One is not born, but rather becomes, a woman' (1953: 295).[2]

A dominant strand that can be identified in this phase of feminism, and which became subsequently very influential, has been termed '**social constructionist**'. On the whole, feminist theorists favouring social construction are concerned with the way women's and men's bodies are differently and unequally imbued with social meanings (see also, Grosz 1994: 16–17). In all the various permutations of social constructionist theories there is at some level a basic distinction made between the material body and its social/cultural representations. So the body is seen as a kind of natural biologically sexed object that pre-exists but is affected by the workings of culture or, as some writers term it, a *tabula rasa*: a blank surface ready to be inscribed. It is this separation of body and culture that defines the sex–gender division. It rests on the belief that, while there are certain natural attributes of the body which cannot be changed (or not without radical surgery), the gendered cultural meanings circulating around and variously inscribing the body can be changed. And, of course, that process of changing cultural meanings to relieve the inequalities of women, in this definition, comprises the feminist project. The blank sheet of the body is not, in itself, of interest within this project since it is a precondition of culture and, of itself, has no meaning, is '**self-identical**'.

One extreme form of social-constructionist thinking is 'sex–role' theory which works on the premise that the gendered patterns of masculine and feminine behaviour, speech, psychology, social interaction, etc. are a kind of scripted role-play organised by institutional forces such as schools and families, and reinforced by the gendered images represented in films, advertisements and literature, and policed by social taboos and codes of behaviour. Feminist intervention in sex–role patterning is often aimed at the swapping or challenging of gendered stereotypes both in institutions (for example, in schools, boys doing cookery classes/girls doing woodwork) and in representations (for example, analyses of 'images of women'; demand for active pictures of women in text books). The emphasis on the idea of 'role-playing' takes for granted a material sexed body that can put off and take on different roles, rather like the cardboard dolls on which you can hang different paper outfits.

As with many explanations and actions developed within the framework of second-wave western feminism, interventionist moves to counter gender stereotyping and sex–role formation rarely take into account the different ways that different groups and individuals have access to mainstream cultural and economic resources within any society. (To emphasise this deficiency is, of course, not to dismiss the importance of such moves.) In 1987 Ann Phoenix represented a position which has since been increasingly voiced in Britain, North America, Australia and Aotearoa/New Zealand: 'By ignoring issues of race and class, current theories of gender, and the research on which these are based, actually address the development of gender identity in the white middle classes': one example of difference that Phoenix points to is in the mainstream (white, middle-class) identification of femininity with a weakness 'meant to elicit a powerful male's protection [which] is redundant for black women (and white working-class women) whose fathers and male peers do not occupy positions of power' (Phoenix 1997 [1987]: 65).

Since her first publication, numerous writers have made interventions of the kind that Phoenix found absent in 1987, but of course many of the earlier texts on which her analysis is based still circulate and are used as references.

While many of the feminist perspectives developing into the 1980s, and often drawing on psychoanalytic theories, appear different both in terms of sophistication and in concept from the idea of 'sex–role stereotyping', it has been argued that they also rest on the unchallenged idea of a biological, natural, sexed body. This is, perhaps, most dramatically enacted in theories of hysteria derived from Freudian psychoanalysis, in which the body of 'the hysteric' appears to be 'written on' by the **unconscious**, thus exhibiting a condition that the person's conscious mind cannot access directly.[3]

There is a pattern throughout earlier western feminist writing of a desire to erase the difference of the female body as far as possible in an attempt to transcend its physical presence in time and space and thus avoid the limitations imposed on it. Some reasons for this will be discussed below.

As Grosz describes it, there is a progression away from this denial of the body in the developing work of late-twentieth-century writers whom she characterises as concerned with 'sexual difference'. They include Luce Irigaray, Hélène Cixous, Judith Butler, Monique Wittig, Moira Gatens, Vicki Kirby and, of course, herself: 'The body cannot be understood as a neutral screen, a biological *tabula rasa* on to which masculine or feminine could be indifferently projected. Instead of seeing sex as an essentialist and gender as a constructionist category, these thinkers are concerned to undermine the dichotomy' (Grosz 1994: 18). Part of this project is to recognise the libidinal aspects of the body, 'a body bound up in the order of desire, signification, and power' (1994: 19): hence titles, across a range of discipline areas like *Sexy Bodies* (Grosz and Probyn 1995), *Erotic Faculties* (Frueh 1996), *Erotic Welfare* (Butler and McGrogan 1993).

Performing gender

In rejecting the idea of the body as *tabula rasa* feminists are faced with the problem of explaining how, in Simone de Beauvoir's terms, one becomes a woman. Monique Wittig entitles her discussion of this question 'One is Not Born a Woman', writing back to de Beauvoir's famous dictum and adding issues of race and sexuality:[4] 'Colette Guillaumin has shown that before the socioeconomic reality of black slavery, the concept of race did not exist, at least not in its modern meaning . . . However, now, race, exactly like sex, is taken as an "immediate given", a "sensible given", "physical features", belonging to a natural order' (1997: 311).

Wittig contends that lesbian existence exceeds the male symbolic order: 'Lesbian is the only concept I know of which is beyond the categories of sex (woman and man) because the designated subject (lesbian) is *not* a woman, either economically, or politically, or ideologically. For what makes a woman is a specific social relation to a man' (Wittig 1997: 316). (More than a hundred years previously, Black American anti-slavery campaigner, Sojourner Truth had used a similar rhetorical device to point out what we might now call the discursive production of femininity and its innately racist and middle-class basis when she asked 'Ain't I a woman?' (extract in Conboy *et al.* 1997: 231–2).)

In *Gender Trouble* (1990), Judith Butler follows Wittig in **queering** the commonsense divisions of masculinity and femininity. Butler draws heavily on some **Foucauldian** theories of discourse. Although Foucault's writing does not address questions of women's different experiences of the discursive processes that he describes as characteristic of the modern period, Butler, like many other contemporary feminist writers, argues for the usefulness of his theoretic frameworks to feminism.

Butler describes gender not as a series of roles, or costumes, hung on to the 'natural' sexed body, but as a continuing performance of interactions between bodies and discourses. Gender, for Butler, comes into being as a particular body repeatedly performs in a stylised sequence which eventually becomes naturalised. For Butler, the key to understanding the **performativity** of gender lies in the transgressiveness of desire. In the commonsense world, a conformity of gender, sexed body, and (hetero)sexuality is assumed and, if not present, is coerced by disciplining measures. However, some individuals expose the artifice of gender by drawing attention to the discontinuity between sexed body, gendered performance and sexuality: 'drag', according to Butler, in its conscious perfomativity, demonstrates the way in which everyone performs gender, becoming more and more adept ('natural') with practice. Like Adrienne Rich, Monique Wittig and other feminist writers, Butler draws attention to the 'compulsory heterosexuality' of society. Female bodies, then, in this construction become not the basic ground on which gender is draped, but a field or site created by the interaction of particular discourses which, of course, are not only those of gender but also of other cultural markers: ethnicity, race, age, class, etc. In developing this theory, Butler draws on the work of Monique Wittig, and also that of Mary Douglas, breaking away from the static division of body/mind that de Beauvoir had accepted, to stress the mobility and changing of bodies through time.

In *Bodies That Matter*, subtitled 'On the Discursive Limits of "Sex"', Butler continues her feminist critique of social constructionism, turning to the other side of the sex–gender distinction (Butler 1993). She argues for the political importance of examining what, and to what extent, can be established of a material presence beyond or outside language. In dualist logic, to be a body rather than a mind is to be outside culture, allied to 'the **abject**'. The abject is a realm outside culture and threatening to reduce culture to chaos: it is shapeless, monstrous, damp and slimy, boundless and beyond the outer limits. It is a realm associated primarily with the adult female body in its perceived fluidity and capacity to change, to bleed, to reproduce. The two theorists most associated with the idea of the abject in relation to female bodies are Julia Kristeva and Mary Douglas. Ideas of the abject will be pursued in Chapter 3.

Within **phallocentric** logic, to become a subject, to become an 'I' with identity, is to reject materiality in favour of transcendence. For de Beauvoir, it was necessary for women to conquer the 'swampy' female body and give the self to the mind. Those who are most associated with the abject, the body and nature, have the most provisional subject status which can always be revoked. Examples might be the problems raised in the workplace by the visibly increasing body of the pregnant woman worker; and the flexible citizen status of Australian Indigenous people until 1965 – legally designated minors for most purposes, but issued with service passports to fight overseas during wartime – and the legacy of this in the present. Butler suggests that it is important to ask what in this materiality is so dangerous to the system that designates it as 'other' and outcast. Feminist inquiry must return to the central question of the body: 'What challenge does that excluded and abjected realm produce to the symbolic hegemony that might force a radical rearticulation of what qualifies as bodies that matter?' (Butler 1993: 16). Or: 'What's the matter with women's bodies?'

Multiplying beyond twos

Binary divisions are endemic to western thought. The writers of 'corporeal feminism' usually start from a discussion of the limitations, for women, of binary thinking in general, and of the mind/ body split in particular. A common reference point is Hélène Cixous' charting of the ways in which 'woman' has accrued a set of subordinate terms throughout western history. Cixous asks '*Where is she?*' in the oppositions that counter Sun to Moon, Culture to Nature, Head to Heart, and she draws a horizontal line, above which is 'Man' and beneath which we find 'Woman' (Cixous 1981 [1975]: 90–8).

In a recent (1998) Australian book review, the feminist author under review was criticised for basing her argument on the assumption that there must be something wrong with binary thinking. The reviewer suggested that this assumption had become the unexamined article of faith (the *doxa*?) of contemporary feminist theory. So, what *is* 'wrong' with binary thinking? Moira Gatens and Elizabeth Grosz have examined the question at length from a feminist–philosophical perspective, pointing out the ways in which the dualism of western thought designates 'woman' as the opposite of 'man' and, in so doing, evacuates the subject of 'woman' of any meaning in her own right. If we follow this thought through, 'woman', as a concept defined by the lack of male attributes, exists only to re-emphasise what 'man' has: 'woman' is an empty space in which to re-write 'man'. If we work within the system that establishes and reinforces this, there is no other way to think 'woman'. Thus, there is a need to think again: to develop new conceptual systems which defeat the history of binary two by twos which are really a disguise of the monolithic (masculine) One.

The work of Luce Irigaray is very important in this process of re-thinking. She describes the place of woman as 'homeless' within the symbolic order because she is shut out from its phallocentric system of representation. In *Ce sexe qui n'en est pas une*, Irigaray develops a reading/writing of woman's body as morphologically different from a man's and escaping the binary division by being in movement and multiple [translated as *This Sex Which is Not One* (1985a)]. What her writing of women's 'two lips speaking together' signifies is multiple and untranslatable, and much debated. Margaret Whitford suggests that this indeterminability is its value, the contribution it makes to rewriting the binary ('it must be this or that') into the multiple ('sometimes it's this, sometimes that, sometimes both . . .'):

> The point is, I think, the *proliferation* of readings. . . . whatever Irigaray may have meant originally when she put the two lips into circulation, and whatever she may maintain now, she is not in control of this image any longer; it has taken on a life of its own and this life is far more significant than any single reading . . . the now seemingly independent life of an image which started off originally as an image of a (mostly unmentionable) part of women's body, but is now thoroughly impregnated with layers of meaning.
>
> (Whitford 1991: 101)

Irigaray's 'two lips' in endless conversation is a very different inscription of 'woman' from that of the *tabula rasa*. Hard dividing lines are replaced by fluid movement in a '*parler–femme*' (which might be translated as 'speaking–woman'):

The female imaginary which Irigaray wants to invoke in both speech and writing appeals to the metaphors or motifs of the female body. As we have seen, the transcendental (masculine) subject of language appropriates only a fantastical image of the (feminine) body, namely one that can be accommodated within the Order of the Same . . . When Irigaray equates fluidity with the flow of blood and the mucous membranes, and the feminine sex with an "excess with respect to form" . . . she is utilizing the subversive potential of the real, bringing to language a *parler-femme* that was previously repressed . . . the underside of feminine sexuality is used to transgress and confuse the boundaries between the real and the symbolic in the articulation of knowledge.

(Williams 1994: 174–5)

In this *parler–femme* 'the real' is not the (masculine) commonsense but a real that is inaccessible to the phallocentric symbolic order as though the abject speaks (for) itself.

Luce Irigaray, from *This Sex Which Is Not One*

But *woman has sex organs more or less everywhere*. She finds pleasure almost anywhere. Even if we refrain from invoking the hystericization of her entire body, the geography of her pleasure is far more diversified, more multiple in its differences, more complex, more subtle, than is commonly imagined – in an imaginary rather too narrowly focused on sameness. 'She' is indefinitely other in herself. This is doubtless why she is said to be whimsical, incomprehensible, agitated, capricious . . . not to mention her language, in which 'she' sets off in all directions leaving 'him' unable to discern the coherence of any meaning . . . For in what she says, too, at least when she dares, woman is constantly touching herself. She steps ever so slightly aside from herself with a murmur, an exclamation, a whisper, a sentence left unfinished . . . When she returns, it is to set off again from elsewhere. From another point of pleasure, or of pain, One would have to listen with another ear, as if hearing *an 'other meaning' always in the process of weaving itself, of embracing itself with words, but also of getting rid of words in order not to become fixed, congealed in them*. For if 'she' says something, it is not, it is already no longer, identical with what she means.

Source: Conboy *et al.* 1997: 252–3.

Within the phallocentric symbolic order where 'woman' is an empty space ready to be written on and in, there is a repertoire of terms and associations to fill in the space. They are, as Cixous has noted, generally imbued with negative or weaker meanings that translate into social repression and oppression. In particular, there seems to be a tendency across cultures to associate woman with nature and man with culture, and this includes the association of woman with the natural body and man with the mind: man above the line, woman below!

Western thinking has been characterised in both pre-Christian and Christian thought by the celebration of the mind at the expense of the body. Three hundred years ago René Descartes invested the human mind with a status beyond and in charge of the natural world, including the human body. This provided the epistemological basis for modern science and, by extension, for modern knowledge more generally by positing a knowing, detached observer (mind) capable of observing and making judgements about the world (nature). When we remember that in the phallocentric binary divisions 'mind' is associated with 'man' and 'nature/body' with 'woman' then it is easy to recognise why feminist philosophers have been so concerned to critique dualism. Irigaray's writing both illustrates and reflects on the problems of constituting 'woman' in opposition to this dualism, since such a move reaffirms women's exclusion from the highly valued realm of rationality. It is a dangerous business to claim as a positive, as Irigaray does, the inconsistencies and incoherences that have traditionally been used to exclude women from the activities of the mind by, for example, pathologising woman as hysterical.

According to Grosz, three major ways in which dualist Cartesian thinking organises current discussions of the body are: first, by the designation of parts of the body or attributes as the subject of life sciences, social sciences and humanities; secondly, through the perception of the body as a tool or machine which is, in itself, inert and requires direction; and, third, through the perception of the body as a communication system, a medium for transmission and reception of messages. For Grosz, it is imperative that new ways of thinking about bodies be developed: 'Insofar as feminist theory uncritically takes over these common assumptions, it participates in the social devaluing of the body that goes hand in hand with the oppression of women' (Grosz 1994: 10).

Summary

- 'The body' has been central to feminist thinking but new concepts of it have recently emerged through the development of 'corporeal feminism'. This development is contested by other forms of feminism: notably, by radical feminists.

- The question 'What is a woman?' challenges commonsense ideas about sexed bodies, and about the construction of knowledge; a movement in feminist thought has been from epistemology toward ontology.

- In answering the question, 'What is a woman?', there has been a tendency to assume an essential femaleness which for some feminists was something to be ignored or minimised, and for others was a cause of celebration.

- The focus of a women's movement around a universal idea of 'woman' has been increasingly critiqued as imperialist: blind to its own exclusions and assumptions. The development of an identity politics organised around a self-defined identity of sexuality, race, ethnicity, etc. challenges this universalism.

- The assertion of women's rights as human rights rests on the humanist ideals of the Enlightenment: the belief in the rights of an individual human subject. Arguably, the late twentieth century is dismantling the idea of the unified human subject; this poses problems for feminism.

- Second-wave feminism, following the work of Simone de Beauvoir, argues for the separation of sex (the natural, given male or female body) and gender (the cultural definitions of masculinity and femininity). 'Social constructionism' relegates the body to no more than a *tabula rasa* for inscription by culture.

- Social constructionist explanations have been criticised for ignoring sexuality and racial difference. Judith Butler (and others) points to the way in which binary gender formation relies on an assumed heterosexuality. She tries to re-think gender as 'performativity': a series of acts repeated until they appear as 'natural' extensions of the body engaged in the performance.

- Butler, like other 'corporeal feminists' works to change the thinking of western philosophy and, particularly, to move beyond the dualism of Cartesian thought. Luce Irigaray and Hélène Cixous also challenge this dualism, attempting to re-inscribe 'woman' in multiple ways that resist the binary oppositions of western thinking. Elizabeth Grosz argues that such a rethinking of and through the body is crucial to feminist politics.

Notes

[1] To be fair, a number of sociologists examining issues of the body have acknowledged, to different degrees and with different emphases, the importance of feminist inquiry to the field. Notable for this are Scott and Morgan, the editors of *Body Matters* (1993), who provide, without sidelining feminist theory as a handmaid of sociology, a good introduction to some feminist perspectives on the body. They point out that, as they went to press, there was an 'explosion' of feminist publication in the field which, of course, they were unable to take into account.

[2] Twenty years later de Beauvoir was to add: 'One is not born a man: one *becomes* a man' (see Keefe 1990: 155).

[3] For a useful introduction to Freudian theories of hysteria and feminist critiques, see Bernheimer and Kahane (1985).

[4] Wittig makes some analogies between slavery and gender oppression. This was an analogy commonly made by early second-wave white feminists, but subsequently criticised for insensitivity to racial differences. (Cf. Anne Summers 1994 in *Damned Whores and God's Police*, an Australian feminist 'classic' first published in 1975).

Further reading

Butler, Judith (1990) *Gender Trouble: Feminism and the Subversion of Identity*. New York and London: Routledge.

Conboy, Katie, Medina, Nadia and Stanbury, Sarah (eds) (1997) *Writing on the Body: Female Embodiment and Feminist Theory*. New York: Columbia University Press.

Grosz, Elizabeth (1994) *Volatile Bodies:Toward a Corporeal Feminism*. St Leonards: Allen and Unwin.

Bell, Diane and Klein, Renate (eds) (1996) *Radically Speaking: Feminism Reclaimed.* Melbourne: Spinifex Press.

Marks, Elaine and de Courtivron, Isabelle (eds) (1981) *New French Feminisms: An Anthology.* Brighton: Harvester Press.

Welton, Donn (ed.) (1998) *Body and Flesh: A Philosophical Reader.* Malden, Massachusetts and Oxford: Blackwell.

Chapter 2

Reproducing bodies

Chapter outline

Introducing some feminist issues concerning pregnancy, including the importance of the different cultural and social sites of maternal bodies:

- Overdetermined pregnant bodies
overdetermination; walking wombs.
- The politics of childbirth
cultural differences; O'Brien's 'philosophy of birth'.
- The pathologising of childbirth
medicine; surveillance; technologies.
- Self and body
alienated labour; pregnant embodiment; phenomenology.
- Representing pregnancy
discourses; metaphors.
- Feminist discourses
new discourses of pregnancy; feminist revisions.

Overdetermined pregnant bodies

This chapter will explore some of the ways in which feminist perspectives have been brought to bear on the pregnant body. As discussed in the previous chapter, it is only recently that there has been, in some areas at least, a range of possibilities for female bodies that has not been totally dominated by the paradigm of maternity. Some of the first organised projects of the second-wave women's movement were directed at securing safe and, ideally, free birth-control for heterosexually active women. The achievement of this goal would not only change the material conditions of women's lives but also the conceptualisation of women as more than 'walking wombs'. It might be argued that the contemporary turn of many feminist writers towards a highly abstracted theory is a luxury enabled by the, qualified, success of this campaign for some women who now have a relative freedom from the daily exigencies of being **overdetermined** as no more than a reproductive body.

Many earlier feminists, for good historical reasons, seem to accept the idea of the reproductive female body as a 'biological trap' that can be evaded but never extinguished, and thus they reaffirm a necessary split between a (superior) mind desiring control, and an (inferior) intransigent, irrational body. Firestone (1970) for example, describes women's reproductive biology as enacting a 'tyranny' which must be overthrown since it is the basis for the sexual division of labour. Mary O'Brien suggests that de Beauvoir saw gestation as 'woman eternally in thrall to contingency' (1981: 75).

My reason for choosing to focus first on the reproductive body is that it encapsulates all those dilemmas for feminism of how to demand multiple ways of being-in-the-world for women when 'woman' as subject seems to have been always marked by that maternal possibility. In the contemporary situation, new technologies have created new dilemmas through the radical ways they widen the terms of maternal possibility and also, for many feminists, point dangerously towards a future, hitherto only imagined in speculative fiction, where gestation can be as separate from the female body as conception now can be. While for Shulamith Firestone in 1970 this seemed like a desirable utopian fantasy, with advantages far outweighing the dangers of male exploitation (which she acknowledged), for many feminists today, the reality of reproductive technology potentially renders woman redundant by taking away her unique power. Emily Martin expresses this concern within the metaphors of economic rationalism: 'If doctors are like managers controlling the work that women's bodies do in birthing a baby, then will they stop short of actually removing the work force, the women themselves?' (Martin 1987: 144). The exploration of reproductive technologies and their perceived risks has been a continuing preoccupation of radical feminists (see, for example, Corea 1985; Rowland 1992; Raymond 1994).

As we have seen, early second-wave feminists sometimes followed de Beauvoir, and other earlier intellectual women, in accepting the binary opposition of mind and body, with the apparently inevitable conclusion that to choose intellect must be to turn away from bearing or rearing children. When, in an interview, de Beauvoir explains, 'I have never regretted not having children insofar as what I wanted to do was write' (1965: 36) she demonstrates the force of the mind/body dichotomy and the power of the elision between child-bearing and child-rearing. For some of the women making this choice it is a matter of regret, while others appear to share the distaste de Beauvoir expresses for the 'swampy' quality of female bodies![1] Again, it is important to put into historical context the ways in which many earlier western feminists endorse the dominant, masculine, ideology of the impossibility of combining maternity with intellectual activity and therefore seem, from a modern perspective, to endorse the very misogyny they were trying to fight. Rather than being an abstract principle, for many the choice of either intellect or maternity was literally a matter of life or death. The eighteenth-century example of Mary Wollstonecraft, the writer of arguably the first major feminist–political treatise,[2] dying from puerperal fever after giving birth, was neither an encouraging nor an isolated one. The case of Wollstonecraft is particularly ironic: her defence of the rights of women to citizenship in part rests on an establishment of the middle-class, educated woman as man's equal by virtue of her separation from the more animal, uneducated serving classes. Yet, it was the bodily function of maternity that she shared, across classes, with other child-bearing women, that killed her – though we should not underestimate the part probably played in her death by the medical profession of the period. The management of childbirth is discussed below.

The politics of childbirth

Turning from eighteenth-century Europe to our own times, dilemmas posed for feminists regarding maternity are still present, and still compounded by issues of class, race, sexuality and other differences. While many women throughout the world (and not just in the so-called Third World) still have little option but to face high-risk pregnancies and births, there are more women than ever before who, because of relative material prosperity, have some access to a range of choices about maternity in both physical and social terms. Among these choices are the option of conceiving without being in a heterosexual relationship, or any relationship, and of being assisted to conceive in numerous different ways and at different times in the life cycle. There are also choices, for those with the material resources, to plan and have monitored virtually every aspect of the developing foetus.

Some of the most heated arguments between contemporary feminists concern issues of maternity – and its prevention. While issues of technologically assisted choice to conceive or prevent/postpone conception tend to be the privilege of the economically secure, there has been increasing exposure of the ways in which involuntary contraception and, sometimes, sterilisation, have been imposed on Indigenous women, poorer women of the 'Third World' and other women deemed for various reasons (deemed by whom?) unsuitable to bear children. Complex ethical issues are at stake when, for example, a western feminist strongly espouses universal programs of zero population growth as essential to women's freedom without acknowledging the different local or individual conditions. Is she, indeed, a late-twentieth-century incarnation of the earlier eugenics movement whose rubric for a 'healthier' human population could be interpreted as a version of white supremacism? Conversely, western feminists have been criticised for campaigning against the use of particular contraceptives in Third World countries, and for ignoring the social and cultural contexts of their use.[3]

There are many examples of these conflicts. Australian activist and writer Roberta Sykes (1984) pointed out to the (largely white) Australian women's movement that she could not endorse the campaign for legalisation of abortion. Her reasons for this were that Indigenous women's experience far from being characterised by unwanted pregnancy has been marked by colonialist practices aimed at the eventual extinction of the Indigenous population: to legalise abortion might be to erode even further Indigenous women's rights to bear children. At the heart of this argument is a scepticism about the power of the law to enact equal rights against the force of historically enshrined social/cultural practices and attitude, and in situations where resources and power are patently unequally distributed (see also Huggins 1994, and Chapter 5).

While many earlier feminists, as we have seen, seem to endorse at some level the assessment that women's oppression is directly attributable to female reproductive biology, others valorised that biology as not only offering a way of experiencing the world that was unique to women, but also engaging women, through that experience, in a knowledge system other than the male-ordered dominant knowledges. Mary O'Brien (1981), for example, works from a binary distinction of a female materially grounded being, against a male abstracted being, based on the difference between male and female participation in conception, gestation and birth. However, she rejects the conventional values (female/inferior; male/superior) historically assigned to those opposites. For O'Brien, the distinction hinges on the radical difference between giving birth as part of a continuum lived in the body from conception through gestation, and male acceptance of paternity as an idea abstracted from the body. O'Brien's work typifies a strong direction in feminist thinking which seeks to undo the separation of epistemology and ontology and valorises a knowing through being. Using a socialist analysis, O'Brien attempts to lay the foundations for a philosophy of birth. Among her memorable contributions is the neat reversal of Freud's pronouncement that anatomy is destiny, to suggest that this, rather than applying to women now more accurately applies to men, since, in contemporary times women have entered history through the availability of effective contraception, leaving men still 'rooted in biology' (O'Brien 1981: 192).

One of the metaphors around which O'Brien constructs her politics of reproduction is Marx' contrast of the human architect with the bee: both build but the human begins with an imaginative project, a theory to be realised. Gendering this metaphor, O'Brien argues that de Beauvoir would seem to align the gestating woman with the bee, as witless actor, and that her own, and other contemporary feminists', task is to move beyond the inevitable and paralysing binaries of that metaphor.

Some difficulties other feminists have encountered with O'Brien's discussion are related to her privileging of child-bearing as the definitive aspect of social interaction and gender relations. Although O'Brien places careful and sustained emphasis on the importance of culture in producing gendered meanings and knowledges, she still returns to the child-bearing maternal body as a central and universal focus somehow beyond culture. Her emphasis on this maternal body begs questions about the knowledges and feelings of non-biological mothers, about those who, for whatever reason, do not bear children, and about those who bear them reluctantly or with feelings of ambivalence. Her argument also rests on broad generalisations about the ways in which human beings experience ourselves as bodies across a multiplicity of situations which may or may not include child-bearing. Arguably, while insisting on the historical materiality of childbirth, it fails to acknowledge fully its own limitation to the particular historical and culturally specific moment of western, late-twentieth-century modernity.

From a late 1990s feminist position, O'Brien's analysis can seem both resolutely heterosexist and over-ready to universalise. Her references to other cultures are based in the structuralist anthropology of Lévi-Strauss, and 'feminism' for O'Brien is implicitly a western phenomenon which reaches out, albeit in a sensitive way, to women in other cultures in a one-way process.

It is interesting to review O'Brien with the hindsight of 17 years. Many of the contemporary feminist theorists of the body continue her project, largely divorced from the socialist frame of reference that informs her analysis, to realise a philosophy of women's bodies that avoids falling into the either/or of idealism or materialism. However, few return to the central presence and experience of the pregnant body. It is interesting to speculate how far O'Brien's (socialist–feminist) warnings have been realised in the emergence of '[a] new class division . . . between those who breed and those who do not' (1981: 193).

Pathologising childbirth

An early theme of second-wave feminism is the way in which, in western medicine, the management of childbirth has been gradually medicalised by a predominantly masculine medical profession. A brief, but highly influential, contribution is that of Barbara Ehrenreich and Deirdre English (1973) which surveys women's role in the western history of birthing. Ehrenreich and English conclude that the rise, in the seventeenth century, of an organised profession dedicated to healing the sick body led to the reconstruction of childbirth as a medical condition, or pathology, rather than as the part of everyday healthy living it had been. Jean Donnison's (1977) study is a more sustained investigation of the medicalisation of birthing and the masculinisation of childbirth knowledge in the post-industrial period. These, and other studies, suggest that part of the process of the professionalisation, in its early stages, entailed the destruction of the power of the women who had formerly enabled childbirth and who now became labelled at best, as superstitious and ignorant, and, at worst, as witches. In more recent times, there have been continuing differences both in philosophy and practice between the, predominantly female, midwifery profession and the, predominantly male, profession of obstetrics.

One of the characteristic moves to power by the (male) medical profession was the development of professional technologies and training in their use: for example, the development of forceps was jealously guarded as a professional secret by its (male) inventor. Foucault identifies the introduction and use of **technologies** of **discipline** and **surveillance** as characteristic of the modern period. The establishment of a coordinated, accredited, medical profession which was, until the late nineteenth century, exclusively male, can be correlated, using Foucauldian theory, with the rise of the medical surveillance and categorisation of the female body as primarily reproductive. From feminist perspectives, the most pernicious effect of this surveillance is the **pathologising** of pregnancy and birth.

While it was increasingly accepted that 'women' need medical intervention and surveillance in order to gestate and give birth successfully, 'women' in this reading really meant – and still means – women of a certain social status. The surveillance with its technology was, on the whole, a commodity to be purchased and its extent and quality still depends, to a large extent, on the capacity to pay. As feminist–historical research has shown, the capacity to pay for medical intervention could be sometimes a disadvantage rather than an advantage before antisepsis was understood, and when along with medical intervention came the possibility of iatrogenic disease: diseases introduced by the very doctors and hospitals intended to decrease maternal and infant risks. However, some earlier feminist analysis of the horrors of medicalised childbirth in the twentieth century can now seem rather extreme and may have contributed to some of the more dogmatic versions of 'natural' childbirth advocacy whereby women faced with complications of pregnancy or birth can feel guilt or failure. In addition, the 'freedom' to choose to opt out of the system, but still maintain low-risk childbirth, may now be the prerogative of the relatively wealthy. A socialist–feminist analysis is sceptical of the ways in which 'choice' may be used in ways that obscure the economic inequalities that govern who can choose, and what range of choice they have.

Paula Treichler (1990) argues for the importance of examining the construction of different meanings around the term 'childbirth' even, or especially, when such an examination throws up uncertainties:

To talk of language, discourse, and definitions sometimes evokes desire for a return to certainty about what is real, but the retrogressive protectionism of certainty is no more the answer than the nostalgic return to a pre-Cyborg, pre-surrogate female maternal body that never was and never will be. The real is always linguistic, unsentimental, and political.

(Treichler 1990: 133)

Treichler's article is a good example of a discussion that focuses both on the production of meanings and the material consequences of those meanings for women's bodies: she draws not only on medical and sociological texts but also on literary sources, most notably the fiction of the Canadian writer, Margaret Atwood. Treichler emphasises the importance of acknowledging the extent to which feminist analyses expose and lay open to scrutiny the power structures of institutions like medicine and the ways in which our lives, as women, are constructed in relation to them.

Ann Oakley is one of the first British feminist sociologists to sustain an examination of the twentieth-century management of childbirth: one of her research innovations being the intensive use of women's own descriptions of their experiences (1979; 1980; 1984). In her pointedly titled *The Captured Womb*, Oakley carries on from the historical work done by writers like Donnison, to ask sociological questions about the ways 'a particular area of social behaviour (pregnancy) comes to be separated off from social behaviour in general and reconstituted as a specialist, technical subject under the external jurisdiction of some expert authority' (1984: 1). Oakley locates the sustained management of antenatal care within the context of the modern state's demands for a healthy workforce. She places emphasis on the British state's demand for an effective, healthy, military force and comments on the ways in which the establishment of comprehensive medicalised antenatal care was often couched in military metaphors. In Australia the emphasis – through a combination of restricted immigration, repression of Indigenous populations, and racially exclusive incentives for producing infants (such as Australia's 1912 maternity allowance) – was on the preservation and expansion of a white population. Oakley (1979; 1980; 1984) and Jane Lewis (1980) in the British context, and writers such as Kerreen Reiger (1985) and Jill Julius Matthews (1984), in Australia, point out that management of antenatal care, combined with infant welfare and, later, educational supervision, reconstructed the mother as guilty if she did/does not accept and implement specialised expert advice for the maximum health of her infant from conception onwards.

Oakley's summary is characteristically balanced and graphic:

> Natural processes are wasteful of human life and humans have invented the resources to do something about this . . . That is one side of the dilemma. The other side is what happens when care is taken to protect the health of mothers and children within the particular socio–political context of a profoundly class- and gender-divided culture, one, moreover, in which the power of professionals to shape people's lives has increasingly escalated to become one central mark of life in the twentieth century. In these circumstances the wombs of women – whether already pregnant or not – are containers to be captured by the ideologies and practices of those who, to put it most simply, do not believe that women are able to take care of themselves.
>
> (Oakley 1984: 292)

It is noticeable, in reading Oakley's *Women Confined* (1980), that while she is concerned to redress what she calls, 'the sociological unimagination', drawing heavily on accounts by women, her major direction is with the medical management of pregnancy and birthing and the actual pregnant bodies rarely appear in their entirety. In 300 pages, only seven (pp. 207–13) focus on 'Change in Physical State' and the quoted comments tend to centre on issues of the discomfort of clothes as the body expands, and the feeling of absence after delivery. This is, perhaps, attributable to Oakley's particular focus in this book on 'female emotional responses to childbirth' but that also may illustrate the difficulties 'the body' has posed as both the necessary participating site of a particular sexed experience – in this case, what is often regarded as the defining female embodied experience – and yet somehow, in itself, beyond representation or interpretation.

A contrastingly embodied but also analytic discussion is Tessa Weare's 'Round in a Flat World', first published in 1979, which concludes: 'Imagining a society where pregnancy was made easy, desirable, delightful, where children were expected in all public places, I realise how far from that we are. At the moment we cannot talk of women having a genuine choice about the way they experience pregnancy or children' (1987: 364).Weare suggests that there is a dearth of meanings and metaphors for women to experience pregnancy: only what she calls the 'NHS [National Health Service] image of motherhood, or 'the Great Earth Mother'. It is salutary to ask how far this has changed in nearly twenty years. Among the conundrums that Weare exemplifies is that of the relationship between 'me' and 'my body': 'I don't feel I can counter my rejection of my physicality by worshipping it. The thought brings out all my fears of being engulfed by my body, becoming only tits, cunt, womb and no me' (Weare 1987: 363). It is not any body, but a quite specifically adult female reproductive one that threatens to 'engulf'.

Self and body

Emily Martin (1987) addresses this issue of how we, as women, inhabit or are the bodies that are also the sign of our female sexuality. Her focus is signalled by her title: *The Woman in the Body.* Among other points of interest, she suggests that the ways in which women describe caesarean-section births offer an extreme example of women's habitual separation of self from body. One of the most arresting demonstrations she gives of this separation, by contrasting it with a more integrated experience, is in the juxtaposition of photographs of two very different births. One set is taken from the view of the traditional obstetrician, whereby the woman is represented as a horizontal figure whose legs, covered in 'sterile drapes', are straddled in stirrups, her vulva swelling with the infant's head, and her upper torso and face totally absent; in the second of the sequence, an attendant totally encased in gloves, hat, gown and mask has just scrubbed 'the vulva, perineum, and adjacent areas'. The second set shows the full body and face of a naked woman standing, supported from behind and with attendants in front, all dressed normally, actively engaged in birthing (Martin 1987: 161, 163).

Martin's gloss on these photographs is interesting. While she endorses the active engagement of the second birthing experience, she also points out that the way in which it is explained by Odent, the participating male obstetrician, is in terms of somehow taking birthing women out of history into some primal 'lower-order' state, part of nature rather than culture. (Perhaps this could be related to Treichler's image of the imaginary 'pre-Cyborg, pre-surrogate female maternal body that never was and never will be'.) Martin proposes: 'Instead of seeing [these birthing women] as engaged in a "natural" lower-order activity, why can we not see them as engaged in higher-order activity? . . . Here, perhaps, are whole human beings, all their parts interrelated, engaged in what may be the only form of truly unalienated labor now available to us' (Martin 1987: 164). Treichler's analysis, however, might suggest that even Martin expresses here a nostalgic and unrealisable desire, since this labour, like all other forms, takes place within the economic material conditions of our society.

The socialist–feminist philosopher, Iris Young centrally addresses the issue of alienation in her discussion, 'Pregnant Embodiment: Subjectivity and Alienation' (in Young 1990: 160–74). Young argues that the experience of pregnancy radically challenges the dualism of western philosophy of the body, including the work of existential **phenomenologists** such as Straus and Merleau-Ponty whom she cites as important for their location of subjectivity 'in the body itself' (Young 1990: 161). Young offers a discussion that moves in and between her own pregnancy and western philosophies of the body, taking care to locate the argument within her own privileged position, as the 'specific experience of women in technologically sophisticated Western societies' (p. 161). She also draws on the work of two, very different, writers of experienced pregnancy, Adrienne Rich and Julia Kristeva.

It is the uniqueness of pregnancy which Young focuses on, particularly in terms of its repositioning of the pregnant woman's body in space and time. However, she also suggests that this uniqueness of pregnancy poses a question for philosophies that are posited on a clear distinction of mind and body, transcendence and immanence, and on the clearly maintained boundary between self and other: 'Reflection on the experience of pregnancy reveals a body subjectivity that is decentered, myself in the mode of not being myself' (p. 162); 'In pregnancy I literally do not have a firm sense of where my body ends and the world begins' (p. 163). One important way in which, Young claims, the pregnant body is at odds with the phenomenologists' description of the body and self, relates to the phenomenological suggestion that 'I' am only aware of my body when it hurts or is damaged: 'These thinkers tend to assume that awareness of my body in its weight, massiveness, and balance is always an alienated objectification of my body, in which I am not my body and my body imprisons me' (p. 164). Young argues that, while the expanding pregnant body can cause discomfort, there are many occasions when its presence is experienced 'with interest, sometimes with pleasure' (p. 165). While there may be alienation from an external viewpoint, as exemplified in the idea of pregnancy as 'expecting' rather than a state of being in its own right, Young suggests that for the pregnant woman, 'she *is* this process, this change' and her sense of the time is different from that of the external observer, since birth is an end as well as a beginning (p. 165).

At the same time, Young admits the prevalence of the idea of the pregnant body as alienated from the self not only in (masculinist) phenomenology but also in feminist writing. She suggests that a contributing factor to this perception is the way that pregnancy is mediated and pathologised by the medical profession. Young argues that there is a misfit between a medical paradigm of the healthy body as 'in a steady state' and the pregnant, and labouring, body. Unlike some other theorists, Young makes practical application of her analysis to suggest that there needs to be a rethinking of what is meant by health and disease: '(M)edicine must shed its self-definition as primarily concerned with curing . . . The alienation experienced by the pregnant and birthing woman would probably be lessened if caring were distinguished from curing and took on a practical value that did not subordinate it to curing' (Young 1990: 172).

Western midwives might argue that this is precisely what distinguishes much of their practice from medical management of childbirth.

How far these analyses of childbirth and of the maternal experience of the labouring body can be transposed to other cultures is highly problematic. In post-colonial countries there are clear tensions and complex relationships between the 'traditional' practices and discourses and the 'biomedical' western models, often also associated with Christianity through the work of medical missionaries. Writers in this field, both from within the cultures and outside, disagree strongly about issues such as the degree of agency and choice exercised by women in their use of western practices and about the desirability or otherwise of maintaining 'traditional' methods. While it may be possible to generalise broadly about ways in which the childbirth experiences of 'western women' are constructed within the discourses of western science (although even here there must be a concern for the differences of class and ethnicity), the ways in which those discourses interact with other cultural discourses need to be explored in their local context. An interesting and useful new intervention in this area is Ram and Jolly's collection *Maternities and Modernities* (1998) located in areas of Asia and the Pacific.

Representing pregnancy

The work of contemporary feminist theorists of 'the body' is characterised by a dissolution of the boundaries between what is conventionally described as 'the real world' and its representation in
language, visual and other imagery. As we have seen, Martin and
Treichler both focus on the ways in which the bodies of pregnant
and birthing women are spoken and written about and portrayed,
in text books, popular culture, and more theoretical texts. These
theorists share the belief that our ideas and the practices that
both conform with and contradict those ideas are discursively produced. That is to say, even what seems the most solidly material
and 'natural' nine-month-pregnant body is 'inscribed' by discourses
about pregnancy, nature, women, birth, etc. The 'woman in the body'
is inextricably part of her particular historical time and space. Thus,
when we discuss and imagine, as Young and others do, the complex ways in which we, as women, experience pregnancy and other
aspects of our bodies, we do so within the discourses available to
us. In the late 1990s, those discourses are complex, varied and contradictory, ranging from the highly theorised philosophical debates
of writers like Julia Kristeva, to the 1991 *Vanity Fair* cover image of
a naked, very pregnant Demi Moore, and including personal and
media pronouncements, speculative representations of pregnant
male bodies, family stories and, of course, medical accounts.

To be a pregnant body in the 1990s is different from being one
in the 1950s, 1850s, 1650s . . . An interest in the specificity of these
differences informs the work of German historian, Barbara Duden.
However, and this is a big however which indicates the major
dilemma with which writers on the body are constantly wrestling,
these discursively produced and experienced bodies seem also
to be 'talking back'. At a basic level, while I may be specifically
spatially and temporally placed within my own particular society
and experiencing my body in appropriately discursively produced
ways, my body is somehow, in and of itself, contributing to and
enacting those experiences. The central problem for corporeal
feminists is how to account for this without falling back into the
mind/body split. In the following discussion I shall touch on
some of the ways in which contemporary feminists have discussed
various discourses of the pregnant body.

Sight has been perhaps the most frequently interrogated of the
senses for feminists. To see implies a separation of the viewer from
the viewed, and this of course has relevance to the discussion of

alienation touched on above. For, if it is possible to say 'I can see myself', what constitutes the boundary between the viewer and viewed? In the 1970s, writers such as John Berger (1972) and Laura Mulvey (1975), within the field of visual arts, instituted a highly influential discussion of the position of western woman as the object of the male gaze. That is, they suggested that the act of looking was gendered masculine: male viewers were characteristically voyeurs of female bodies. (This was, as critics pointed out, an implicitly hetero-sexist analysis and firmly based within twentieth-century western culture.) Berger argues that when women look at themselves in the mirror they are not looking for themselves but as the monitors of heterosexual desirability. Mulvey explores the idea of the male voyeur in terms of cinema, arguing that the viewing position of the Hollywood cinema audience is always masculine.

Similar ideas about the voyeurism of a masculine perspective have been used to explore the representation of women's bodies in medical texts and other 'scientific' accounts. In *Speculum of the Other Woman* (1985b), Luce Irigaray takes up the central medical instru-ment of gynaecological surveillance as paradigmatic of the ways in which female embodied experience is subjected to masculine vision.

Until recently, the pregnant female body has presented some-thing of a site of resistance to this voyeurism. Its increasing size as a female body occupying space in a way independent of masculine desire, tacitly but loudly contests dominant gender ideologies. It is, as Weare's title 1987 [1979] graphically proclaims, 'Round in a Flat World'. There are still residues, in western culture, of the desire to keep the pregnant body out of the public domain, most notably the workplace. This is evocatively summed up in the title of a report of the New South Wales Anti-Discrimination Board (1993), 'Why Don't You Ever See a Pregnant Waitress?'.

In addition, while the speculum can, of course, be used to invest-igate the vagina and outer cervix, the inner site of the pregnancy has been hitherto invisible. However, new technologies have changed this, enabling the uterus and its contents to be scrutinised and monitored. Arguably, this changes not only the management of pregnancy but also the perception of her pregnant body by both the woman herself and others. This is not only of academic interest but also impinges on legal and social decisions about pregnancy and foetuses.

Some writers (e.g., Oakley 1984; Jacobus 1990) have suggested that the pregnant female body visibly and increasingly confronts men with their own lack of a definite and indisputable link to the next generation. The construction of patrilineal/patriarchal laws and management of women's pregnant bodies from early religious regulations to contemporary debates around surrogacy and reproductive technologies might be seen as an elaborate attempt to erase or usurp this expression of uniquely female power.

For Mary Jacobus, drawing on Julia Kristeva's psychoanalytic analysis, the representation of the Christian Virgin Mary epitomises this erasure: 'Reproductively speaking, the Virgin's role becomes that of sublime incubator for the Word' (Jacobus 1990: 21). In 'Stabat Mater', Kristeva (1985) explores her own experience of pregnancy to stress not the vulnerability or difficulties of being a pregnant body, but rather the ways in which the body is increasingly invested with a power of its own, which is somehow in excess of available descriptions and analyses. One of the problems of such analyses is that they seem to buy into the idea of female ontology as somehow outside culture. While this could be seen as the power of transcendence, this power only has any material use for women if it is acknowledged and valued by the cultural world. The fact that it invariably is not acknowledged or valued, with the consequent devaluing of women themselves, provides the platform on which feminism is based.

Julia Kristeva from 'Stabat Mater'

The weight of the 'non-said' (*non-dit*) no doubt affects the mother's body first of all: no signifier can cover it completely, for the signifier is always meaning (*sens*), communication or structure, whereas a mother–woman is rather a strange 'fold' (*pli*) which turns nature into culture, and the 'speaking subject' (*le parlant*) into biology. Although it affects each woman's body, this heterogeneity, which cannot be subsumed by the signifier, literally explodes with pregnancy – the dividing line between nature and culture – and with the arrival of the child – which frees a woman from uniqueness and gives her a chance, albeit not a certainty, of access to the other, to the ethical. The peculiarities of the maternal body make a woman a creature of folds, a catastrophe of being that cannot be subsumed . . .

Source: Suleiman 1985: 99–118.

A number of recent analyses have examined the visual representations (and lack of representations) of pregnant bodies in the context of new technologies. Carol A. Stabile (1994), in a provocatively titled chapter, 'Shooting the Mother', offers a material analysis of changes in fetal photography from its first emergence in the mid-1960s to the 1990s. Her thesis is that there is a perceptible shift in the representation, both visual and verbal, of the foetus that transforms it from a dependent, even parasitic, relationship to its mother's body, into an autonomous person.

The visual representations of the 1960s, according to Stabile, link the foetus, the subject of the fetal photography, with its mother's body through, for example, the inclusion of the placenta, while the accompanying text reaffirms that 'the mother is more than mere surface or screen'; this text tends to endorse a portrayal of 'mother' as 'a sentient, sympathetic, and self-sacrificing presence' (Stabile 1994: 80). By the 1990s, however, Stabile detects a marked shift in both photography and text:

> The earlier atmosphere of liberal tolerance . . . has given way to a dark, amorphous background, from which all evidence of a female body, as well as any connection to the maternal environment, have disappeared . . . Instead of being a symbiotic link between woman and embryo, the placenta becomes a modem that permits communication between two distinct, and separate environments. Thus, both visually and textually, the embryo/foetus enjoys a thoroughly autonomous status.
>
> (Stabile 1994: 80–1)

Stabile follows her analysis of fetal photography, purportedly from within the maternal body,[4] with a discussion of the representation of the pregnant body from outside. She draws on the example of Demi Moore's cover portrait to explore 'the pregnant body's ability to shock and horrify the spectator' (Stabile 1994: 84). She points out that the adverse response to the cover was disproportionate when viewed within the context of western culture's saturation with images of naked female bodies: 'What repelled and shocked viewers was the vast expanse of white, pregnant belly' (p. 84). Stabile's point of comparison is that the external photograph represents a powerful and, to some extent sexualised, photograph of a woman, while the internal photographs work hard to erase that woman, and with her, her power. Her comment also indicates briefly but pointedly the ways in which there is a racial inflection to this: there is much less reticence about rendering visible the pregnant bodies of 'primitive' women in publications like *National Geographic*. Stabile suggests that, for feminists, visual representations such as that of Moore are problematic in so far as they might seem to return women to an ahistorical function totally determined by biology and, essentially, mindless. One could add that this notion of mindlessness is often reinforced by pregnancy manuals that show only the torso, literally decapitating the woman.

Pictures such as that of Moore, and the responses they evoke, are indicative of the complexity of the issue of women and pregnancy for feminism. On the one hand, it might well be argued that such pictures should be increasingly circulated to demystify the pregnant body and keep it legitimately within the public arena and thus empower it. On the other hand, through publication it enters a nexus of representations of female bodies and could be seen to reinforce the conventional notion that *all* female bodies are fundamentally determined by their reproductive potential.

Feminist discourses

Another way of naming this problem is to talk about the available discourses for experiencing and discussing pregnancy. Kristeva, in the article mentioned, uses her own experience to suggest that twentieth-century western culture is woefully lacking in such discourses for women. Part of this lack is attributed to the decline of Christianity in general, and more specifically, to the decline of the Virgin Mary as popular and universal icon of femininity (see also chapter 3 below). It is important to note that Kristeva is not unreservedly endorsing the usefulness of such an icon: indeed, she perceives it as part of the social control exercised by the Church. Kristeva herself is one of the few contemporary feminist theorists to engage, albeit in a philosophical and psychoanalytical way, rather than material way, with pregnant bodies. A brief excursion through the indexes of some of the most frequently cited contemporary theorists of 'corporeality' reveals no reference to 'pregnancy', 'birth' and fleeting references to 'maternity'. Even more interesting is that a recent radical–feminist anthology, that proclaims in its title that it is 'reclaiming feminism', has a similar lack.

Beyond feminist theory, it is worth conducting a short empirical exercise to examine what is on offer under the heading 'pregnant/ body' in any library catalogue. When I tried this in a university research library, I came up with 212 references. There were 10 feminist texts, a very large number of standard physiological texts directed at medical students of obstetrics – many with titles such as 'The gravid uterus' – 15 'so now you are pregnant' manuals, and several texts with titles like 'Management of pregnant ewes'. None of these, apart from some sections of a couple of the feminist texts, could refute Kristeva's description of a dearth of active contemporary discourses for pregnant women themselves.

Donna Haraway is one of the theorists who most interestingly looks at issues of technology and representation beyond the kind of technomania/technophobia documented by Stabile. Her analyses are always based within the material conditions of living beings. In common, however, with other writers on technologies of gender,[5] she also tends to concentrate on the foetus rather than on the pregnant body for attention. This highlights the issue of how hard it seems to look historically at pregnant bodies as more than an ontological ahistorical state of suspension or 'expectancy'.

Haraway, also, draws attention to the ways in which the development of technologies of surveillance erodes the traditional authority of the pregnant woman and thus changes her relationship both to her own body and the developing foetus: 'Quickening, or the mother's testimony to the movement of the unseen child-to-be in her womb, has here neither the experiential nor the epistemological authority it did, and does, under different historical modes of embodiment' (Haraway 1997: 177). This point is also made, more extensively, and in rather different terms by Barbara Duden: 'No wonder that an inner touch experienced only by women has gone unobserved and unnoted' (1993: 80–1). Iris Young (1990) also uses the experience of quickening as the marker of the expansion of self for the pregnant woman.

Haraway evokes the central image of the speculum to trace feminism's historical engagement with it, appropriation of it as a tool for envisioning our own bodies, and the need, in the new contexts of the present and near future technosciences, to develop 'the right speculum for the job'. Haraway's work offers ways of maintaining commitments to freedom and justice questions within rather than against new technologies:

> Feminist technoscience inquiry is a speculum, as surgical instrument, a tool for widening all kinds of orifices to improve observation and intervention in the interest of projects that are simultaneously about freedom, justice, and knowledge. In these terms, feminist inquiry is no more innocent, no more free of the inevitable wounding that all questioning brings, than any other knowledge project.
>
> (Haraway 1997: 191)

One of the few feminist writers to explore women's own experience of their pregnant bodies within a theorised framework, and to provide the historical perspective, is Barbara Duden (1993). Duden writes, and is translated from German, in a way that is both scholarly and accessible; her historical preoccupations with the constructedness of experience are at the service of her contemporary feminist concerns. 'What interests me is how women's flesh felt in earlier ages' (1993: 2); moreover: 'How did the female peritoneum acquire transparency? What set of circumstances made the skinning of woman acceptable and inspired public concern for what happens in her innards?' (1993: 7).

A noticeable aspect of her writing is the materiality or carnality of the words she and her translator use: 'flesh', 'skinning'. Like Haraway and others, Duden argues that a marked shift has occurred in the discursive construction of pregnancy, with a resultant 'transparency' or erasure of the female pregnant body in favour of the 'life' of the foetus, with its resultant political implications. Like Stabile, she points to the advent of fetal photography ('The Nilsson Effect') and the sonagram as the significant break in perceptions of pregnancy that, by privileging sight over other senses, bring about the disempowering of the pregnant woman.

Duden brings to this an analysis informed by consciousness of class and ethnic differences. She gives the example of rural, Puerto Rican women living in the urban United States whose pregnant bodies are 'read' and translated back to them in ways which are at odds with their cultural knowledges: 'In ways that she [a specific Puerto Rican woman] cannot fathom, expert professionals claim to know something about her future child, much more than she could ever find out by herself' (Duden 1993: 29).

In looking at some contemporary discussions of pregnant bodies, we engage with some – perhaps *the most* – pressing questions for feminism. At a philosophical level there are the questions of how pregnancy, as a (to-date) uniquely female power can be theorised in ways that do not return women to a negatively defined, ahistorical, identification with nature. In addition, there are the questions of identity and the ways in which the self and body relate, which are brought into question by pregnancy. For Iris Young, for example, the experience of pregnancy leads her to argue for a positive rethinking: '(P)regnancy can be better understood as an expansion in the borders of the self than as a collapse of its structure' (See Diprose 1994: 115). The majority of these discussions centre on the ways in which modern technologies and their context within an increasing cultural privileging of sight, conventionally associated with 'the male gaze', create new discourses for pregnant women, so that, as Duden says: 'Pregnant women today experience their bodies in a historically unprecedented way' (1993: 51). For some of these writers, these new discourses have complex material effects, legally and medically, which are also inscribed with ethnic and class differences.

Summary

- The pregnant body raises some of the most difficult questions for feminist debate because it embodies the cultural identification of women with childbearing and nature: the identification of women with nature which provides the rationale for most, if not all, oppression of women.

- Relatively few feminists engage with the complexities of the question and even fewer attempt to articulate and theorise the experience of pregnancy and childbirth as continuing states within time and space (rather than as an ahistorical state of being in nature).

- Pregnancy and childbirth are, in the modern western era, increasingly monitored and put under surveillance by the medical profession and the state.

- One of the most significant changes in this monitoring is the use of technologies to view the inside of the uterus and its contents.

- This surveillance and monitoring have different political implications in terms of class and ethnicity.

- The use of these systems of monitoring has drastically changed pregnant women's perception and experience of their bodies.

- Discourses of pregnancy and childbirth from the perspectives of pregnant women themselves are limited and usually invisible.

- It is therefore a feminist project to investigate and develop new discourses based on women's embodied experience.

- The experience of pregnancy radically challenges conventional ideas about identity and the self: this dissolution of boundaries has occasioned some re-thinking about these two concepts, notably in the work of Young and Kristeva.

Notes

[1] de Beauvoir's expressed revulsion for the physicality of an adult, reproductive female body echoes the terms of Jean-Paul Sartre's description of the female sex as 'obscenity', in common with other things that 'gape open' (Sartre 1992; first published 1956). The association of adult female bodies with the jungle, swamp, etc. has a long history; it is taken up at a psychical level by Freud with his description of woman as 'the dark continent'.

[2] Mary Wollstonecraft's *A Vindication of the Rights of Woman* (1975; first published 1792) elicited misogynist criticisms directed at her betrayal of proper female reticence ('hyena in petticoats') and being unnatural (or perhaps, too natural!).

[3] See, for example, the *Spare Rib* articles on the debate around the injectable contraceptive Depa-Provera (1975–85) (O'Sullivan 1987: 164–75); Chilla Bulbeck offers a valuable and inclusive summary of some of these debates with a useful set of up-to-date references (Bulbeck 1998: 97–112).

[4] There were some ambiguities in the actual provenance of the early photographs: the majority seem to have been of autopsied foetuses with only a few taken in utero. See Stabile 1994: 78–9. Haraway offers a complementary but differently focused discussion of these photographs (1997: 178–9).

[5] See, e.g., Petchesky 1987; Hartouni 1997.

Further reading

Duden, Barbara (1993) *Disembodying Women: Perspectives on Pregnancy and the Unborn*. Trans. Lee Hoinacki. Cambridge, Massachusetts and London: Harvard University Press.

Martin, Emily (1987) *The Woman in the Body: A Cultural Analysis of Reproduction*. Boston: Beacon Press.

O'Brien, Mary (1981) *The Politics of Reproduction*. Boston, London and Henley: Routledge & Kegan Paul.

Oakley, Ann (1984) *The Captured Womb: A History of the Medical Care of Pregnant Women.* Oxford: Basil Blackwell.

Young, Iris Marion (1990) 'Pregnant Embodiment: Subjectivity and Alienation'. In *Throwing Like a Girl and Other Essays in Feminist Philosophy and Social Theory.* Bloomington and Indianapolis: Indiana University Press.

Chapter 3

Bodies on the threshold

Chapter outline

An exploration of the concept of **abjection** in relation to women's bodies with particular reference to issues of fertility, menstruation and menopause: some of their discursive formations and their place in the understanding of women's bodies. Some feminist revisionings.

- Monster bodies   abjection; liminality; discourse.
- Fertile swamps   fecundity; (in)fertility; and pregnancy.
- Menstruating bodies   taboos; pollution; representation; narratives.
- Menopause   pathologising; medical regulation; HRT.

Monster bodies

Abjection, a key concept for some contemporary discussions of the female body, was introduced in chapter 1. This term implies a dissolution of boundaries and certainties, fluidity and movement. In ordinary conversation it also carries with it ideas of subservience and domination which make it, like many terms, problematic for feminism. Who wants to identify as being in a state of abjection? The complementary associations – ones which a number of feminist film theorists have been interested in exploring – are with horror.

'Abjection' is a **liminal** state, and it is this positioning of women, on the threshold, or 'in-between', that some writers, notably Julia Kristeva, suggest can be reappropriated for women instead of being used against us. Kristeva (1982) emphasises abjection as dynamics rather than as stasis: while cultures work by regulations and rituals to contain the abject, the abject is continuously evading containment. The pregnant body and the breast-feeding body most obviously enact aspects of abjection, in continuous changing of shape and size, dissolution of boundaries between self and other and, from a phallocentric viewpoint, in absolute female 'otherness'. Some of these aspects are shared by the menstruating body. Barbara Creed (1993) and others, drawing heavily on psychoanalytic theory, suggest that films like *Alien* and its sequels represent in a speculative form some of these fears and resulting imaginary constructs of the female reproductive body. The negative associations underlying fear of this body become materially represented in such films with associations of bodily fluids and waste, death and a ravaging, rather than nurturing, maternity. The violence and horror of the images are in proportion to the power of the force they seek to confine and negate.

Since abjection is most apparent at extreme, visually evident, moments of the body's changes, so childbirth and menstruation would seem to require the most complex and sustained rituals and rules of containment. These ideas are not only part of complex academic theory but also observable all around us. A recent (1998) BBC short radio play made comic use of the potency of the birthing body when two heavily pregnant members of an all-women's dart team faked labour pains to put their (male) opposition off form. Childbirth is neither easy nor without mess but the anxieties around the physical site of birth are often disproportionate to, and at odds with, the physical event. Similar anxieties can be seen around the representation and actuality of menstruation where the concerns of consumerism to circulate images to sell 'sanitary products'[sic] still have to represent menstrual blood by unspecified, blue fluid.

Many of the technologies by which the medical profession has become the primary manager of women's bodies could be interpreted as managing the essential monstrosity of women's bodies: a point taken up by Rosi Braidotti in her article, 'Mothers, Monsters, and Machines' (in Braidotti 1994), and extended to the collection, edited by Lykke and Braidotti, *Between Monsters, Goddesses and Cyborgs* (1996).

In this chapter, I want to look at some further ways in which women are materially organised: as 'fertile' and 'infertile' bodies; as menstruating bodies; and as 'menopausal' bodies. These are the bodies that as women we variously, simultaneously, and at different times, 'are': so what discourses and ways of experiencing ourselves are available?

Fertile swamps

As discussed in Chapter 2, for many feminists the ability of women's bodies to reproduce has been regarded as a negative rather than as an asset. When de Beauvoir repeats Jean-Paul Sartre's metaphor of 'swampiness' as a descriptor – or when other women, some of them child-bearing, bemoan the absence of images for maternity other than the 'earth mother' with its connotations of over-flowing figures: big tits and belly, small head – she evokes the negative identification of nature with reproductive women. In numerous discourses, to be a 'real woman' is to be 'fertile' and to be fertile is to be moist, fluid: swampy.

However, as in many issues around the question of what being female means, the position of male-to-female transsexuals can highlight the ways in which 'fertile' is not a 'natural' state but one culturally inscribed. Some transsexuals have expressed the desire to bear children and, while this has previously been only imaginable in the realms of speculative fiction, now, as in other areas of technology, this is becoming realisable. As one writer on the projected process envisages it: 'the embryo could be placed in a pocket of peritoneum in the omentum where it could be retained in position by suturing a flap of peritoneum over it' (William A.W. Walters 1989, cited in Squier 1995: 128). Walters' medical terminology is a long way from swamps, fecundity and earth mothers. The possibility of abdominal 'pregnancy' in a formerly male body, along with other forms of medically mediated reproduction, raises crucial questions for feminism. If we position 'femaleness' in a particular biological body, then what constitute the necessary parts and functions? At the centre of these debates is the question of where we perceive the boundaries of the female reproductive body to be situated and the allied question: if, culturally, 'fertile' female bodies are imagined as 'swampy', would women benefit from a technological take-over of fertility that would substitute the discourse of surgery for that of swamp?

For some radical feminists the answer is clearly 'no': the 'natural' female body is a primary ground of self-definition. A central pre-occupation of radical feminism has been an attack on the spectrum of reproductive technologies that has arisen over the last thirty years and, to a lesser extent, on the 're-assignment' of male bodies, as patriarchal, misogynist attempts to remove unique female reproductive power from women (e.g., Corea 1985; Rowland 1992; Raymond 1994). Other feminists are less certain. Some might argue for the importance of reproductive choice, on the basis of individual freedom, and this would include the choice to consume or not consume the products of medical technology; others might argue in a line following from de Beauvoir and Firestone, that, since the central issue of woman's child-bearing has been the key to her oppression, any moves to change its meanings may offer positive as well as negative possibilities for women. As with other debates about the management of women's bodies, the concerns about these technologies are different for different groups and individuals. A socialist–feminist response to appeals about autonomy and choice must always return to the issue of what limits and conditions are placed on that principle of choice within specific economic and social contexts where resources are not equally distributed.

There can be little doubt that the constantly changing material conditions brought into being by new technologies necessitate revision and reconsideration of previously held positions. One might ask, for example, what the impact of viable 'male abdominal pregnancy' would have on Mary O'Brien's argument that the continuum of gestation culminating in birth is what distinguishes female and male experience of parenting. Furthermore, the necessary severing of gestation from vaginal birthing in the case of a re-assigned male body, in its extremity enables us to detect some problems in arguments that do not adequately accommodate the range of *women's* maternal experience that includes caesarean and other surgically mediated delivery, adoption and fostering.

Whatever one's view of reproductive technologies, there can be little question that the meanings of 'fertility', 'birth', 'pregnancy' and 'mother' are all more publicly in flux than they have been hitherto.[1] While mainstream medical research has been more interested in the possibilities of 'male pregnancy' and, many feminists would argue, in the elimination of women's bodies from the process of reproduction, there has been a strong lesbian–feminist interest in the possibilities of 'gynogenesis' (cloned female-only reproduction). While the technologies are still in the arena of speculative fiction, a number of writers have used its possibilities to underline the ways in which the supposedly natural progression of 'scientific discovery' is actually determined politically.

Elizabeth Sourbut (1996) draws attention to the lack of interest in developing the possibilities of gynogenesis compared with the interest in 'male pregnancy'. She suggests that the possibility taps into the existing fears of (monstrous) female reproductive power, not only at an unconscious level but also in terms of social fears of the challenge to conventional family organisation it poses. Sourbut argues that this can already be seen in the fears surrounding 'lesbian mothers'. The technologies and resultant social reorganisation of the family could engender 'a monstrous hybrid creature which threatens the ideological basis upon which society is structured' (1996: 228).

Sourbut, like many contemporary feminists investigating the power structures behind new technologies, engages with the ways in which the material changes and effects on people's lives are inextricable from the discourses in which these changes are generated and to which they, in turn, contribute. We speak of our bodies in different ways from the ways we did, if we were alive then, in the 1960s, and so on. A pregnant woman, with access to most up-to-date medical technologies in the early 1970s, who again became pregnant in the early 1990s, would experience a very different pregnancy in terms of what she knew, or thought she knew, and what she thought she *should* know. Similarly a woman who wants to be pregnant in the 1990s and is not becoming pregnant has a different relationship to that state of being and a different choice of potential actions than she would have had in the past.

Deborah Gerson (1989) explores the term 'infertility', suggesting that this is one important area omitted by Emily Martin (1987) in her discussion of contemporary discourses of women's bodies. In common with many of the radical feminist discussions of the 'reproductive industry', Gerson points out that the terms central to the industry have become part of public utterance without an accompanying scrutiny of the assumptions and concepts they embody. Like Sourbut, Gerson is concerned to point out that 'infertility' is not a transparent description of a biological state but embedded in social and political beliefs. Frequently, it is 'a (heterosexual) couple' that is described as 'infertile', but the treatment that ensues is directed, in the majority of cases, to the female partner. As Gerson unpacks the term: 'the diagnosis of infertility, measured and studied by medical and social scientists, represents an accounting of the "failure" to conceive of those persons who are actively trying to conceive at the same time that they are socially designated as sanctioned to conceive' (1989: 49). It is this link of the biological body to the social body that creates many of the questions debated about 'rights' in the field of reproduction.

A large number of contemporary feminists are concerned, in rather different ways, with the 'monstrous' and abject body of pregnancy. The ability of many, but not all, adult female bodies, to reproduce can be interpreted as the site of unique power and, consequently, as the site of a multitude of fears and anxieties for men. Various ways of explaining this have been produced, many of them drawing on psychoanalytic theories which suggest that at the root of the fear is the apparently undifferentiated state of pregnancy whereby the individuality of a single self has been permeated by another. To simplify: this fear involves an anxiety, triggered by the sight of a pregnant woman, that it might be possible for the individual self, the 'me' that has developed since birth, to return to a state of non-being: in essence, a fear of death. It is 'the terror of non-differentiation. The threat of the maternal space is that of the collapse of any distinction whatsoever between subject and object' (Doane 1990: 170). Some feminists argue that this fear is translated into a desire by men to take over the single power of women – reproduction – and also assert its obverse, the power to inflict death. The 'mastery of nature' as expressed through modern science could, therefore, be seen as fuelled by this anxiety and desire, imaged powerfully in the fictional character of Victor Frankenstein and the many 'mad scientists' who follow him through western literature and film. The surgeon who articulates a possible pregnancy as 'the insertion of an embryo in the omentum', the obstetricians who 'manage' childbirth so that the delivering mother is virtually absent (see Martin 1987) and the reproductive technologists who engineer pregnancies in the containing body of a woman have all been described as the heirs of Frankenstein. The point is graphically made in a widely circulated media photograph of an early 'test-tube baby' in the arms, not of its mother or father, but of the officiating technician. It is important to remember, however, that much of the analysis and discussion of abjection, male fears and anxieties about women's reproductive powers, and the application of these theories to modern medical practices and discourses, are framed by contemporary, western cultural preoccupations and may take on different meanings, or be irrelevant, within other cultural contexts.

Menstruating bodies

There are numerous anthropological studies of other societies' taboos around pollution, most of them concerned with the polluting or abject properties of adult female bodies. The marker of female adulthood with its accompanying dangerous entry into the abject, is taken to be the onset of menstruation. In Mary Douglas's analysis, menstruation is, like childbirth, a liminal and therefore abject condition where the female body is perceived (by men) as changing shape and transgressing from the 'natural' human state whereby blood, and other bodily fluids, are contained. Douglas, in *Purity and Danger* (1966), is concerned with the reasons why menstrual, rather than other bleeding, is perceived with a disgust or fear vastly out of proportion to its actual ability to infect or harm. Following Douglas, Julia Kristeva (1982) distinguishes between bodily fluids that are considered to be polluting and those which are not. Menstrual blood is associated with excrement, in Kristeva's analysis, as fluids that are perceived as 'defiling'.

It is, of course, interesting to note how western anthropologists seem to have been fascinated by *other* people's 'pollution' rituals and taboos, and to have focused so determinedly on *women*'s bodies as their object of study. Arguably, this says more about western epistemologies than about the cultures studied. The focus on specific parts of women's bodies and the racial inflections of such studies have been increasingly commented on (Gilman 1985; Schiebinger 1993). Western-feminist anthropological studies have often been drawn on to support various feminist–political arguments such as the case for universal patriarchal oppression of women. For example, in the case of menstruation practices, western-feminist analysis had tended to point to the use of menstrual huts in many Pacific Island cultures as evidence of male fear of female pollution. Recently, the intervention of Pacific Island women and a more receptive listening on the part of some western feminists have identified the need to look also at some of the possible advantages for women who labour intensively in subsistence economies of a regular 'time out'.

In addition, there is a need to be attentive to the range of discourses in which these practices are situated (see Jolly 1998: 16). Some of these discourses construct a very different notion of the body, in relation to specific social, geographic and spiritual space, from that of western culture. Ram (1998a; 1998b) points out that ideas of pollution and abjection rest on the centrality of the body as a non-permeable entity which certain conditions, primarily of the female reproductive body, breach. She argues that few western theorists pay attention to the body's relationship to those spiritual beliefs which may be of paramount importance to the people studied, tending to dismiss them as passé.[2] This has important significance, for example, when looking at ideas of the body's non-permeability, since in many of the world's cultures, both male and female bodies are considered to be highly permeable between the spiritual and material worlds.[3] Such a re-casting of ideas of permeability demands a rethinking of 'pollution' and 'abjection'.

Coming a lot nearer home, we can see that in contemporary western cultures there are many constraints and fears surrounding menstruation. It remains one of the few areas of women's bodies to be almost unspeakable and unrepresentable. Barbara Creed (1993), in the context of film studies, comments that even when genres like Hollywood film's 'maternal melodrama' which purport to deal with the 'real world' expand the range of women's topics available for representation menstruation is not among them.

Until recently, there was a number of areas of 'abjection' surrounding women's bodies that either could not be visually represented at all or were reserved for carefully policed and marked areas of representation with their own codes: medical text-books, 'serious' documentaries, pornography, horror films. The list is an interesting one! As I write, the area of childbirth has been thrown open to a very public gaze by the first birth to be transmitted on the Internet. However, apart from the explicitly feminist art productions that directly confront the social silences by, for example, the presentation of used menstrual tampons – a particularly outspoken instance of the body speaking back – there has, to my knowledge, been no mainstream public rendition of, or expression of interest in, the menstruating body.

Menstrual blood, like birth, offers an area of the body in a sense out of control: and the language and imagery of the 'sanitary product' industry is one organised around that idea of containing danger and embarrassment. We are not usually embarrassed if we cut our finger and bleed, so what is it about menstrual blood that causes such concern? As with childbirth, menstruation is not an issue (!) that is highly theorised in contemporary feminism. In the early stages of second-wave feminism, consciousness-raising groups were very concerned with a reclaiming of women's bodies. This included not only encouragement of self-use of the speculum but also the removal of taboos surrounding menstruation, such as the notorious suggestion that women taste our own menstrual blood. There were also less controversial attempts to challenge the idea that menstruating women were debilitated and thus incapable of sustaining high-powered jobs or engaging in physical activity. Not surprisingly, the workplace and the advertising industry have been much more enthusiastic to espouse the latter idea – when it suits the needs of industry.

Penelope Shuttle and Peter Redgrove (1978) offered an early full-length recuperative investigation which draws on Jungian psycho-analytic theory to explore elements of myth around menstruation; it is evocatively entitled, *The Wise Wound: Eve's Curse and Everywoman*. Elements of second-wave feminism also attempted to give more positive values to menstruation by suggesting the development of celebrations for the onset of puberty: it is interesting to speculate why this did not catch on, either as a possible new avenue for con-sumerism (a menstrual industry parallel to the wedding industry?) or as popular practice for young women (see Lovering 1995; 1997).

One of the few contemporary detailed feminist studies of menstruation is Sophie Laws' *Issues of Blood: The Politics of Menstru-ation* (1990) which is explicitly grounded in social–constructionist approaches intermingled with radical feminism. Laws seeks to offer an alternative to psychoanalytical discussions that favour terms like 'taboo' by exploring male attitudes to menstruation and replacing the notion of 'taboo' with 'etiquette'. This implies replacing ideas of irrationality that resist explanation and thus resist intervention, with ideas of rational social regulation that can be changed.

The public discourse of menstruation is dominated by medical models which emphasise almost exclusively the link of menstru-ation to childbearing and thus reinforce the idea of 'woman' as primarily reproductive. A corollary of this is what Adrienne Rich (1980) has called 'compulsory heterosexuality'. Laws argues the need to return to the beliefs and ideas of 'people in society' in order to identify the lived practices. She suggests that her findings demonstrate an acute difference between 'laymen' and masculine medical writing on menstruation, whereby the former view men-struation primarily in (hetero)sexual rather than in reproductive terms: that is, in terms of their own sexual access, and the sexual difference represented by menstruation, for example, in terms of workplace competence. Laws goes on to argue the need for further explorations beyond the medical models to open up the multiple ways in which women experience and conceptualise menstruation beyond its reproductive signification. Lovering's (1997) research into young British women's understanding of menstruation and puberty demonstrates a similar commitment to the validity of the interview process and the legitimacy of the spoken word as source of knowledge.

The move to incorporate experience and to investigate women's (and men's) experience as they express it themselves is a characteristic of certain strands of contemporary feminist research, particularly that committed to social change. It is also closely linked to the feminist enterprise of giving voice to the silenced. Thus, there are many feminist books and articles with titles that refer to 'voices', 'removing the silences', 'speaking out' etc., or which reclaim negative terms. One recent example is the collection, *Off the Rag: Lesbians Writing on the Menopause* (Lynch and Woods 1996).

Like 'childbirth', 'menstruation' does not figure largely in the indexes of corporeal–feminist writers. Elizabeth Grosz, however, offers some interesting perspectives, not only on the ways in which menstrual blood is signified as abject but also on the induction of young women into their role as potential mothers:

> Women's bodies do not develop their adult forms with reference
> to their newly awakened sexual capacities, for these are
> dramatically overcoded with the resonances of motherhood.
> Puberty for girls marks the development of the breasts and the
> beginning of menstruation as an entry into the reproductive
> reality that is presumed to be women's primary domain.
>
> (Grosz 1994: 205)

Grosz paints a graphic and depressing picture of the ways that the menstrual markers of a young woman's puberty are enmeshed in a signification of stains, loss of control, and leakage which draws her back into the dependency and inadequacy of infancy rather than forward into self-contained adulthood: 'the impulsion into a future of a past that she thought she had left behind' (Grosz 1994: 205). (How far this analysis is culturally specific needs to be considered, bearing in mind Kalpana Ram's warnings (see above p. 50)).

To give a material instance of this concept, consider the ways that women's 'sanitary products' are marketed in a product niche that includes disposable infant nappies and adult incontinence pads. For Grosz, as for many other feminists, it is the enmeshing of sexed bodies within these systems of signification that gives them an irreducible specificity. Like vaginal childbirth, menstruation and the cultural significations of 'woman' that surround it are unavailable to the body that is not female: 'There will always remain a kind of outsideness or alienness of the experiences and lived reality of each sex for the other . . . At best the transsexual can live out his fantasy of femininity – a fantasy that in itself is usually disappointed with the rather crude transformations effected by surgical and chemical intervention. The transsexual may look like a woman but can never feel like or be a woman' (Grosz 1994: 207). While medical interventions, surgical and chemical, can inhibit and change the processes of menstruation in women's bodies, they cannot induce menstruation in a surgically constructed 'woman'.

Gloria Steinem, from 'If Men Could Menstruate'

So what would happen if suddenly, magically, men could menstruate and women could not?

Clearly, menstruation would become an enviable, boast-worthy, masculine event:

Men would brag about how long and how much . . . Street guys would invent slang ('he's a three-pad man') and 'give fives' on the corner with some exchange like, 'Man, you lookin' *good!*' 'Yeah, man, I'm on the rag!' . . . Men would convince women that sex was *more* pleasurable at 'that time of the month.'

Lesbians would be said to fear blood and therefore life itself, though all they needed was a good menstruating man. Medical schools would limit women's entry ('they might faint at the sight of blood').

Of course, intellectuals would offer the most moral and logical arguments. Without that biological gift for measuring the cycles of the moon and planets, how could a woman master any discipline that demanded a sense of time, space, mathematics – or the ability to measure anything at all? In philosophy and religion, how could women compensate for being disconnected from the rhythm of the universe? Or for their lack of symbolic death and resurrection every month?

Menopause would be celebrated as a positive event, the symbol that men had accumulated enough years of cyclical wisdom to need no more.

Source: Steinem 1984: 338–9.

Looking at very different discourses, Emily Martin investigates the ways in which contemporary medical texts, both professional and popular, over the last two hundred years, influence perspectives of menstruation through the metaphors and descriptors they habitually employ. Martin (1987) draws attention to the relatively

recent scientific separation of the sexes and to the ways in which
new discourses arose to define sexed biology (see also Jordanova
1989; Laqueur 1990; Schiebinger 1993). This critical examination
of what is normally taken for granted as 'straightforward description' reveals the constructedness of our experience. It is a variant
on the long-established feminist practice of using reversal and **irony**
to expose inequities and imbalances, and to demonstrate that there
is no transparent 'natural'.

Martin (1987) surveys the nineteenth-century's pathologising
of the female body, and observes the development of a specific
vocabulary for female reproductive organs framed by the metaphor
of wasting and spending. By the twentieth century the female reproductive system has become imaged as a productive system that,
at menstruation, has failed to produce. Havelock Ellis, a writer on
sex at the turn of the century, describes women as 'periodically
wounded', with the suggestion that all menstruating women are
inevitably debilitated: 'even in the healthiest woman, a worm, however harmless and unperceived, gnaws periodically at the roots of
life' (Ellis 1904, *Men and Women*, cited in Martin 1987: 35). Moving
into our own times, Martin cites a number of contemporary medical
authorities who conflate 'woman' with her reproductive organs;
in one 1986 US textbook, then in its seventh edition, Martin finds
this description: 'female reproductive functions can be divided into
two major phases: first, preparation of the female body for conception and gestation, and second, the period of gestation itself'
(Arthur C. Guyton 1986, *Textbook of Medical Physiology*, cited in
Martin 1987: 44). Just as Steinem speculates on the social changes
that might be evident 'If Men Could Menstruate', so Martin takes
the conventional descriptions of menstruation as waste, negativity,
and the equally politically charged, if more poetic, 'menstruation is
the uterus crying for a baby', and recasts them. What if medical text-
books used positive, productive images: 'Constriction of capillary
blood vessels causes a lower level of oxygen and nutrients and paves
the way for a vigorous production of menstrual fluids. As part of the
renewal of the remaining endometrium, the capillaries begin to
reopen, contributing some blood and serous fluid to the volume
of endometrial material' (Martin 1987: 52).

In a more recent discussion, Martin (1997) points to the work
of a Berkeley biologist, Margie Profet, who has proposed a new
way of envisaging menstruation within the context of contemporary research into the body's immune system. Menstruation, in this
new vision, is 'a mechanism for protecting a female's uterus and

fallopian tubes against harmful microbes delivered by incoming sperm'. In addition to remarking on the interesting re-visioning this entails in itself, Martin speculates on the reasons why a positive recasting of menstruation ('instead of a useless and disgusting debris, an important part of (woman's) flexible and responsive immune system') met with such vehement rejection by the medical establishment (Martin 1997: 23–4).

The menstrual body and its products are generally perceived, at least in western culture, not only with some degree of distaste but also as a signifier of (re)productive 'proper' womanhood. Medical discourses attempt to manage this area, as other areas of women's bodies, through surgical and chemical control and by a process of monitoring which, Martin and others suggest, is heavily modelled on images of the body as machine and doctor as mechanic. These discourses represent menstruation as waste product, an image which depends for its effectiveness on the identification of adult women ('real women') with fertility. For many feminist theorists, medical practices of surveillance and management, in the sphere of reproductive health as in other areas, are closely linked to the demands of consumer capitalism. Some analyses explore the ways in which the advertising industry, based on appeals to the visual, negotiates the twin and apparently contradictory demands to extend markets while also preserving cultural conventions, when selling 'sanitary products'. Many of the advertisements appeal to ideas of control, management and hygiene while also emphasising the alleged capacity of their products to erase any of the social and physical discomforts of menstruation. While earlier marketing names favoured connotations of feminine discretion ('Modess'), contemporary ones signal the removal of an irritating obstacle or impediment ('Libra'; 'Stayfree'). One strategy that has provided copious fodder for comedians is to suggest that use of a tampon can miraculously enable you to engage in a whole range of activities like sky-diving and windsurfing. As in other areas of feminist cultural critique, a potent technique is to expose the inconsistencies and contradictions inherent in such images and scrutinise the discourses and contexts of their transmission.

Menopause

If menstruation in western culture is constructed by official discourses as a signifier of adult women's, primary, reproductive function and its appearance is seen both as a confirmation of a functioning reproductive body and of that body's current 'failure' to produce a baby, what is menopause and what are the discourses available to us? Elizabeth Grosz suggests that there is now a veritable flood of material: 'the growth of literature on menstruation and menopause since the feminist awakenings of the 1960s and 1970s is truly astonishing' (Grosz 1994: 198). She contrasts this with the silences, 'the unspoken of the male body'. Grosz's point gestures toward a key problem for feminist analysis in dealing with issues of visibility/invisibility and speech/silence. While feminism argues for the rendering of the invisible and silent as visible and articulate, there is the concomitant risk that this (over)exposes women in still further ways to the male gaze. While the growth of literature on women's 'corporeal flows' may be astonishing, there is no guarantee at all that the bodies envisioned and, in effect, brought into being by that literature, will be necessarily positive ones for women. One example of a highly contested, relatively new, field of scrutiny and management is 'menopause' and the use of Hormone Replacement Therapy (HRT).

It is virtually impossible to speak of menopause without also discussing menstruation. Although the term 'menopause' is used to encompass a wide range of different changes over time to women's bodies (none of which changes is uniformly experienced by all women), 'menopause' is physically marked as having occurred, only by the permanent cessation of menstruation. 'Menopause' is an invisible absent event!

Susan J. Wolfe from 'Non-menopause: A Chronology'

I went to see him [a specialist] in mid-April, by which time I had had the current menstrual period for fourteen days. I suggested that menopause might be a factor in the other symptoms I was experiencing. And that's when he did the magic test that told me and the medical world that I was not menopausal, and that all these symptoms were obviously in my *mind* . . . the FSH, follicle stimulating hormone test. It seems that when you cease to produce enough estrogen, this hormone becomes elevated in a last-ditch attempt to convince your body you may still bear the young of the race. And if you have a low FSH reading, your estrogen should still be fine: ergo, you are not menopausal. But he suggested that if I were contemplating estrogen replacement, I should see my family practitioner or a gynaecologist.

Source: Lynch and Woods 1996: 193.

The development of a category of 'menopausal women' with which we ourselves identify is a remarkable example of how discourses construct and organise experience and do so in different ways for different groups of women. Bettina Leysen points out the imprecision of the supposedly precise medical science of menopause: 'What symptoms are characteristic of menopause? The only symptom experienced by all women is cessation of menstruation. Over four hundred effects of oestrogens are known, but there is no consensus in medicine about the menopausal syndrome' (Leysen 1996: 174). Germaine Greer (1991) makes a similar point, drawing attention to the ways in which many of the body's processes, including aging and menopause (or 'the climacteric', a term which has a rather different ring to it) are not transparently open to medical science. Wendy Rogers suggests: 'The symptoms for which hormone replacement therapy offers respite are not unique to or solely attributable to the cessation of menstruation. It is as if menopause has been built up into a fearful event just so that it can be controlled and regulated' (1997: 231).

For the majority, but not all, of child-bearing women in western cultures, menopause (as defined medically) will be achieved at some considerable distance from our last pregnancy. Many of us can confidently expect to live at least a quarter of our lives after our last period. This was not the case for most women before this century and remains different for many groups of women in all societies. Many women for a variety of reasons will not experience their final period within the context of child-bearing at all: these include celibate women, some but not all lesbian women, women who have chosen not to bear children, women who have accepted that they will not, for whatever reason, bear children (these groups are not, of course, mutually exclusive). The meaning of menopause in modern late-capitalist society is to a large extent coopted into consumerism. In a society where regularity of menstrual periods is important, the change in frequency during menopause has tended to become pathologised along with the concomitant rise of a menopause industry. Susan Wolfe's personal account of engagements with the medical profession in the United States (and she makes the point that these were expensive engagements enabled by her relative middle-class security) illustrates, among other things, how thoroughly 'oestrogen replacement' or HRT has become entrenched in western thinking. Much contemporary medical debate and its feminist critiques focuses on this particular development to the extent that 'menopause' and HRT have become synonymous. Some recent feminist commentators show how this particular discourse has come into being.

For Bettina Leysen, HRT and the menopause industry are a female-gendered part of the contemporary emphasis on prolonging life and defying mortality: 'The message of popular culture is to be fit, healthy and active at whatever age or stage in life' (1996: 173). Leysen suggests that opinion is as divided among feminists, as among different medical authorities, about the function of meno-pause and how it should be regarded: as a normal element in women's life cycle that does not usually require any treatment or management, or as a deficiency disease in need of a cure. The dif-ferent feminist opinions tend to reflect, again, the extent to which the idea of a 'natural' female body is held to be an asset or a prob-lem. (They also tend to be somewhat coloured by the individual's particular experiences of menopause!)

From one point of view, the injunction to use HRT can be placed within the spectrum of a decentralising trend in politics whereby the onus for health is placed on the individual. The logic goes: if we know that HRT can restore bone mass but fail to use it, then we are culpable of knowingly risking osteoporosis and becoming burdens on the public health system. Leysen observes that there has been a considerable expansion of the number of older-life-stage conditions supposedly prevented or retarded by HRT. She contrasts the present emphasis on old-age health and individual health care, with the early 1960s menopause industry's preoccupation with the alleged capacity of HRT to extend women's heterosexual attract-iveness. The writings of the time, epitomised by Leysen's 1966 title *Feminine Forever*, clearly equate femininity with heterosexual avail-ability, with the additional, sometimes explicit, corollary that a post-menopausal woman must be unfeminine and unattractive. This links to the kind of medical representations of woman, as described by Emily Martin, which represent her as either a potentially or an actually reproductive body. In this imaginary, a post-menopausal woman is essentially redundant machinery. Unlike some other cul-tures in which women who have survived their reproductive years acquire some status and a respect for their knowledge, western society on the whole has no formal space or position for them, despite some valiant radical feminist attempts to create mythical connections to 'crones' and 'wise women'.

Given the non-place for menopausal women in contemporary society, and what is arguably an increasing emphasis on youth-fulness, and individual responsibility for well-being (equated with 'staying young'), it is not surprising that there should be a great degree of ambivalence and debate among feminists about how to respond to our menopausal bodies. While, as Elizabeth Grosz observes, there is a mass of literature on menopause, there are relatively few personal accounts and what exists does not really reflect the diversity of experience either at an individual or a cultural level.[4] *Off the Rag* (Lynch and Woods 1996) and Germaine Greer's *The Change* (1991) go some way to filling this gap in the records.

A more recent intervention in the field is a collection of essays on the whole influenced by phenomenological approaches to the body (Komesaroff *et al.* 1997). Several contributors combine a theorising approach with subjective accounts, most notably the opening essay by Fiona Mackie, 'The Left Hand of the Goddess: The Silencing of Menopause as a Bodily Experience of Transition'. Mackie's project is to offer a different discourse of embodied experience to the prevailing position of 'women in modernity' who 'as menopause approaches, confront an entire governing code that decrees their placement according to prevailing values operating greatly to their disfavor' (1997: 22).

Fiona Mackie, 'Menopause as Spacetide'

If you have resisted becoming a junkie of the fixed and unified self, with its frozen and paralyzed body, then the organism's resistance, diffusion, quiet seepage across the fixed lines of its enclosure is delicious, a delight – an ally in the serious game of that refusal. Like a trace, in silver slippers, the process arrives with a smile. The energy flow shifts across centers, between limbs, and I know that something is coming . . .
And so, the struggle is engaged, for whose world will allow them to shift toward *being*, against the endless pressures to *do*, push, rush; annihilating bodily sensations as one races forward, bound to a linear time, frozen in the face of the future, through the teeth of rage? Whatever had been one's praxes toward preserving life, against this deathdrive of 'the normal', they are joined now by a companion: body asserting itself within language, against its exile . . .

Source: Komesaroff *et al.* 1997: 22.

Coney (1994), Leysen (1996) and van Wingerden (1996) all draw attention to the ways in which osteoporosis has been constructed as a new area of social concern in the west, in parallel with the development of HRT. Sandra Coney's primary emphasis is on the interconnectedness of the medical profession and pharmaceutical industries with their need to promote and expand markets for their products. Ineke van Wingerden follows the more discursive methods of Emily Martin, by examining the genesis of a female post-menopausal body prone to osteoporosis. Starting from Donna Haraway's proposition that bodies are produced by particular apparatuses, and that feminism needs to understand and intervene in the processes of production ('The Bio–politics of Post-modern Bodies' in Haraway 1991), van Wingerden explores the experience of a group of women in The Netherlands who attend a clinic for bone metabolism. She combines this with engagement in an Internet discussion group.

Van Wingerden considers the multiple ways in which the clinic outpatients are drawn into different discourses and ways of viewing their bodies and, in particular, how they are inducted into defining themselves as potentially 'at risk' of osteoporosis. Being 'at risk' becomes here (as also with regards to other conditions such as breast and cervical cancer) part of the identity, 'menopausal woman': this is evidenced by the vocabulary of the women at the clinic and in the Internet group. Among the implications of this study are the ways in which this management and re-orienting women's bodies through medical surveillance and management produces a different body which may be at odds with some of the women's own perceptions. That is to say, the 'bone-mass body' which is given priority is produced independently of the woman's own perceptions of pain, which the management may or may not alleviate. In identifying this perceptual contradiction, van Wingerden suggests an inadequacy in both Rosi Braidotti's and Judith Butler's poststructuralist accounts of 'body matters' for feminist practice in health areas: an absence of consideration for pain and the feeling body's difference from the discourses in which it is otherwise officially constituted (cf. Susan Wendell's discussion of pain, Chapter 7). This is, perhaps, a good example of what corporeal feminist Vicki Kirby (1997) is interested in: the body that writes/talks back.

Contemporary western feminist discussions of menstruation and menopause draw variously on discourse analysis, interview, and empirical research in attempts to reveal the constructedness of our experience of what might appear to be the most 'natural' and inevitable of bodily processes. In so doing, they again throw up issues of feminist politics around what, if at all, in essence constitutes the female body. Most markedly in the case of 'the menopause industry',

opinions are sharply divided about the degree and level of intervention that is consistent with a feminist praxis. By looking at the
two, allied, areas of menstruation and menopause (which might be
conceptualised as presence and absence) we can readily identify
some of the contradictions that women must constantly navigate.
On the one hand, menstruation is perceived largely in our society
as messy, 'a curse' and, at one level, a sign of women's inferiority,
but it is also the sign of fertility and its irregularity or long term
absence (outside pregnancy) is pathologised. Simply, to be an adult
woman and menstruating marks her as fertile (good) but also not-
male/permeable/polluting (bad). This is complicated, as Laws'
research indicates, by the apparent discrepancy between 'laymen'
and medical discourse: the former seeing women primarily as sexual
partners whose accessibility may be impeded by menstruation, while
the medical discourse constructs menstruation almost exclusively
in terms of reproduction. All of this has ramifications in terms
of the needs and self-identification of women who are not heterosexual or sexually active (but still menstruating). It also impacts on
the choices made by the medical profession and funding bodies
when determining which areas of menstruation and women's life
cycle to research. For example, there is relatively little interest in
the very painful condition of endometriosis.[5]

In terms of menopause, there is an almost total medicalisation
of this stage of women's lives with very limited alternative discourses
available. Imagining an older woman's body and subjectivity in wider
and more varied terms is, at present, very difficult in western society:
a void summed up by the identification of menopause as a cessation
and absence.

Summary

- Abjection has been an important concept in contemporary
  western feminist thinking about the body.

- Abjection is primarily identified with the fluids and processes
  specific to the adult female reproductive body: in particular
  childbirth and menstruation.

- The identification of a 'normal' adult woman as fertile also
  implicates her in being 'close to nature' and 'swampy': both
  conditions associated with the irrational, and with various
  states of fear and uncertainty.

- New technologies of 'fertility' present a complex issue for feminism in both offering some release, through their 'machinery', from this traditional association, but also propelling maternity further into the 'Frankenstein' framework of phallocentric science and medicine.

- Menstruation has been identified as one of the prime areas of 'taboo' and abjection.

- Recently, there has been some sustained critique of earlier feminist anthropologists, and some more contemporary feminist theorists, for their assumptions of universality when applying ideas about abjection to the menstrual, and other, practices and beliefs of different cultures.

- In western culture menstruation is primarily still constructed in terms of a nuisance to be regulated. This is reinforced by the discourses of advertising.

- Analysis of contemporary horror films suggests a more complex set of associations reflecting unconscious fears.

- Discourse analyses of medical texts reveals shifts in the metaphors used to explain and describe menstruation.

- Menopause discourse links menopause inextricably with HRT, illustrating the pathologising of this stage in women's lives and the power of consumerism.

- While there has recently been an expansion of material on menopause and menstruation, there is relatively little that speaks from the position of women themselves.

Notes

[1] The emphasis on 'publicly' needs to be made. The meanings of these terms have been variously interpreted for political reasons, particularly in racial contexts, before the advent of new technologies. 'Mother' and 'reproduction' for example, were used very differently by slave-owners when talking about their slaves and their wives (see, e.g., Patricia J. Williams 'On Being the Object of Property' in Conboy *et al.* 1997: 155–75). 'Mother' also meant something very different to the Indigenous women who had their children removed, and to the authorities who removed them (see, for example, Barbara

Cummings (1990) *Take This Child . . . From Kahlin Compound to the Retta Dixon Children's Home.* Canberra: Aboriginal Studies Press)
[2] Ram offers an interesting comment on Kristeva's 'Stabat Mater': while Kristeva's argument is based on the demise of the cult of the Virgin Mary, in many post-colonial cultures this remains a strong article of faith (Ram 1998a: 292 and elsewhere in Ram 1998a and 1998b).
[3] Compare also Judith Macdonald's discussion of differences in (her own) western and Solomon Island perceptions of the body, 'The Body of the Land – The Bodies of the People: Gender in Tikopia', in de Ras and Grace (1997).
[4] Susan Bell (1990) comments on the lack of collection of direct, experiential material on menopause from women's personal writing.
[5] See Caroline Hawkridge's *Living With Endometriosis* (1996).

Further reading

Komesaroff, Paul, Rothfield, Philipa and Daly, Jeanne (eds) (1997) *Reinterpreting Menopause: Cultural and Philosophical Issues.* New York and London: Routledge.

Coney, Sandra (1993) *The Menopause Industry: A Guide to the 'Discovery' of the Mid-Life Woman.* North Melbourne: Spinifex Press.

Douglas, Mary (1966) *Purity and Danger: An Analysis of Pollution and Taboo.* London: Routledge and Kegan Paul.

Laws, Sophie (1990) *Issues of Blood: The Politics of Menstruation.* Houndmills: Macmillan.

Lovering, Kathryn (1995) 'The Bleeding Body: Adolescents Talk About Menstruation'. In Sue Wilkinson and Celia Kitzinger (eds) *Feminism and Discourse.* London: Sage.

Chapter 4

Cutting bodies to size

Chapter outline

Further discussion of feminist critiques of the ways in which women's bodies are 'disciplined' both by themselves and cultural institutions, with particular reference to the examples of eating disorders and cosmetic surgery. The feminist appropriation of some Foucauldian theories and the importance of cultural difference.

- Males in the head
- Eating disorders or self-starving norms?
- Critiquing the clinic

- Under the knife

- What choice?

heterosexual economy; discipline; interiorisation; imaginary bodies.
compliance or resistance; discourses.
issues of difference; reclaiming narratives and rewriting 'anorexia'.
plasticity; anthropometry; postmodernist theory and its limits.
'cultural dopes'; deconstructing 'nature'; cosmetic surgery as performance art.

Males in the head

Much feminist work on the disciplining of bodies draws on the theories of Michel Foucault, and particularly on his text *Discipline and Punish: The Birth of the Prison* (1977). Terms such as 'discipline', 'docile bodies', 'surveillance' and 'genealogy', signal an affiliation with Foucauldian theory.[1] In the next two chapters, we shall explore some of the current feminist theorising on the ways in which contemporary western society disciplines women's bodies within a **heterosexual economy** and the central issue of how far, and in what ways, women accept and/or contest this disciplining. This chapter continues from Chapter 3 in discussing feminist interest in the less formal disciplinary institutions, including the ways in which women are encouraged to discipline our bodies within the 'male gaze' (cf. Chapter 2), with a focus on the particular instances of 'eating disorders'[2] and cosmetic surgery. Chapter 5 will explore feminist interest in some of the more formal social institutions that practise discipline and surveillance of women's bodies.

The increase in both 'eating disorders' and cosmetic surgery among women in western societies suggests, for most feminist commentators, the continuing constraints of the heterosexual economy. For some, it is evident that, as women gain more civil status, particularly in the workforce, cultural forces acting in the interest of masculinity will seek to cut them down to size again. Both an obsession with slenderness and cosmetic surgery (itself, often used to change body size) are, arguably, determined in one way or another by ideas of what men desire.

The ways in which the dominance of male heterosexual desire organises the body perceptions of young women is the focus of an important recent British study arising from two related projects, investigating risk and AIDS (Holland, Ramazanoglu, Sharpe and Thomson, *The Male in the Head* 1998). This feminist examination of personal accounts by young women negotiating their heterosexuality underlines that for most of them there is a clear, if not always totally articulated, nexus between their body size and appearance, heterosexual availability, and their sense of self.

The empirical research on which *The Male in the Head* draws was concerned with examining the ways in which 'risky' sexual practices, in the context of AIDS, could be seen as part of pervasive cultural constructions of sexuality. This perspective tries to counter the more common approach of pathologising AIDS as a problem of specific minorities (gays, Haitians, intravenous drug users, etc.). As will be seen in the discussion of 'eating disorders', a characteristic of much feminist research into areas of health adopts this strategy of re-thinking an area identified and categorised as 'aberrant' or 'abnormal'.

The researchers identify some gaps in both mainstream and feminist analysis, particularly in the theorising of heterosexuality. 'The Male in the Head' of the title represents a privileged masculinity that informs heterosexual relationships (in this case of young men and women in Britain, across different class and ethnic groups). This masculinity is a powerful impetus to monitoring, including self-monitoring, since it seems to be **interiorised** as a (perhaps the) dominant value by the young women themselves. Holland *et al.* compare it to the description by Sandra Bartky of women's place in patriarchal systems: 'a **panoptical** male connoisseur resides within the consciousness of most women: they stand perpetually before his gaze and under his judgment' (cited in Holland *et al.* 1998: 19) and to Monique Wittig's metaphor of 'the straight mind' (cf. Adrienne Rich's idea of 'compulsory heterosexuality' (Rich 1980)). The young women interviewed in the study tend to disassociate from their own bodies and thus do not practise, in their embodied experience, some of the 'safe sex' techniques that intellectually they are aware of and espouse. The study offers a powerful example of feminist praxis: combining theory and practice to suggest new ways of thinking and operating in a situation of immediate social significance.

The young women's disassociation can be characterised in two different ways. First, there is the woman's active constitution of her body and construction of her femininity in terms of what is perceived as desirable by men, rather than in terms of what may contribute to *her* desires. Secondly, there is her denial and repression of her material lived female body where and when its presence conflicts with the imaginary feminine. This body is a powerful presence that resists repression, as the authors of *The Male in the Head* graphically express it: 'Although the body which engages in sexual activity is always socially constituted and managed, it is also always material, hairy, discharging, emitting noises, and susceptible to pleasure and pain. This materiality is in danger of erupting into men's space and so has to be carefully regulated' (Holland *et al.* 1998: 8). At its most extreme, this regulation constitutes total self-erasure whereby the woman becomes no more than an orifice for male penetration. How men are inducted into these ideas of femininity and into their own masculinities has clear implications, for example, for the analysis of male sexual violence against women. Kerry Carrington's examination of the multiple rape and murder of a young Australian woman, *Who Killed Leigh Leigh?: A Story of Shame and Mateship in an Australian Town,* argues for the continuing need for a feminist analysis of masculinity and for the discussion of such cases in the context of socially pervasive ways of thinking about women, rather than as individual, and single, aberrations.

The processes of active constitution of femininity emerging from the young women's interviews discussed in *The Male in the Head* offer a good example of the power of the '**imaginary body**' as a body image distinct from, but highly influential over, the 'real' material body and its behaviour. Elizabeth Grosz suggests the usefulness, for the production of a new feminist theory of corporeality, of Schilder's theories of body image, formulated in the 1920s and 1930s. She offers the reservation, almost inevitable for feminists drawing on male theorists, that Schilder himself makes no mention of sexual difference (Grosz 1994: 82–3). This is how she describes Schilder's understanding of the body image: 'The body image is a map or representation of the degree of **narcissistic** investment of the subject in its own body and body parts' (p. 83). However, this map is not static but shifts and moves around, thus providing a means for coordinating into an apparently unified field (the self) the different sensations that a body's separate parts experience. Importantly, the body image is not coterminous with the body: 'there seems to be a time lag in the perception and registration of real changes in the body image' (p. 84). Grosz refers to anorexia, 'where the body image remains at the level of the preanorexic subject's weight' (p. 84). The idea of an imaginary body has also clear applications to the increasing use of cosmetic surgery as a radical alteration of the physical body.

As in Emily Martin's account of women, pregnancy and labour (see Chapter 2), the interviews in *The Male in the Head* (Holland *et al.* 1998) indicate an alienation or separation of the young women from their bodily experiencing selves, as distinct from the body appearance constructed and organised for outside view. This was particularly evident in terms of the heterosexual interactions which were the focus of the study. Thus, the young women in the study lacked vocabulary to describe their own sexual pleasure or, indeed, to give a personal description of themselves from inside, even when invited by direct questioning: 'In no instance did they respond in terms of a physical image. In general they had difficulty in answering this question at all, but when they did manage to do so, tended to speak of their personality or character or what their friends thought of them' (Holland *et al.* 1998: 111). This contrasted with the 'tremendous amount of careful thought and energy . . . invested in their physical presentation of self' (p. 111). This production of self, for many of the young women, seemed to construct an image of sexual knowledge and availability at odds with their actual experience and desires: 'The images which they devise . . . may be understood differently by the young women from the way in which they are read by the men who view them' (p. 110). In this commun- ication gap, given the powers invested in masculinity, abuse and danger can flourish: 'The overwhelming conclusion that came from the interviews was that femininity constituted an unsafe sexual identity' (p. 6).[3]

One of the strategies that some young women seem to adopt, albeit largely unconsciously, as a counter to the multiple risks they face, is to change body size:

> Young women can also attempt to take control of their body
> through anorexia, through celibacy, or through constructing
> themselves as unattractive to men. One young woman said she
> was a virgin at 21 and explained this in terms of the intersections
> of class and race in her own history, and the impossibility of her
> having a sexual relationship with the available black or white men.
> She gave an account of intentionally putting on weight and
> wearing unattractive clothing to avoid the complications
> of the sexual market place.
>
> (Holland *et al.* 1998: 119–20)

There are, of course, numerous different feminist analyses and discussions of the many ways in which women obey the injunctions of 'the male in the head' to change and adapt our bodies. One of the central points of debate among feminists is over the centrality of the heterosexual injunction and how far women can choose to take on some of the practices of body management for ourselves, even when we are all inevitably implicated in this heterosexual economy. Additionally, as commentators like bell hooks continually remind 'white' feminists, the female bodies, the 'ourselves', subject to these injunctions come in many different shapes, colours and forms, and claims for the universality of our experiences as *women*, need con- stant scrutiny and questioning. In this chapter, I shall focus on two areas that have particular prominence in our current culture and have, correspondingly, attracted a high degree of feminist attention and debate: eating disorders and cosmetic surgery.

Eating disorders or self-starving norms?

The idea of starving oneself is not peculiar to late-twentieth- century western capitalist society, nor entirely confined to women. However, as mentioned in the previous chapter, perhaps the dominant practice of body discipline for contemporary western women relates to body size. While this seems to be overwhelmingly related, as in other forms of management of women's appearance, to heterosexual attractiveness, it also carries with it, like the management of menopause and HRT, injunctions of individual responsibility for well-being – as opposed to being a burden on social health resources – and it is inextricably linked to consumer capitalism. There is a huge and thriving industry in products and processes promising to assist in the self-disciplining of the body: diet plans, cosmetic products, exercise machines, exercise programs, self-help books – and more.

However, this self-disciplining is not all to do with well-being, and a key element of Foucauldian analysis is the demonstration of inherent contradictions and discontinuities in the apparently seamless 'natural' order. The area of 'eating disorders' offers one such contradictory site. In many ways, the bulimic body which consumes but then purges food offers an exemplary paradigm of consumer capitalist society – constantly ingesting and expelling, never (ful)filled – but it can hardly be described as part of the general endorsement of well-being! The woman exhibiting anorexic behaviour would seem to be one of the most exemplary of docile bodies of our society in terms of exerting an inexorable will over recalcitrant flesh. Yet she is penalised by being classified as psychiatrically disordered when she has most obeyed society's injunctions. In her attempt to erase her body she seems to expose the ultimate logic of being a 'good girl' and a 'dutiful daughter'. As Noelle Caskey describes it: 'It is the literal mindedness of anorexia to take "the body" as a synonym for "the self", and to try to live in the world through a manipulation of "the body", particularly as it is reflected to the anorexic by the perceived wishes of others . . . Will alone produces it and maintains it against considerable physical odds' (Caskey 1985: 184). (When I first read this I was also coincidentally listening to an arts program on BBC radio. In a segment on ballet, a ballet master said, among other 'disciplinary' instructions to a class of 13-year-olds: 'I can't bear to see your fat arses – cover them up'.) However, for some feminist writers, particularly those writing in the early 1970s, anorexic behaviour is not at all a sign of extreme docility but of rebellion and refusal of precisely the kinds of femininity that Holland *et al.* see many of their young female interviewees conforming to. Perhaps it is possible to have it both ways and see 'the anorexic body' as very precisely embodying the constant contradictions women try to live with from day to day.

British writer Morag MacSween's *Anorexic Bodies: A Feminist and Sociological Perspective on Anorexia Nervosa* (1993) combines a review and critique of different analyses of anorexia with the voices of women both from in-depth interviews and open-ended question-naires. Her approach is similar to that used by the authors of *The Male in the Head* (Holland *et al.* 1998) in exploring the dissonances and congruency between academic or clinical literature and experi-ence as reported at first-hand. MacSween offers a particularly clear example of a feminist interest in the ways that anorexic bodies seem to address central issues of the different conceptualisation of male and female bodies and, in particular, the notions of openness and abjection discussed in Chapter 3. One continuing analysis offered for the over-representation of women among those treated for anorexia, and apparently borne out by many of the first-hand accounts, is revulsion towards the adult female body, perceived as lacking boundaries, leaky and incomplete. In this analysis, anorexia is construed as the attempt to create boundaries and effect closure or, in other words, to defeat abjection. This analysis is frequently brought to bear in the cases of women with anorexia who have sur-vived sexual abuse and assault. MacSween, like most recent feminist writers on the topic, seeks to remove anorexia from a category of individual pathology and reposition it within a broad contemporary cultural context of gender formations and power relations.

This context is riddled with complexities, as epitomised by some of the introductory comments of Susan Bordo, a leading United States feminist cultural-studies theorist. Bordo refers to her own engagement in a weight-loss program:

> I know . . . that although my weight loss has benefited me in a variety of ways, it has also diminished my efficacy as an alternative role model for my female students. I used to demonstrate the possibility of confidence, expressiveness, and success in a less than adequately normalized body. Today, my female students may be more likely to see me as confirmation that success comes from playing by the cultural rules . . . Even though my choice to diet was a conscious and 'rational' response to the system of cultural meanings that surround me . . . I should not deceive myself into thinking that my own feeling of enhanced personal comfort and power means that I am not servicing an oppressive system.
>
> (Introduction to Bordo 1993: *Unbearable Weight*, 31)

Appropriately for a writer so strongly influenced by Foucault, Bordo emphasises the interconnectedness of power relations, and their ambiguities, but as her use, in the above quotation, of the term 'oppressive' suggests, she is also careful to return to questions of unequal social power in terms both of gender and 'race'. Thereby she resists the charges of moral relativism often levelled at writers who employ poststructuralist theory.

Bordo's *Unbearable Weight* (1993) offers a ten-year development of her feminist research into the cultural constructions of women's body size through a collection of essays, many of which have appeared elsewhere. She is one of the most influential and much-cited writers in this field. Her work, in its engagement with philosophy, poststructuralist theory and cultural analysis and its inclusion of highly theoretical approaches alongside personal and political observation is, in many ways, paradigmatic of the intellectual trajectory followed by many western feminists through the last decade.

The relatively early essay, 'The Body and the Reproduction of Femininity',[4] situates her more specific and detailed explorations of cultural meanings in areas such as contemporary advertising, within her philosophical frame of reference. As is characteristic of contemporary western feminist philosophers, Bordo emphasises the centrality of dualism within western culture, tracking back its influence, and implications for women, to that culture's origins in classical Greece. Elizabeth Ellsworth (1982) sums up this position effectively, in her description of the Classical Greek 'founding father' of western philosophy, Plato: 'His misogyny is part of his somatophobia [fear of the body]: the body is seen as the source of all the undesirable traits a human being could have, and women's lives are spent manifesting those traits' (1982: 118). Bordo offers a more explicitly Foucauldian approach by providing a genealogy for contemporary ideas of the body, which includes discussions of the parallel, but differently inflected, development of hysteria as the late nineteenth-century western 'female malady', and of anorexia as the late-twentieth-century embodiment.

Dualism, for Bordo, has not only dominated mainstream western thought but has also prevailed within feminist thinking. She argues for the need to move away from an earlier (1960s–1970s) dualist construction of feminism as a defined oppositional force based on categories of 'oppressors and oppressed, villains and victims' (1993: 167). Foucauldian analysis, she suggests, by reconstituting power as a nexus or web of connecting forces that operate in specific ways within a specific time and location, opens up possibilities of negotiation and movement which the absolute oppositional categories lack. These possibilities have their own specific limits and constraints.

Bordo argues that anorexia nervosa epitomises the condition of contemporary western society, playing out the contradictory and interwoven forces of our particular place and time. She offers an account of the emergence of a taxonomy of 'eating disorders' that constitutes them as clinical conditions and those who exhibit them as clinical subjects. Feminist clinical practitioners, like Susie Orbach, who, Bordo argues, maintain a commitment to the clinical approach and operate within the clinical frame of reference, reinforce the perception of the conditions as 'aberrant' and 'bizarre'. For Bordo, the significance of the conditions extends far beyond the clinical category of individual victim in need of a cure. She follows both Mary Douglas and Foucault in seeing the individual physical body as also embodying the collective 'social body': 'The anorectic thus appears, not as the victim of a unique and "bizarre" pathology, but as the bearer of very distressing tidings about our culture' (Bordo 1993: 60). It is Bordo's extended project, over the ten years represented by this collection, to be the news reader and interpreter of those messages about culture.

Critiquing the clinic

In exploring the construction of a pathology of eating disorders, Bordo draws on similar strategies to those used by Emily Martin and other contemporary feminists engaged with an exploration of the medicalisation of the female body. She in no way denies the individual suffering or the inevitability of medical intervention when eating problems threaten life, but insists that social and political action for change depends on moving beyond the individual and understanding the processes in which she is embedded and through which her experience is constructed. Bordo's examples, therefore, tend to be drawn not from the extremes of clinical practice but from 'ordinary' life.[5] In discussing the ubiquitousness of injunctions to be slim, particularly in advertising, she concludes:

> Watching the commercials is a little girl, perhaps ten years old, whom I saw in Central Park, gazing raptly at her father, bursting with pride: 'Daddy, guess what? I lost two pounds!' And watching the commercials is the anorectic, who associates her relentless pursuit of thinness with power and control, but who in fact destroys her health and imprisons her imagination. She is surely the most startling and stark illustration of how cavalier power

> relations are with respect to the motivations and goals of
> individuals, yet how deeply they are etched on our bodies,
> and how well our bodies serve them.
>
> (Bordo 1993: 164)

The phrasing of this last sentence is solidly Foucauldian in its detachment of the idea of power from notions of conscious individual
intention, and thus from a dualist opposition of culprit/victim,
oppressor/oppressed.

In a very useful, clearly written overview of the development
of feminist perspectives on anorexia, Australian Matra Robertson
(1992) concentrates on the discourses of 'eating disorders'. Like
Bordo, she sees 'anorexia' as a construction of modern medical
practice concerned with objectifying individuals into a discipline of
symptoms, classifications and 'cures'. Robertson seeks to distinguish
how, as a construct, 'anorexia' has accrued cultural meanings different from those accorded to earlier forms of 'self-starvation':
'"Anorexia nervosa" has become a complex combination of folk
term and medical category. The term "anorexia" is filtered to
women through biopolitical channels, so it becomes a means of
structuring and making sense of non-eating behaviour' (Robertson
1992: 19). It is, for Robertson, of high significance that the term
'anorexia' has been so completely assimilated into popular usage
from the clinical discourse in which it originated. Again, in common with Bordo, Robertson argues that this popular acceptance
of the term as a catch-all label forecloses debate or analysis of the
wider implications of a cultural imperative to control body size,
especially in women.

While Bordo comes from an academic, philosophical back-
ground, Robertson's interest and concern comes directly out of
health-worker counselling experience, and she constantly argues
for the need to reclaim the experience of 'self-starvation', and
recovery, from a clinical discourse that isolates self-starving women
as psychiatric cases. For Robertson this is a highly gendered issue
whereby women are given more responsibility (and blame) for
maintaining healthy bodies than men. In particular, she points to
the identification and cordoning off of eating disorder as a female
psychiatric problem, as distinct from 'life-style' physical problems
attributed to male bodies:

> While self-starvation is certainly life-threatening, mortality statistics
> indicate that heart disease is the major cause of death in New
> South Wales. How is it that men with beer bellies, as they court

death (according to the medical literature) by excessive drinking and eating, are not also generally referred to psychiatrists? The dominant discourses regarding the body position men and women in different places.

(Robertson 1992: 17)

In arguing the need for a re-thinking and a new discourse she effects a bridge of praxis between the extreme positions of theory *or* practice. One of her central concerns is the way that the pathologising of 'self-starvation' as a clinical condition can overdetermine an individual as 'the anorexic':

> There is a distinction between feminist therapists who try to establish alternative treatments for the constructed entity 'the anorexic', and feminists who work alongside self-starving women in deconstructing the totalised object – the anorexic . . . Weight restoration to save a woman's life and stabilise her nutritionally is a first priority . . . Yet it is vital that in the process the woman with the weight-loss symptoms is not obscured, and that an anorexic identity is not created for her.

(Robertson 1992: 77)

Integral to Robertson's concerns here is the perception that issues of identity seem to be central to many experiences of 'self-starvation'. Some of the earlier feminist therapists, like Susie Orbach and Kim Chernin, worked from Freudian-derived theories – most commonly, object-relations theory – focusing on the ways in which children achieve, or fail to achieve, independence from maternal figures. Robertson suggests that they still assert an authoritative clinical perspective: 'It is rare in any analysis of anorexia nervosa to hear the voice of the woman who is being treated for anorexia' (p. 51). For much of her book, Robertson substitutes the words 'self-starver' and 'self-starvation' for 'anorexic' and 'anorexia' as a strategy for destabilising the ways that western culture has fully interiorised and naturalised the clinical 'objective' designation, and to restore embodied meanings.

While reading Robertson together with Bordo, the power of Robertson's strategy struck me. Bordo offers as one example of the cultural ubiquitousness of 'slenderness', a comment by film-star Sylvester Stallone that 'he likes his women "anorexic"' with the result that 'his then girlfriend, Cornelia Guest, immediately lost twenty-four pounds' (Bordo 1993: 60). Suppose we substitute 'self-starved' for 'anorexic' in that statement – there is a shift to the bodily processes and damage that 'anorexic' erases, an inclusion of an ethical dimension that 'anorexic' obscures.

Other erasures are brought about by such clinical approaches as the profiling, for predictive purposes, of 'types' most likely to develop eating disorders. In terms of racial stereotyping, Bordo observes that a tendency to rely on slightly out-dated statistics can ignore the increase of eating disorders across ethnic and 'racial' groups since the statistics identify the condition as predominantly affecting middle-class and 'white' women. This can impact directly on the experience of women seeking help: 'To imagine that African American women are immune to the standards of slenderness that reign today is . . . to come very close to the racist notion that the art and glamour – the culture – of femininity belong to the white woman alone' (Bordo 1993: 63). Bordo illustrates this with the experience of a young Black woman who approached her school counsellor about weight problems and was told not to worry because it wasn't a 'black issue': 'Saddled with these projected racial notions, the young woman, who had struggled with compulsive eating and yo-yo dieting for years, was left alone to deal with an eating disorder that she wasn't "supposed" to have' (p. 63). In the British context, there is some evidence that Black women in 'mixed race' hetero-sexual relationships conceal or change their body size to conform to 'white' expectations (Weekes 1997).[6]

While many feminist researchers are now far less ready to dismiss the usefulness of quantitative methods than they used to be, most would still suggest the need for great care and selectiveness in reliance on statistical tools, and the importance of a reflective con-sideration of their research methods and methodologies. A very recent study of anorexia by Australian Catherine Garrett (1998) is typical of such an approach. Garrett acknowledges the limits of her sample of participants but also analyses the extent to which they conform to or diverge from existing clinical statistics.

Garrett's study introduces a different dimension to anorexia. While most other feminist studies concentrate on psycho-social and/or cultural aspects, Garrett reintroduces ideas of spirituality. Foucauldian–feminist analyses have tended to position the spiritual as an historical, culturally specific, dimension of earlier forms of self-starvation: notably in the case of early Christian mystics. Garrett argues for its relevance to the contemporary condition. In this she reflects an observable development over the last decade of a femin-ism which has found a spiritual dimension lacking in many forms of western-feminist thinking.[7] In concentrating on narrative, Garrett seems to address directly Robertson's concerns about the absence in the literature of the voices of women being treated for anorexia.

Current feminist interest in the phenomenon of 'eating disorders' continues the ongoing feminist project of challenging the practices and the discourses of medical and related clinical sciences as they categorise and objectify women's bodies. While some feminist analysts continue to work within clinical frameworks, while introducing some gendered, cultural perspectives, others attempt to deconstruct those frameworks and challenge their terms of reference. One of the main forms this deconstruction takes is the replacing of clinical and popularised-clinical terms by a more embodied vocabulary. As Margrit Shildrick observes in another context, if medicine were to take on cultural interpretation as a central factor this would necessarily change the model: 'If there is neither a fixed reality of health and disease, nor yet a natural body to restore to good health, then what is at stake when health professionals intervene in the lives of individuals?' (Shildrick 1997: 57).

Under the knife

Women's dieting and its development into 'eating disorders' can be seen, from certain feminist perspectives, as the extreme embodiment of women's interiorisation of injunctions concerning body shape. That is, the women themselves enact the disciplinary regimes on their own bodies.[8] Apart from the extreme interventions of force-feeding and the deliberate with-holding of food, the majority of adults in western societies have control over our food intake. Surgical interventions may constitute a somewhat different relationship of the self to the body and of the imaginary and physical bodies being managed, in so far as they require the submission of the body to another: the surgeon and his [sic] technologies. Another difference may lie in the relative reversibility of dieting: a notorious feature of 'normal' diets is the high degree of recidivism whereby the body seems to desire to return to its pre-diet shape. In much of the diet literature, metaphors are used that evoke ideas of a battleground and stress the need for the dieter to be vigilant against 'sneaky' attempts of the fat to return! These metaphors for parts of the body (fat) as enemy and Other are mirrored in the terms that women with 'eating disorders' seem to refer to their entire bodies, as Another who must be punished and distanced.

Surgery effects a much more permanent alteration and presents a set of contradictions around the idea of **plasticity**. In these contradictions and their interpretation, some contemporary feminist debates about the usefulness or otherwise of postmodernist theories can be located. Plasticity, according to Susan Bordo, is paradigmatic of our period of late modernity: the body as 'cultural plastic' has replaced the older model of the body as a machine ('"Material Girl": The Effacements of Postmodern Culture' in Bordo 1993: 215–44). Similarly, Kathy Davis (1995) places cosmetic surgery as characteristic of 'the cultural landscape of late modernity: consumer capitalism, technological development, liberal individualism, and the belief in the makeability [sic] of the human body' (pp. 28–9). On the one hand, a belief in the plasticity of the body argues for an open-ended range of possibilities of change: of being, as the advertisements promise, anyone you want to be. On the other hand, 'plastic' has become synonymous with rigidity and indestructibility: as the many failures of silicon breast-implantation has all too painfully inscribed literally on the bodies of women. Davis draws attention to the historical process whereby surgical practices that were developed as extreme, and often risky, remedies for severe health problems are now common, but still dangerous and painful interventions in healthy bodies.

In Bordo's analysis, the emphasis on personal freedom to choose, characteristic of certain areas of postmodernist thought, masks the lived experiences of bodies marked by economic, 'racial' and other differences. She is sceptical of the usefulness for feminism of a postmodernist cultural analysis that argues that '(w)hat the body does is immaterial, so long as the imagination is free. This abstract, unsituated, disembodied freedom . . . celebrates itself only through the effacement of the material praxis of people's lives, the normalizing power of cultural images, and the sadly continuing social realities of dominance and subordination' (Bordo 1993: 275). In this she shares a concern of material feminists to separate what Teresa Ebert has called 'ludic postmodernism' from those aspects of postmodernist thought that seem applicable for feminist–political purposes (Ebert 1996).

What choice?

Bordo, as in all her writing, turns to contemporary cultural examples to illustrate her argument and to reinsert the materiality of bodies. Citing a particular session of the American Phil Donahue talk-show, Bordo explores the way a discourse of individual choice that has become naturalised among both the white and Black women in the audience works to suppress the minority attempt to insert a, mildly, political perspective. Bordo's main point is that, while 'choice' appears to be egalitarian, there are dominant preferred patterns of 'beauty' and 'normality' that are, on examination, caucasian and which impose their own parameters on those 'choices'. In her introduction to *Unbearable Weight*, Bordo asks rhetorically, 'Does anyone in this culture have his or her nose reshaped to look more "African" or "Jewish"?' (Bordo 1993: 25).

Many contemporary feminist writers share with Bordo a commitment to exposing the extent to which supposedly neutral or universal ideas of 'beauty', which of course contribute significantly to the construction of the imaginary body, have quite clear reference points in the white mainstream culture which is the principal culture purveyed by global media. bell hooks has written extensively on the pervasiveness of this white imaginary body, with particular reference to its meanings for African–American women. She offers a further perspective on the matter of Black women's relationship to body-size and shape, by drawing attention to the ways in which the bodies of Black women as entertainers (singers, models and actors) in mainstream cultural production are altered and produced to serve a racialised imagination (hooks 1992). As one example, hooks explores the ways that the singer, Aretha Franklin, has constructed herself and has been constructed, as presented in a PBS documentary: 'Much space was given in the documentary to white male producers who shaped her image' (p. 69). bell hooks goes on to suggest that the film 'can be seen as a visual narrative documenting her (Franklin's) obsessive concern with the body and achieving a look suggesting desirability. To achieve this end, Franklin constantly struggles with her weight' (p. 70). Even more extreme, hooks suggests, are the surgical interventions used to manipulate 'racial' features to the particular dictates of the white culture's desire for sameness or difference at any particular moment.

While 'white' entertainers similarly alter lips, breasts, and other features to the dictates of the fashionable feminine, hooks argues that 'non-white' women have an additional imperative, produced by their exoticised and sexualised position within the white imagination. Barbara Omolade (1983) argues powerfully for the centrality of the history of slavery in the particular material dissection and commodification of African–American women's bodies. Similarly, one could argue that the specific history of Indigenous

Australian women has created a quite specific relationship for them to mainstream contemporary culture's fashioning of 'the body' (see Brook 1997).

Analyses of differences among women in 'racial', ethnic, economic and other terms, draw attention to the limitations on the freedom of choice implied by terms like 'elective' and 'corrective' surgery. Similarly, such analyses suggest the utopian impossibility of some postmodernist gestures towards a totally free play of identity. For Anne Balsamo (1996) cosmetic surgery 'literally transforms the material body into a sign of culture' by tailoring it to conform. Balsamo's focus is on the ways that new technologies can still be inscribed within traditional gender and racial orders and thus aid in the establishment and maintenance of norms. In discussing cosmetic surgery, she uses as a reference point the contemporary reapplication of **anthropometry** to the realm of elective surgery, and draws attention to the normalising effects that this reapplication

---

From Jacqueline Urla and Alan C. Swedlund's 'The Anthropometry of Barbie'[*]

(T)he anthropometrically measured 'normal' body has been anything but value-free. Formulated in the context of a race-, class-, and gender-stratified society, there is no doubt that quantitatively defined ideal types or standards have been both biased and oppressive. Incorporated into weight tables, put on display in museums and world's fairs, and reprinted in popular magazines, these scientifically endorsed standards produce what Foucault calls 'normalizing effects', shaping, in not altogether healthy ways, how individuals see themselves and their bodies. Nevertheless, in the contemporary cultural context, where an impossibly thin image of women's bodies has become the most popular children's toy ever sold, it strikes us that recourse to the 'normal' body might just be the power tool we need for destabilizing a fashion fantasy spun out of control. It was with this in mind that we asked students in one of our social biology classes to measure Barbie to see how her body compared to the average measurements of young American women of the same period.

[*This article centres on an application of anthropometric measurements to 'Barbie' and associated dolls.

Source: Terry and Urla 1995: 293.

produces. Anthropometry has a politically dubious history of being put to the service of eugenicist beliefs. Balsamo stresses that she is not attacking the practice of anthropometry as itself necessarily racist or misogynist (she points out that data can, for example, be used in formulating traffic safety standards) but argues that its applications demand some scrutiny when they are used to universalise cultural assumptions that are culturally specific.

Through technologies such as digital imaging, surgeons can offer multiple potential versions of 'you': but, Balsamo reminds us, these are multiple rather than infinite. In the surgeon's selection of possibilities, enabled by anthropometric data, choices have already been made that favour particular western models. Balsamo offers a number of examples from cosmetic-surgery literature; Bordo's comments about styles of noses makes the point graphically clear. When the cosmetic-surgery industry argues for technology's role in achieving 'regularity' or sameness it makes a clear, though usually non-explicit, reference to a western cultural model. Balsamo refers to the increase of a form of blepharoplasty – eyelid surgery – among women of 'Asian' origin, and the ways in which the literature of cosmetic surgery seems to try to deny its cultural biases while at the same time endorsing them (Balsamo 1996: 62–3).

Balsamo argues that the production of these ideal images through technology is gendered as well as eurocentric: there are differences in application for male and female bodies undergoing cosmetic surgery. For Balsamo, the images are not only racially inscribed but also produced within a heterosexual economy which moves to fragment and designate, for heterosexual use, the female body. A concomitant effect, of central concern to Balsamo's feminist analysis, is that women come to devalue (further) that material body which, as Holland *et al.* (1998) so vividly describe, disrupts and transgresses against ideal femininity.

Balsamo has been accused of failing to give adequate recognition to the economic dimensions of cosmetic surgery. According to Pippa Brush (1998), Balsamo's suggestion that there needs to be a re-orienting of feminist perspectives on cosmetic surgery towards a view of it as 'fashion surgery' erases the reality that cosmetic surgery costs money. Balsamo's position, for Brush, is too close to the kind of postmodernist feminism that Teresa Ebert terms 'ludic'. Brush, like Ebert, is deeply suspicious of any appeals to an individualist freedom of choice that seem to minimise economic realities. In partial defence of Balsamo it might be pointed out that, while the costs of surgery are very high in most western countries, there has been a perceptible expansion of its availability beyond the realm of what one US magazine calls 'Knifestyles of the Rich and Famous' (Bordo 1993: 246). Popular women's magazines in Britain and Australia have recently introduced readers' advice columns on 'nose jobs', 'tummy tucks', etc.

The question then arises, to what extent are 'we' as consumers of such magazines and, possibly, of cosmetic surgery, victims of the industry and of patriarchal constructions of femininity? How far does surgery offer a way for us to be agents of our own destinies and how far does it disempower us?

Opposed positions on this question are presented by Kathryn Pauly Morgan (1991) and Kathy Davis (1995). Morgan emphasises the disciplinary nature of cosmetic surgery. Like Balsamo she points to its homogenising of women's shapes and forms. She too suggests that the choices offered about appearance are heavily policed and that deviance is punished, so that, to avoid punishment, we must correctly interpret what is the 'right choice'. For Morgan, as cosmetic surgery gradually becomes normalised, women who do *not* seek cosmetic surgery will be at risk of being ostracised and labelled deviant. (This could be compared to the way in which national campaigns that place responsibility for 'well-being' on individuals render those who do not consume treatment like HRT, culpably irresponsible.)

Morgan also employs ideas about the validity of women's own reported experiences of cosmetic surgery in terms which recall earlier feminist notions of 'false consciousness'. Thus, women who report positively about cosmetic surgery must be constructed as deceived, coerced and victimised. In this model there is a clear polarisation of what Morgan offers as the 'good' feminist position and its opposite, with little or no room for negotiation.

Kathy Davis (1995), in a controversial and detailed study of cosmetic surgery, takes issue with Morgan on a number of points, of which one of the most pressing is her allegation that Morgan discounts women's own words. Davis suggests that there needs to be a clear difference made between research that is based largely on media reports and quotations and research based, like her own, on face-to-face interview and recording: 'Morgan does not reflect on the textual practices and discursive formations which construct women's voices in the media' (1995: 167). That is, Davis raises a central concern of contemporary feminist research methodology: to distinguish the different discourses organising the expression of

experience. Davis sees Morgan as using selected material to promote a pre-existing political platform that cosmetic surgery is wrong.
She contrasts this with her own approach which she characterises
as open-ended and concerned with finding out why women opt for
cosmetic surgery. She names this, memorably, as the task of moving
away from the idea that women are 'cultural dopes'.

One particularly interesting aspect of Davis' research is its
site within the medical institution of The Netherlands. As Davis
emphasises, The Netherlands was, at the time of her research,
virtually the only country to offer cosmetic surgery as part of its
national health system. This meant that some of the issues about
access and economics could be eliminated from the study, giving
it a wider application across a range of different women than could
be the case elsewhere.

While Davis pays tribute to the important work done by feminist
cultural analysts like Bordo, in providing a scrutiny of the practices
and ideologies of cosmetic surgery, she feels something still needed
to be explored: 'While I am now armed with a critical perspective
on cosmetic surgery, I am left empty-handed in terms of how to
take women who have cosmetic surgery seriously' (Davis 1995: 58).
In addressing this problem, and paying attention to the women's
own explanations, she consciously engaged in what she calls 'a kind
of feminist balancing act' (p. 5). She laid herself open to charges of
'going soft' on cosmetic surgery (despite the fact that she positions
it 'as one of the most pernicious expressions of the western beauty
culture') by suggesting that for individual women, even given the
oppressive ideologies and power issues involved, it may be the best
thing to do in their particular situations (p. 5). As she records later
in the book, many feminist critics failed to be impressed by her
sense of balance.

Davis identifies Dorothy Smith, Iris Marion Young and Sandra
Bartky as feminist theorists who take women's explanations seriously: Smith for her ideas of women's agency; Young for her
emphasis on women as 'embodied subjects'; and Bartky for her
designation of women's 'ambiguous ethical position' (Davis 1995:
59–64). Davis' own study seeks to combine these perspectives.
One of the most interesting suggestions that Davis develops from
her observation and conversation with the women undergoing or
seeking surgery, is that part of the agency they develop (in Smith's
terms) is as narrators of their own story. This is similar to the
emphasis placed by Garrett (1998) on narratives of recovery from

eating disorders. Davis discerns recurrent narrative patterns in the women's stories which characteristically place the woman herself as the heroic protagonist of an epic, in which she must success-fully overcome obstacles (like the medical inspector) in order to complete her quest.

While the quest's immediate object is the surgical operation, Davis argues that it is also about making over the self as, in Young's terms, an embodied subject: 'Cosmetic surgery was presented as part of a woman's struggle to feel at home in her body – a subject with a body rather than just a body' (Davis 1995: 161). She main-tains that the stories of many of the women reveal an awareness of the different ways that the surgery can be interpreted: the 'ambiguous ethical position' (Bartky) in which they have placed themselves. In focusing on the active seeking of cosmetic surgery as a means of assertion rather than submission as a 'cultural dope', Davis relocates 'beauty' as one aspect rather than the single goal. In so doing, she offers a way out of the ideological trap of 'the beauty myth' which at once both urges women to conform to its ideals and accuses us of narcissism when we do.

At the very centre of much of the feminist debate and interest in areas such as cosmetic surgery and eating disorders is the ques-tion of what, if anything, constitutes a 'natural' female body. As we have seen in previous chapters, Elizabeth Grosz has argued that this should be dismissed as a non-question, in order for feminist theory to develop new conceptualisations of body, identity and self. However, as Pippa Brush (1998) discusses, the phantom natural body inhabits many of the current analyses whether as a moment of nostalgia or as a desired material site, and the ways in which we speak about bodies is historically saturated with ideas of origins and foundations – what Grosz has called, 'the body as a kind of natural bedrock' (Grosz 1994: 144).

If terms and discourses are so heavily saturated with a particu-lar conception of the body then perhaps, the actions of surgery could perhaps speak more loudly and radically if they were not, themselves, so thoroughly bound up in the medical models of our time. The work of some performance artists, in particular, the French artist Orlan, attempt to embody this through their work. Orlan has offered a public explanation that the ongoing series of cosmetic surgery she has undertaken, directed, filmed and offered for view is her confrontation with the idea of self as stable and the body as natural. Arguably, Orlan's feminist agency rests in her devising and organisation of the operations, so that the surgeons, rather than controlling her, become her tools. The filming of the processes and their immediate after-effects (bruising, distortion and pain) keep in sight the materiality of the operations, which the standard literature and promotion of cosmetic surgery disguises or minimalises. Further, Orlan's overall plan is to reproduce isolated facial parts from icons of European feminine beauty: it is possible to interpret this as a satirical deconstruction both of that aesthetic and the natural (Auslander 1997; Brush 1998).

In examining the ways that women perceive and seek to radically change our bodies, contemporary feminists differ in the extent to which they consider the women to be constructed by and, at worst, oppressed by discourses of heterosexuality and femininity. The emphasis on 'compulsory heterosexism' means that there is an absence in many of the accounts, of lesbian women's narratives regarding both cosmetic surgery and 'eating disorders'. In exploring the embodied experiences of women with 'eating disorders' and those seeking cosmetic surgery, contemporary feminist researchers emphasise the importance of women's narratives and seek to distinguish them from objectifying clinical discourses. This focus on narrative is part of a move to localise and particularise the experience and materiality of women, by rewriting the terms and concepts.

Summary

* Much contemporary feminist discussion of women's management of body size is influenced by some of Michel Foucault's theories of disciplinary surveillance as a marker of the modern period; women's bodies as a principal site for medical surveillance; and the need to reconceptualise power as interconnected webs rather than polar oppositions.

* Central to many feminist analyses of this area is the belief that women's bodies are organised by a heterosexual economy in which 'beauty' is defined as heterosexual attractiveness and women 'interiorise' the surveillance of an imagined male observer.

- This 'beauty' is not abstract but situated in specific western values which organise the lives of those in western societies, and other cultures through global media.

- Concepts of 'imaginary bodies' and questions of identity formation inform many contemporary feminist approaches to this area.

- Interpretations of 'anorexia' highlight the contradictions of its development, some seeing it as extreme docility and others as rebellion. Characteristics of anorexic behaviour include attempts to negate the (perceived) permeability of the female body.

- Susan Bordo's approach is representative of a materialist–feminist analysis that has some but highly selective engagements with poststructuralist theories. For Bordo, 'anorexia' needs to be rethought and positioned, not as an aberrant or bizarre pathology but as paradigmatic of contemporary culture.

- Other writers have also argued for the importance of re-naming and repositioning 'eating disorders' and the women who have them. This constitutes a challenge to medical models and their tendency to categorise and 'objectify' their subjects.

- Both dieting and cosmetic surgery can be seen as ways of materialising the 'imaginary body'. Feminists debate to what extent the women who diet/elect for surgery are actively generating a 'new self'.

- Cosmetic surgery is becoming increasingly normalised in western society: a number of problems are identified by some feminist theorists with this process. Some like Balsamo, locate this process in the rise of new technologies of surveillance. Others situate it primarily within contemporary late-capitalist economics.

- As in other areas of feminist research, there is a strong emphasis on the power of narrative both as a site of recovery and of the active constitution of an embodied subject.

- The particular examples of 'eating disorders' and cosmetic surgery as extreme interventions in the body enable and necessitate consideration of what constitute 'natural' bodies: a question at the heart of much feminist thought.

Notes

1 A useful survey of the uses, and problems, of feminist appropriation of Foucauldian approaches can be found in Caroline Ramazonoglu's edited collection, *Up Against Foucault: Explorations of Some Tensions between Foucault and Feminism* (1993) London and New York: Routledge. The editor's introduction offers a quick tour of some of the issues for feminism and a basic definition of some Foucauldian terms.

2 The vocabulary of 'anorexia', 'eating disorders', etc. is called into question by feminist analysis, as the following discussion will explore.

3 It is interesting to compare this with Carrington's analysis of the Leigh Leigh murder in which, she stresses, the young women who attended the beach party preceding the rape and murder did not appear to be emphasising their femininity in this way. Indeed, she speculates that the 'provocation' that the young men perceived to be offered by Leigh Leigh was her 'unfeminine' active expression of desire for one of them, and her refusal of indiscriminate sex. This raises questions about how far any sexual identity is 'safe' for women.

4 The original published form of this essay (in Jaggar and Bordo's collection, *Gender/Body/Knowledge* 1989), was much more explicit about its Foucauldian context. It was originally subtitled, 'A Feminist Appropriation of Foucault'. The subtitle is dropped for the *Unbearable Weight* publication.

5 Bordo does, however, draw on some first-hand accounts of specific aversive reactions to body shape, size, and functions such as menstruation. These are individual experiences rather than clinical case-notes.

6 In emphasising the priority of issues of colour, Weekes qualifiedly allows: 'on the whole Black women may not suffer greatly from the problems of anorexia' (1997: 115). Bordo's analysis might suggest the usefulness of including the word 'yet'.

7 This dimension can be observed, for example, in certain areas of eco–feminism in alignments with 'New Age' philosophies, and it has, of course, always been a focus for feminists within the more established religions.

8 Or, perhaps, again this should be expressed as 'our' if we follow the belief that all women in our society are, to at least some extent, influenced by these injunctions.

Further reading

Balsamo, Anne (1996) 'On the Cutting Edge: Cosmetic Surgery and New Imaging Technologies'. In *Technologies of the Gendered Bodies: Reading Cyborg Women*. Durham and London: Duke University Press (pp. 56–79).

Bordo, Susan (1993) *Unbearable Weight: Feminism, Western Culture, and the Body*. Berkeley: University of California Press.
(See particularly, 'Whose Body is This? Feminism, Medicine, and the Conceptualization of Eating Disorders' pp. 45–69; 'Hunger as Ideology' pp. 99–134; 'Anorexia Nervosa: Psychopathology as the Crystallization of Culture' pp. 139–64.)

Davis, Kathy (1995) *Reshaping the Female Body: The Dilemmas of Cosmetic Surgery*. New York and London: Routledge.

Morgan, Kathryn Pauly (1991) 'Women and the Knife: Cosmetic Surgery and the Colonization of Women's Bodies'. *Hypatia*. 6.3 (Fall): 25–53.

Robertson, Matra (1992) *Starving in the Silences: An Exploration of Anorexia Nervosa*. North Sydney: Allen and Unwin.

Urla, Jacqueline and Swedlund, Alan C. (1995) 'The Anthropometry of Barbie: Unsettling Ideals of the Feminine Body in Popular Culture'. In Jennifer Terry and Jacqueline Urla (eds) *Deviant Bodies: Critical Perspectives on Difference in Science and Popular Culture*. Bloomington: Indiana University Press.

Chapter 5

Public bodies

Chapter outline

The absence of women as subjects of the law and within the discourses of 'human rights'. Feminist critiques and strategies within the law. Issues of cultural difference.

- The body politic — metaphors of the body and the state; 'neutrality' and law.
- Public/private — private and public subjects of the law; sexual/social contract.
- 'Benchmark man' and rationality — the male-gendered body as subject of the law; gendered 'reasonableness'.
- Rights and the body of the citizen — gendering 'human rights' in international law.
- Women subjects of the law — problems of 'writing' embodied woman into the law.
- Questions of voice — cultural difference and cross-cultural issues of law; feminist 'world-travelling'.

The body politic

In western thought, the metaphor of the body politic regularly occurs from Classical Greek times to the present. This metaphor images the governance system of a society (the state) as a human body in which various groups or organisations function like the limbs, internal organs, etc., each with its specific functions that contribute to the whole. Western feminism, in analysing and critiquing this metaphor, has concentrated on two particular areas: first, the exposure of the body evoked in the metaphor as not neutral but sexed-male; second, the establishment of human bodies as political rather than only natural. The feminist work in these two linked areas has, of course, immense implications for new ways of perceiving how different bodies are organised and dealt with in those systems and organisations dominated by the illusionary metaphor of the neutral body – in particular, the legal system. Jo Bridgeman and Susan Millns (1995: xix) observe that this feminist analysis has revealed women 'to be alien to the legal system: foreign bodies inhabiting a hostile terrain'. Similar claims are made of the political system, as a region in which women are, at best, foreigners – our bodies always signalling our difference from the (male) body politic. The law purports to be disinterested and above the constraints of the embodied individual and yet, as Carol Smart observes: 'Law has been deeply interested in things corporeal' and claims the right to make judgements regarding them (1989: 92).

For Moira Gatens, the body politic is organised by fantasies and desires around an imaginary masculine body. This single model invests the institutions with a dynamic that draws everything back into sameness and erases difference, with profound and often injurious consequences for those whose bodies do not approximate the model:

> Recent feminist work has shown that the neutral body assumed by the liberal state is implicitly a masculine body. Our legal and political arrangements have man as the model, the centre-piece, with the occasional surrounding legislative insets concerning abortion, rape, maternity allowance, and so on. None of these insets, however, takes female embodiment seriously . . . Man is the model and it is his body which is taken for the human body; his reason which is taken for Reason; his morality which is formalized into a system of ethics.
>
> (Gatens 1996: 24)

Gatens joins other feminist analysts of silences in arguing that the dominance of this model in public life means that women's voices cannot be heard: 'Who can decipher the language of a hysteric, the wails of a hyena, the jabbering of a savage – apart from other hysterics, hyenas and savages?' (Gatens 1996: 26) Echoing Luce Irigaray's description of 'woman' as literally unspeakable,[1] Gatens continues: 'Our political vocabulary is so limited that it is not possible, within its parameters, to raise the kind of questions that would allow the articulation of bodily difference: it will not tolerate an embodied speech' (p. 26). If this idea is carried through into the specific example of women entering party politics, then it renders it virtually impossible for an 'embodied female' voice to be heard at all: indeed, Gatens speculates that a realisation of this may have led to the withdrawal of a female US presidential candidate, Pat Schroeder, from the 1987 elections.

One of the most heated debates between contemporary feminists concerns the usefulness of 'poststructuralist'/'postmodernist' theories for feminist politics. Gatens' argument might be seen as fuel for the anti-postmodernist arguments in that it seems to deny the possibility of any effective engagement for change in existing political institutions. How then is it possible, if at all, to address this dilemma? Some of the essays collected by Judith Butler and Joan W. Scott, in *Feminists Theorize the Political* (1992) attempt an answer by exploring different ways in which the **decentring of the subject** can be applied in a different kind of feminist analysis of traditional areas of feminist concerns around the body, such as rape and abortion. Gatens' concern, in *Imaginary Bodies*, is with the importance of developing an adequate ethics that acknowledges its own history – rather than relying on appeals to ahistorical and immutable values:

> Ethical systems which acknowledge their historical forms of embodiment highlight their own genealogies, their own historical and social production. As such, we are *accountable* for the present in that we are *responsible* for those present possibilities which become actual through our actions. Far from this state of affairs plunging us into a postmodern desert where it is no longer possible to say anything or judge anything, it opens the possibility of engagement with others as genuine others, rather than as inferior, or otherwise subordinated, versions of the same.
>
> (Gatens 1996: 105)

Again, this concern for genealogies of female experiences and female bodies aligns Gatens with Irigaray. Gatens shares, with the contributors to Butler and Scott's collection, a concern to move outside polarities of oppression and resistance into a rethinking of the conditions which produce specific injustices. Her most recent publication, 'Institutions, Embodiment and Sexual Difference' is the first chapter in a collection very firmly grounded in the material conditions of women's lives (Gatens and Mackinnon 1998). Here, she centrally challenges the structural organisation of western society into 'public and private' spheres: a set of binaries in which 'the private' is subordinated, feminised, and denied political validity. A need to deconstruct these binaries is also at the heart of much feminist-law analysis, as reflected in edited collections by Margaret Thornton (1995b) (Australian) and Jo Bridgeman and Susan Millns (1995) (British).

For many writers concerned with issues of law and the allied field of citizenship, there is a need for a critical examination of terms such as 'rights' which underpin both western-democratic legal discourse and much of the discourse of 'liberatory' politics. For these theorists, 'rights' has a suspect history in western humanism, which needs to be acknowledged through the construction of genealogies. The challenges offered to existing legal and political systems by proposals to rethink their foundational terms is, it is argued by their proponents, a much more radical and momentous process than any attempt to change aspects of the systems from within. Furthermore, such a move is bound to be resisted and disarmed because of the homogenising inertia of the systems, described by Gatens above, and the force of the interests invested in them. This analysis in terms of the legal discipline and its institutions has parallels with the claims made by Shildrick and others, that isolated interventions in the medical and related disciplines need to be replaced, or at least accompanied by, larger reassessments of the assumptions and philosophy underpinning them.

Such a reassessment is also important on the part of western feminist analysis itself, as Bridgeman and Millns' comments about diversity indicate. While, arguably, the analysis of western democratic government and legal systems is internationally relevant because of the dispersion of those systems through colonisation, writers familiar with other political and legal systems argue the need for diverse perspectives to be considered with some recognition of their different cultural contexts. The 'woman of legal discourse' is not singular, all laws are not western nor are all political systems modelled on western democracy. Even where the west has been most influential, in the colonial and ex-colonial context, differences apply. The legal and political systems of the colonising country, supposedly identical 'at home and abroad', are inflected differently in terms of the perceived race of the body in question. And the same is true of how those systems deal with the 'foreign bodies' of immigrants. In former colonies establishing nationhood there are further questions about how women are constituted as citizens, or otherwise, in these new systems.[2]

Public/private

The pervasiveness of the public/private divide in denying women equal status in the law and political arena has been one of the primary targets of western feminist analysis since the eighteenth century. Human rights discourse developed in conjunction with liberal democracy, at the centre of which is a supposed commitment to a separation of civil society from the domestic. As Thornton explains, this commitment is more an abstraction than a reality: 'The fiction of non-intervention has served to disguise the multifarious ways in which the polity has fashioned the family and gender relations. Needless to say, the characterisation of the family as an unregulated sphere has been the impetus for trenchant critiques by feminist scholars' (Thornton 1995a: 5).

Heavily implicated in the separation of separate spheres is a belief that the traditional family is somehow natural rather than social. Thus, ideas about women's 'natural' function as mother, the 'natural' authority of a male head of household, and 'natural' heterosexuality, among other beliefs about nature and women's bodies, reinforce the liberal state's reluctance to intervene in 'private' arenas that it defines as natural, and to regulate those which it defines as unnatural. This produces anomalies whereby, for example, the human right to bodily integrity, as articulated by the United Nations, does not seem to apply *in toto* to women within the home.

Ngaire Naffine (1995) offers a cogent summary of the logic by which women, relegated to the private, were historically not 'subjects of the (western) law' at home or away:

> The private subject of the law . . . was therefore the husband and father. Law countenanced and enabled the realisation of his personal freedom by giving him sexual access to, and property in, a wife. . . . The legal object (as opposed to the subject) of life in the private was therefore the wife, who played a particularly crucial role . . . To make it possible for the man to realise his personal and sexual freedom in the private, it was essential that she (his wife) did not (for how could he be free to do as he pleased if she had the right to say no?).
>
> (Naffine 1995: 27)

While the twentieth century has seen trends towards declaring men and women equal subjects of the law, the beliefs underlying the original legal status quo still colour judgements, most notably

in the case of 'domestic violence' cases.[3] In some western jurisdictions it is only recently that the concept of marital rape has
been recognised. One notorious example of the time lag between
attitudes and legislation is the case oft-cited in recent Australian
feminist–legal literature of a male judge who commented, during
the prosecution of a man on six counts of marital rape, in 1992:
'There is, of course, nothing wrong with a husband, faced with his
wife's initial refusal to engage in intercourse, in attempting, *in an
acceptable way*, to persuade her to change her mind [my italics]'
(cited in Graycar 1995: 271).

Margaret Thornton points out that arguments based on a notion
of separate but equal spheres fall down, because the separation
of the spheres, rather than being a natural and self-evident division, depends on the defining powers of the *public* realm which,
she argues decides something is 'private' or 'public' depending
on how far it wants to intervene in that area (Thornton 1995b:
'Introduction' 11).

'Equal-but-separate' also has links to the idea that the state's
legitimacy is based on the idea of a social contract. The whole notion
of a contract is premised on the consent of partners who are equal.
Carole Pateman's *The Sexual Contract* (1988) examines ways in which
the 'social contract' disguises how it is based on the maintenance of
male power and, ultimately, on the subordinated bodies of women,
to which men are guaranteed access. Gail Mason (1995) points
out that Pateman's analysis needs to be supplemented by an inter-
rogation of the specifically heterosexual nature of this contract:
if the public/private divide and the 'social contract' are based on
male access to women's bodies, where does this leave the lesbian
body in relation to the law? The metaphor of 'coming out' appears
to address directly a crossing from private into public. As Mason's
analysis suggests, such a crossing will have multiple meanings
depending on the specific body that is 'coming out' and there is
a danger that the public declaration of what has been a private
identity will help to construct a homogenous 'lesbian-as-subject-
of-the-law': 'a public lesbian body exclusive of all but the most
privileged lesbians: those with the class, race and bodily prerogative
to speak and to be heard' (Mason 1995: 88).

A great deal of western-feminist energy has gone into blurring
the divide of private and public, arguing both for the inclusion
of women as equal actors in public life, and for the expansion of
protective legislation into the private sphere. Both these moves,

however, as the analysis of Mason and others shows, can reinforce the power and ascendancy of the public over the private. Writers on and from different cultures increasingly argue for the need to look at the specific articulations of domestic and public in their particular contexts. Joanne Sharp, for example, points out that in eastern Europe feminism has a very different inflection and focus because of the very different nexus between state and home. Thornton (1995a) similarly argues that a collapse of the boundaries of private/public may not be a straightforward gain for feminism, because of the tendency of the public to draw the private into itself, rather than vice-versa. To bring abortion, for example, into the public arena and under scrutiny enhances the power of the state and of lobby groups to make material decisions about the bodies of women independent of the women's own desires.[4] This is not only evident in the case of legislation outlawing abortion, but in cases where, for example, the state has made a decision perceived to be in the interest of a foetus.

As Anne Morris and Susan Nott (1995) describe it, the law has no place for a pregnant woman as an autonomous person with rights but reassigns her 'as a vessel for a new person' (the foetus) who, in effect, becomes a ward of the court. That is, her private status, and the rights to bodily integrity invested in it, are superseded by her public designation as an incubator of new citizens. Morris and Nott point out that, in the United States, women have been prosecuted for failing to take advice on 'proper' pregnancy life-styles, and some have been given longer-than-standard jail sentencing during pregnancy to monitor their pregnancies.[5] As the many feminist writers on reproductive technologies and surrogacy expose, pregnancy is one of the areas where the modern state seems to have very little problem in deciding the personal is political, not in the way that feminism required, but by erasing women's pregnant bodies and focusing on the foetus and, in some surrogacy cases, on the 'father' (see for example Raymond 1994; Rowland 1992; Treichler 1990). This mirrors the ways in which medical technologies and their discourses have moved towards an imaging of the foetus in isolation (Stabile 1994; Petchesky 1987; and see Chapter 2 this text).

A discussion of the increasing regulation of women's pregnant bodies, as a class, can mask the ways in which some women's bodies have always been less private than others as regards the law. While the social contract could be said to disguise its dependence on the sexual contract of a public (male) and private (female) sphere, both of these contracts could also be seen as resting, in colonial societies, on a racialised economy that does not fit neatly within either. Thus, the bodies of enslaved men and women were traded in the public domain and had, in the eyes of the law, no private identity. If the bodies of white women had some degree of safety in the domestic sphere, this was arguably at the expense of the bodies of colonised and enslaved women who were constituted somehow outside public and private, in the domain of 'the wild' as either the sexually exotic or as breeding-stock (see, for example, hooks 1992; 1990; Ware 1992). The legacy of colonial history is still embedded in the law, both nationally and internationally. 'Minority' women have questioned the universality of such terms as 'rights' and the differences of racial identity that apparent universality conceals (Behrendt 1993; Mohanty *et al.* 1991).

Archana Parashar points out that the western definitions of public and private tend to relegate religion to the private, but that this is not relevant to many women in Third World countries – nor indeed, to the lives of many in the west: 'Religion is an integral part of one's personality in both private and public spheres' (Parashar 1995: 231). However, Parashar argues, the role of religion and the individual's relationship to it in many newer nation states is being changed in ways that elude the conventional public/private analysis. For example, there is an ongoing redefinition of female Muslim identity in Indian law as a result of the state's provision of maintenance rights for divorced women.[6]

In contemporary western countries there remain differences in the ways that some women's bodies are (dis)regarded by the law, and/or in the degree that women have access to legal redress for violations of the right to choose (informed consent). Many of these differences can be traced to the law's reluctance to admit some bodies into the circle of 'rational adult' and thus, to the right to privacy. One case in point is the court's endorsement of, or reluctance to interfere in, the sterilisation of women regarded as 'unfit' to be mothers. The women most commonly targeted by these practices are those with 'learning difficulties' and/or from the lowest economic groups and/or racial minorities. Kirsty Keywood (1995) offers a detailed analysis, in the British context, of the ways in which the rationale for sterilising a woman with learning difficulties, when it is 'in her best interests', is based on a set of problematic assumptions about female sexuality and pregnancy. She argues that underlying the court's willingness to allow sterilisation in these cases is a set of beliefs and fears about the basic irrationality of *all* women's sexuality.

'Benchmark Man' and rationality

'Benchmark man' is the term coined by Australian writer Margaret Thornton (1995a) to label the invisible man who is the assumed subject of western legal and political discourses. He is the model described by Gatens and characterised by her, and others, as, above all, rational. Genevieve Lloyd (1984), one of the first contemporary feminist philosophers to identify him and trace his historical development, calls him 'The Man of Reason'. He is, in brief, the exemplar of how far human beings (men) can transcend nature (women). It may appear paradoxical that this exemplar is invisible, but of course this invisibility is the guarantee of his transcendence: the denial of flesh and of time. It is therefore one of the primary tasks of feminism to bring this invisible being back down to earth and reincarnate him, thus (re)constituting him as a subject in history with particular properties.

Once reincarnated, in his all-too-solid flesh, Benchmark Man, for Thornton, reveals that (in the Australian legal system) 'he is Anglo–Australian, heterosexual, able-bodied, supports a mainstream religion, if any, is middle-class and can be located within the middle to the right of the political spectrum' (1995a: 200). While these characteristics may have their variations within other countries, the set of privileges they represent will be remarkably similar.

Benchmark Man haunts western political and legal discourse and, as the term 'benchmark' suggests, other bodies are measured against him and usually found wanting. This is not simply of academic interest but, as the growing collection of feminist–legal case studies indicates, has serious implications for the ways in which women's lives are affected by legal decisions. Thornton is clear that, while she supports and argues for the increased representation of women on the bench and in the courts, this is not in itself sufficient, since the women who have arrived there have been, themselves, trained in the ways of Benchmark Man. Regina Graycar comments: 'Despite the relatively recent entry of women into the profession, and their increasing numbers . . . legal doctrines and legal reasoning appear to have remained almost completely impervious to perspectives other than those of the (dominant) White, middle-class male' (1995: 267–8). Indeed, it could be argued that for women to succeed in any discipline or organisation, we must always to some extent engage in a drag act that mimics both that imaginary male and his beliefs about femininity.[7]

Benchmark Man is used, Thornton argues, as the standard by which those appearing before the courts are found to come within the ambit of the law and are judged. To take one example, the body of a pregnant woman embodies her difference from the supposedly neutral 'man of reason' and offers a challenge to the whole concept of neutrality enshrined in the idea that 'human' can generically include 'woman' and 'man' equally. Zillah Eisenstein (1988) offers examples of how this can operate to discriminate against women in the workplace when the law acts on the supposition that the 'non-pregnant' is the subject of the law. She cites the North American case of some women being excluded from disability insurance systems on the grounds of pregnancy. The Supreme Court ruled that this did not contravene anti-discrimination legislation on the grounds that their exclusion was based on 'a physical condition' rather than sex! Furthermore, the disability insurance system was entitled to divide 'potential recipients into two groups – pregnant women and non-pregnant persons. While the first group is exclusively female, the second includes members of both sexes' and, therefore, is not discriminatory! (Eisenstein 1988: 66–9).

The most important attribute of Benchmark Man is 'reasonableness', sometimes also termed 'commonsense'. (How far does the Supreme Court's judgement indicate anybody's definition of commonsense?) Supposedly objective judgements are made about people's behaviour and motives based on the judge and jury's notions of what is reasonable and acceptable. Vicki Schultz offers a number of examples of 'commonsense' being used to legislate on women's place in the North American workforce: 'The conservative story rests on a simple syllogism: women are "feminine", non-traditional work is "masculine", and therefore women do not want to do it . . . "Commonsense tells us that few women have the skill or the desire to be a welder or a metal fabricator," said one judge' (Schultz 1992: 307).

As numerous feminist commentators have observed, western justice systems rely on a faith in 'the rational actor' and his [sic] commonsense. Gatens (1998) points out that an important component of this 'rational actor' is, on analysis, a tendency to act individually in pursuit of self-interest. Such rational, self-interested actions are posited on a relative freedom of agency.

> ### Rationality and the case of battered women who kill
>
> Marie Fox (1995) gives an extended analysis of how the use of
> a 'rational normality' as the basis for legal judgement can be
> used to the disadvantage of women who have been assaulted
> by partners and, in particular, those who have killed abusive
> partners. Fox points out that women in such cases are caught
> in a number of contradictions that can be traced directly to
> the body of the woman as anomaly/alien in the legal system.
> Fox cites Canadian Bertha Wilson's point that there is a big
> problem with an appeal to 'the ordinary man' as a benchmark
> of reasonableness when dealing with situations that men do
> not ordinarily find themselves in such as that of battered spouse
> (1995: 175). But there are also problems inherent in establishing
> a benchmark of ordinary or reasonable woman to apply in such
> cases.
> In the first place, legal assumptions about women, as we have
> already discussed, are enmeshed in cultural and social beliefs
> about gender which will inevitably influence the definitions.
> In the second place, an emphasis on the state of mind of the
> woman who has killed a battering spouse reinforces a mind/body
> dualism that discounts and renders invisible the material injuries
> inflicted on her *body*. This erasure is already in place through
> what Fox calls 'the oxymoronic term "domestic violence"' which
> contains within it a history of special pleading for the privacy
> of the home and the autonomy of the male head of household'
> (p. 188). The plea of 'diminished responsibility' at the time
> of the killing is, Fox argues, problematic since it feeds into
> prevailing stereotypes of women as hysterical, irrational and
> vulnerable; furthermore, if once established as a favoured
> defence, it might disadvantage those women who cannot evoke
> it because they have acted with deliberation, are intelligent,
> and/or in their appearance and manner contradict notions
> of passive, vulnerable femininity.

Rights and the body of the citizen

If the idea of the 'rational man' is one cornerstone of western legal
systems and of the political systems in which they are embedded,
equally important for western democracy – and now enshrined
in international law) – is the idea of human rights. 'Rational

Man' recognises a set of common human rights. In common with other liberatory movements of the last two centuries, feminism has asserted the claim for 'equal rights' based on rational appeals for fair play. These appeals rely on evidence of the ways in which women, even when legally recognised as citizens, are discriminated against. The establishment in many states of legislation addressing discrimination on the grounds of sex might be seen to be a measure of the success of this strategy. Why then are some contemporary feminists arguing about the value of a 'rights' discourse? Some of the reasons are discussed below.

'Human rights' are evoked in two major ways: as the base line of what any human being is entitled to – what might be called a 'natural right'; and as one of the factors in the State's contract with its citizens. 'Natural', as Eisenstein (1988) describes, suggests some kind of absolute value system beyond and independent of specific cultures and states. Documents like the United Nations Universal Declaration of Human Rights (1948) enshrine certain basic principles. (Hilary Charlesworth (1996) points out, however, that even though the Declaration was a statement of principle, rather than a treaty requiring implementation, eight countries abstained when it was put to the vote – so much for universality![8]) As we have seen in all the fields discussed so far, generalisations based on 'human' are haunted by the presence of an embodied man and take his experience as the benchmark or measure of experience. One problem with 'human rights' discourse is that it obscures embodied differences such as sexuality, age, 'race' and, of course, gender. As numerous commentators have pointed out, 'woman' is constructed as provisionally rather than incontrovertibly 'human'. This presents a dilemma: to accept the degree of invisibility attendant on being tacitly included in 'human' or to risk reinscribing 'woman' as always only provisionally human by singling out her particular embodied conditions.

Elizabeth Grosz argues that two main directions of second-wave feminism (she chooses to label these 'egalitarian' and 'social constructionist') have shared a preference for the first course, which brings with it a denial or suppression of body differences, 'neutralization of the sexually specific body' (1994: 15–17). While Grosz does not address directly issues of 'human rights', it would follow from her argument that appeals for women's equal rights within the terms of a 'human rights' manifesto are doomed because the sexed specificity of women's bodies *is* different from men's and cannot be accommodated within a discourse in which 'human' is haunted by a male body. Karen Engle suggests that the 'obsession with women's marginality . . . eclipses questions, as well as critiques, about the core. So concerned are we to be included that we assume the doctrine to be good. Our only critique is that we are not part of it' (cited in Charlesworth 1995: 253).

Hilary Charlesworth's work on international law and the United Nations centrally addresses these questions (Charlesworth 1995; 1996). Charlesworth (1996) examines the impact of campaigns to include women's issues as a related but specific component of United Nations' definitions of human rights, focusing on the significance of the public/private division. Underpinning the operations of United Nations is an attempt to draw a line between the areas open to international regulation and those deemed to be the business of the individual states. The United Nations defines various areas as the sovereign responsibility of the state within its own borders, analogous with the right of the head of household to oversee that household's affairs. Just as, in the domestic sphere, this division fails to protect the interests, and bodies, of women, so in the international arena, women are less than fully defended by those appeals to 'human rights' that allegedly include us. Charlesworth draws attention to the ways in which each side of the private/public divide, inscribed as it is with quite different sets of power relations, governs the areas designated as 'women's'.

How gender differences work in practice can be illustrated by Charlesworth's example of the 'universal' human rights law regarding torture. 'Torture' in human rights legislation is quite clearly defined as a public act. For an action to be viewed as torture, an extraordinary act of violation of the body, and thus breach United Nations' establishment of a basic human right, it must be performed by a public official. Charlesworth emphasises that, while this of course will cover the experience of some women, it fails to give any recognition to the kinds of 'ordinary' violence characteristically enacted against many women which often, in terms of bodily effect, are indistinguishable from what is more commonly regarded as 'torture'. Inge Agger (1994) draws on the words of refugee women from numerous countries, to embody what 'torture' can mean across multiple contexts, restoring the embodied experience from silence. Chilla Bulbeck (1998) points out that there is a gradual shift towards recognition of sex-specific conditions producing refugees, but that this recognition is discretionary on the part of each member state of the United Nations. That is, it is seen as a domestic/private rather than a universal/public issue.

Another much-discussed example, in the critiquing of the universality of 'human rights', is that of rape, and particularly of rape in war. Rape has been recognised by the United Nations as a war crime but it tends to be defined in a quite specific way which fails to acknowledge that, as Bulbeck puts it: 'Women have so often been raped as part of the process of war that it can hardly be described as "extracurricular"' (1998: 190).

The question of rape is a particularly clear site for looking at the ways in which women's bodies are viewed and how this makes problematic both the idea of a universal, disinterested, legal system and the usefulness for feminist politics of 'human rights' discourse. The distinction made by international law of 'war-crime' rape and rape in peace time could be traced to the underlying belief that women's bodies and sexuality belong ultimately not to ourselves, but to a man, and to the state. As Sharon Marcus (1992) observes 'the most deep-rooted upheaval of rape culture would revise the idea of female sexuality as an object, as property, and as an inner space' (1992: 399).

Feminists disagree about the usefulness of separating out rape-as-war-crime from other forms of rape. Some fear that such a separation might reinforce prevalent ideas about women as property – of individual men and of the state – rather than help to effect a 'deep-rooted upheaval of rape culture'. The separation aligns the violation of women's bodies, *in war*, with other acts of pillage aimed at destroying or appropriating the enemy's property and makes it into a case for special horror, removing attention from its continuum with the pervasiveness of 'rape culture' in peacetime.

Given that the discourse of national politics is replete with metaphors of the body, and of invasion as the 'rape' of the nation, it is hardly surprising to see the metaphor made literal on the bodies of women. The act of rape not only defiles enemy property but literally invades the nation's body in terms of potential pregnancies. Bulbeck, drawing on the work of Kabeer (1991) and Stiglmayer (1994), cites two recent examples: Pakistan's occupation of Bangladesh in 1971 and ensuing use of mass rape ' "to improve the genes of the Bengali people" '; and the practice of 'ethnic cleansing' in the former Yugoslavia. Natalie Nenadic (1996) offers an example of a radical feminist appeal for a recognition of women's different experience to be enshrined in law. Addressing the Hague War Crimes Tribunal, she argues for a separate category of genocide to be embodied as 'femicide': 'Women are targeted as women in every genocide whereas genocidal sexual atrocities constitute one part ... of a larger continuum of global and historical crimes against women' (Nenadic 1996: 460).

Feminist arguments over the usefulness of 'human rights' discourse in the advancement of women's issues centre on the problems of inclusion and separation and, in doing so, expose the ways in which female bodies are in excess of the category 'human' in western legal and political discourses.

Women as subjects of the law

In the traditional western construction of the law and the citizen, women had no place in their own right and could not speak on their own behalf. Women's bodies were 'covered' by their nearest male relative or the state acting on his behalf. To recognise women as subjects and to listen to women's voices – rather than dismissing them as 'the language of a hysteric, the wails of a hyena, the jabbering of a savage' (Gatens 1996: 26) – would be to alter materially the discourse and practice of the law. While in British, and other legal systems, there have been moves to change the gendered-masculine terminology of legal discourse, 'there has been no concomitant endeavour to rethink the defining characteristics of law's subject ... Putting the word "she" in a piece of legislation is simply not enough, for it leaves in place all the cultural baggage that renders that word simply a token addition' (Naffine 1995: 29–30).

Naffine offers as a particularly telling example of the law's tendency to assimilate different bodies back into the singular model of 'benchmark man', the introduction of anti-discrimination legislation. Drawing on the work of Catharine MacKinnon, Naffine points out the 'awful paradox of sex discrimination legislation': women must prove they are the same as men in order to be eligible for the same treatment. Thus, it is those women who can most approximate 'Benchmark Man' in terms both of perceived characteristics such as class and race, and of life-style, who are most likely to benefit from anti-discrimination legislation. The issues affecting women that are most specific to our sexed bodies are the areas in which the law is least effective in protecting women or allowing women autonomy.

When women enter the law, either as a profession or as litigants, our bodies mark us as different while the official legal discourse insists on its neutrality. The contradictions are clearly marked in, for example, the dress regulations of some law firms which advocate that women members wear (tailored) skirts, endorse the use of 'discreet' make-up, but also proscribe 'feminine' markers such as long earrings. Anything which draws direct attention to the sexed, and sexual, nature of the female body erodes the woman's always-provisional credibility as an equal participant in the public sphere. As Margaret Thornton describes the historical distinction of public/man and private/woman: 'Conventionally, a "public woman" was a prostitute, a figure of derision, in contrast to a "public man", a figure of approbation who acted in and for the universal good' (1995b: 'Introduction' 13).

To draw attention to the sexed body in the legal context seems immediately to position women as the sexualised other of the public and private good: it is a sexed body out of place, beyond the confines of the male contract. Rape cases highlight this by allowing exhaustive investigation of the sexual history of the woman who allegedly has been raped, in effect giving her the burden of proving that she fits a category of sexually virtuous woman, as though this is necessary to legitimate her story. Once her body has been identified as the site of sexual activity, albeit *forced*, her full entitlement to be an equal subject of the law is called into question. This becomes particularly clear in the general lack of sympathy and belief extended to women raped and otherwise assaulted in the course of sex-work, even in states where sex-work is legalised. Naffine argues persuasively for the need for feminists to engage with legal culture in two major directions: first, to ensure that the law does identify the gaps between the lives of women and the law's traditional interpretations of them; and second, to envisage new interpretations and what a law with fully developed female subjects might look like.

Part of the second project must be the deconstructing of the narrow definitions of women before the law which influence and control judgements. In order to find a place for women under the law, the law assigns them special designations: one example, as we have seen, being 'The Pregnant Woman'. Regina Graycar (1995) indicates some of the ways in which these stereotypes function to maintain the status quo and deny the lived materiality of women's lives. In determining compensation, for example, for a full-time, unpaid carer's loss of capacity to work in the home, prevalent notions of 'The Housewife' come into play. These notions are neatly encapsulated in the ironic title of one of Graycar's own articles,

'Hoovering as a Hobby: The Common Law's Approach to Work in the Home' (*Refractory Girl* 1985; cited in Graycar 1995: 262).

Questions of voice

Western feminism has increasingly stressed the importance of speaking for ourselves and thus creating new discourses and new subject selves, in a challenge to the singular dominant discourse of the male order. However, this feminism has been challenged from many directions as itself creating a homogenised western woman and offering her up as the singular and universal subject of feminism. Hazel Carby, in 1982, concluded her injunction 'White Women Listen!' as follows:

> Black women do not want to be grafted onto 'feminism' in a tokenistic manner as colourful diversions to 'real' problems. Feminism has to be transformed if it is to address us. Neither do we wish our words to be misused in generalities as if what each one of us utters represents the total experience of all black women . . . In other words, of white feminists we must ask, what exactly do you mean when you say 'WE'?
>
> (Carby 1997 [1982]: 52)

Homogenisation resides in the failure to hear or to listen for specific and personal stories from different experiences; in a blindness to the privileges of whiteness; in a refusal to recognise the legacy of colonialism; in a compartmentalising of all different experience into a generalised category – what Karen Engle's has called 'The Exotic Other Female' (cited in Beveridge and Mulally 1995: 253–4). Just as the lived and speaking bodies of women in their material presence offer the strongest challenge to masculinist constructs such as the public/private division, the speaking bodies of women in their diversity most radically challenge eurocentric feminism's hierarchies. This has strong implications for the project of re-constituting woman as subject of the law (both nationally and internationally). What does the body of this singular woman look like? What colour is her skin? How has wealth or poverty, good or poor diets, exercise or lack of exercise formed her body? In embodying women as subjects of the law western feminists must avoid constructing a singular 'Benchmark Woman'.

One example of a particularly fraught bodily site in both international and national legal debates is that of surgical incision of female genitalia, commonly referred to as 'female circumcision' or 'female genital mutilation'. The term itself is a matter of dispute, being largely a western classification of a number of different practices carried out in non-western cultures. To discuss and pronounce in public upon what are often called 'private parts' transgresses all notions of a private and public divide and raises profound questions about 'rights' and their basis in the notion of an autonomous individual.

At the international level, there have been moves both from western nations and from internal pressure groups to outlaw such practices universally, and a corresponding resistance to such moves. At the national level, in ex-colonial independent states there are dissensions over an ascendant political group's right to regulate what may be important cultural practices for another group, and similar arguments occur in countries with high levels of immigration. These debates raise complex issues of body rights, autonomy and cultural identity. At an international level, there have been clear divisions of opinion over the United Nations' authority to rule on issues of 'tradition' seen as part of the internal, domestic concerns of a state.

A radical–feminist approach on the whole discounts claims that respect for cultural specificity should take precedence over concerns for female bodily integrity. At the other end of the spectrum, Lois Bibbings (1995) focuses on discursive constructions, and the ways in which a label such as 'mutilation' construes the body of 'the other woman' as part of a separate frame of reference linked to eurocentric designations of the exotic and barbaric with a corresponding valorisation of western practice and belief. As Chilla Bulbeck points out, such eurocentrism is endemic in the west: 'So ingrained is the racism of this approach that you will often see media reports in which white western men (or women for that matter) contrast "our" liberated women with "their" oppressed women . . . so that apparent commitment to women's rights becomes a container for racism' (Bulbeck, 1998: 80). Bulbeck approvingly cites the work of Isabelle Gunning (1992) and her strategy of 'world-travelling' for westerners as a 'mechanism for avoiding both pre-given universals and sinking into a self-censoring relativism'.

An important difference in legislative approaches can be seen around the question of whether or not genital surgery is an issue of women's rights or more broadly a health issue, and the concomitant feminist question of which issue to emphasise when lobbying against the practice. Western feminists crusading against the practices have been accused of imposing a western-feminist priority of sexual rights in cultures where other issues may be seen to be much more pressing or relevant (Mohanty 1991). Lois Bibbings (1995) argues for a re-thinking on the part of western feminists on similar lines to Isabelle Gunning, and focuses on pointing out similarities between many of the explanations and justifications of western 'body-modifiers' and those of 'Third-World women'. By undoing the classificatory divisions of 'them' and 'us' (barbaric/civilised) Bibbings avoids the need to appeal to notions of 'false consciousness' or, as Kathy Davis more graphically terms it, in her investigation of women who elect for breast transplants, 'women as cultural dopes' (1995: 37).

In order to dismiss the idea of 'false consciousness' it is not also necessary to deny the constraints that operate on women's lives and the ways in which our ideas about the body are enmeshed in culture. One of the problems for western feminism has been its own embeddedness within western notions of individualism and autonomy which are often at odds with other cultures' emphases on community. As critics like Kalpana Ram (1993; 1998a; 1998b), Chandra Mohanty (1991) and Archana Parashar (1995) point out, some of the most notable gaps in western-feminist appreciation of other women's perspectives arises from their marginalising of religious/spiritual dimensions and discounting of other cultural factors which may be central to those women in their communities. Other writers emphasise the dangers of an indifferent cultural relativism in the face of rising fundamentalist religious movements of all faiths (Saghal and Yuval-Davis 1992; Patel in Mirza 1997).

In the context of legal and political definitions women's bodies speak a difference that exposes the partiality of systems that owe their legitimacy in the western tradition to claims of neutrality and truth. Feminist debates, both within feminism and against the various systems, reveal the ways in which these systems are imbued with assumptions about gender, race and other aspects of embodiment that locate them within specific time and space. In contesting these assumptions in the context of law, as in the context of other powerful institutional discourses such as medicine, there is always the risk of assimilation and homogenisation. This, as the proliferation of feminist voices attests, does not negate the importance of specific campaigns to change the subject. Feminisms, as Jan Pettman (1996) describes, are not stable or transparent in their meanings or affiliations, but 'the site of contestation, and of negotiation of multiple identities in relations that are increasingly globalised in implication and effect' (213).

Summary

- Feminist analysis argues that 'the law' is organised around, and in favour of, an abstract fantasy male figure with the result that women's embodied presence is marginalised or separated from the law.

- This raises questions about how far it is possible or desirable for feminists to make specific and local appeals for women to be made more equal in the law.

- Further questions arise from debates within feminism around notions of the decentred subject (usually associated with poststructuralist analysis) and the dangers of women becoming increasingly categorised by the law into narrow definitions.

- Feminist analysis has been directed at deconstructing the public/private division in terms of the power relations embedded in the relegation of women to the domestic/ private sphere.

- The value of 'coming out' from the private is of arguable benefit to some groups of women.

- The absent 'fantasy' male figure, 'Benchmark Man', can be reconstructed with quite specific privileged attributes which influence the law's judgements.

- The assumptions and beliefs held by 'Benchmark' are normalised as 'commonsense' and universalised to the exclusion or marginalisation of the differently embodied.

- Feminist campaigns for 'equality' under the law are vitiated by the need to prove women equal to men: that is to deny difference.

- At the international level, as well as the state, this creates a problem for feminists in whether or not to argue for women's rights to be included within, or treated as separate, from 'human rights'.

- Just as western women have argued that women's embodied experience is invisible and unheard in western law, so women of other cultures have questioned the homogenising tendency of western feminism.

- Contemporary feminisms in relation to the law are confronted with the practical problems discussed in theory: of how to accommodate differences and ideas of decentred subjectivity within structures and institutions which are essentially monolithic and singular.

Notes

[1] Irigaray suggests that the embodied presence of women, if spoken and heard, would offer a challenge that could not be assimilated, and would take away the single, homogenising legitimacy of 'law' (1985a). In some of her later writing, she directly addresses ways in which civil rights discourse might be invoked to persuade legal systems to recognise the difference of women's bodies (see Bridgeman 1995).

[2] Jacqui Alexander offers the example of the development of legislation outlawing homosexuality in Trinidad and Tobago and the Bahamas. She points out that such legislation in effect bars her, as an 'out' lesbian, from full citizenship in the new state: 'heterosexuality becomes coterminous with and gives birth to the nation' (1994: 10).

[3] Feminist commentators draw attention to the ways in which the term itself rests on, and reinscribes, a private and public divide: a woman's body being assaulted in her home by a partner is constructed differently from her body when assaulted by someone outside her family. It is the relationship, rather than the location that seems to determine what is 'domestic' about the violence.

[4] It is important to note that when Thornton and similar feminist commentators critique and deconstruct legal concepts and practice in this way they are not advocating that feminists should desist from engagement with law reform regarding abortion. Rather, they are pointing out the complexities of the power relations involved.

[5] Morris and Nott (1995) emphasise that the definition of whether or not a foetus constitutes a legal 'person' varies between jurisdictions.

[6] See Parashar (1995) and, for a fuller discussion, Zakia Pathak and Rajeswari Sunder Rajan, 'Shahbano'. In Butler and Scott 1992: 257–79.

[7] For ideas of 'drag' and the ideas of bodies continuously enacting repetitions that include gender, see Butler (1990; 1993) and Chapter 6.

[8] Bulbeck offers an additional perspective on the abstentions: 'six were communist countries arguing that economic, social and cultural rights were equally important' to the *individual* rights at the heart of the UN Declaration (1998: 70).

[9] It is important to reaffirm that the common western equation of genital surgery with Islam is another instance of homogenisation. Raqiha Abdalla (1982) argues that the practices are not part of any

official religion. Fatima Mernissi (1991) uses detailed interpretation of the Koran to argue that gender inequality is not part of its doctrine.

Further reading

Fox, Marie (1995) 'Legal Responses to Battered Women Who Kill'. In Jo Bridgeman and Susan Millns (eds) (1995) *Law and Body Politics: Regulating the Female Body.* Aldershot and Brookfield: Dartmouth.

Gatens, Moira (1998) 'Institutions, Embodiment and Sexual Difference.' In Moira Gatens and Alison Mackinnon (eds) *Gender and Institutions: Welfare, Work and Citizenship.* Cambridge: Cambridge University Press.

Graycar, Regina (1995) 'The Gender of Judgements: An Introduction'. In Margaret Thornton (ed.) *Public and Private: Feminist Legal Debates.* Melbourne: Oxford University Press.

Marcus, Sharon (1992) 'Fighting Bodies, Fighting Words: A Theory and Politics of Rape Prevention'. In Judith Butler and Joan W. Scott (eds) *Feminists Theorize the Political.* New York and London: Routledge.

Naffine, Ngaire (1995) 'Sexing the Subject (of Law)'. In Margaret Thornton (ed.) *Public and Private: Feminist Legal Debates.* Melbourne: Oxford University Press.

Parashar, Archana (1995) 'Reconceptualisations of Civil Society: Third World and Ethnic Women'. In Margaret Thornton (ed.) *Public and Private: Feminist Legal Debates.* Melbourne: Oxford University Press.

Chapter 6

Performance and spectacle

Chapter outline

Performing in public places puts the female body on display in ways that contradict many of the constructions of femininity. These contradictions enable some transgressive feminist performances. Femininity itself may be considered as a drag performance or masquerade.

• Making a spectacle	contradictions of performance, spectacle, and femininity.
• Masquerades of femininity	masks; gender performativity; drag.
• Feminist readings of bodybuilding	narcissism; eradicating femininity; race/class issues.
• Histories of healthy bodies	sport and fitness; disciplining health; eugenics.
• Bodies in space	
• Inhibited intentionality	phenomenology; movement.
• Staged performances	queering; Takarazuka Revue; circus; performance art; transgression.
• Everyday performances	teaching bodies; bodies of knowledge.

Making a spectacle

The public spectacle of a woman's body enacts an antithesis to the identification of femininity with the private and domestic body.

Theories of the disciplining functions of the 'male gaze' suggest that she enters public (masculine) space as a potentially disruptive, transgressive body and it is her position as spectacle (making a spectacle of herself) under the view of the masculine eye, that disciplines her back into line, returns her into a docile body. Feminist theorists are interested in the ways that women evade or subvert that disciplining.

There are any number of disciplinary technologies to regulate a woman's body in public space, across the spectrum from constituting her purely and explicitly as sexualised object of the male gaze in table-top dancing, to the attempt to cloak her body differences totally through a comprehensive clothing which in a sense creates a private space, space-bubble, for her body to move within, even when 'in public'. Across the spectrum in the public sphere, 'woman' is configured as irreducibly female and in relation to men.[1] The different meanings of this relationship in specific locations will have their own political interpretations which have not always been recognised in western-feminist critiques. Issues of cultural difference and accusations of western-feminist neo-colonialism have been raised, for example by Muslim critics of western interpretations of 'the veil' (e.g., Mernissi 1987).

Women, then, could be said to be always performing when in public: needing to 'watch herself'. A woman designated as a performer has been equated in the west with promiscuity and sexual availability: leading to cross-cultural misunderstandings when western colonialists encounter women dancers and other performers in different cultures. Women in performance as actors, dancers and other entertainers, athletes, body-builders are, by definition, drawing attention to their bodies: a question for feminism is, how far can they do this and also have autonomy? To become and remain subjects they must negotiate not only the regulatory conventions of performance but also the ways in which the disciplining male gaze attempts to reduce them to no more than the docile (hetero)-sexualised object of desire. Western-feminist cultural theorists have argued fervently about the degree of transgressiveness and agency available to women performing explicitly and knowingly to a male gaze: the 'Madonna' industry in cultural studies offers extended engagement with this debate (e.g., Schwichtenberg 1993).

Public spaces other than those designated for entertainment and sport also demand an element of putting on a performance. Barristers in court and teachers and lecturers in the classroom and lecture-theatre perform to an audience.[2] In terms of women's engagement in public activities where we are supposedly equal to men in the workplace, the conditions of entrance are often marked by prescriptive dress and body regulations intended to de-emphasise female sexuality and submerge it in the general erasure or denial of body perceived as 'professional', but in fact gendered masculine. The power of these regulations, both in workplace settings and other public arenas, is understood even by very young women.[3]

The term 'performance' captures within its meanings the idea of offering up the body/the self to public consumption, and of being assessed on the adequacy of the performance. It also puts a question-mark over the 'authenticity' of what is being offered. 'Performance' is conventionally something constructed, something with a gap between what we see and what we think might be its, invisible, origin. However, the theorising of performance in post-structuralist analysis calls into question any such boundary between 'staged' performances as a separate sphere and everyday enactment or performance of self, and in so doing problematises authenticity, identity and origins. This collapsing of definitions that divide performance spaces from the everyday has informed much contemporary praxis in the arts.

This idea of performance as everyday activity, with its implications for what constitutes identity has preoccupied the contemporary feminist theorist, Judith Butler (1990; 1993; 1997). Butler is concerned not with the traditional separation of performance as a specialised public act for an audience in the context of entertainment, but with the idea of 'performativity': ways in which bodies more generally perform themselves, specifically as regards gender. Jane Gallop (1988), similarly, is interested in what could be called the textuality of performing bodies – often in the context of teaching and the academy – although her interpretation is different from Butler's. Recurrent in Gallop's work, and recently a central focus of contributors to her edited collection, *Pedagogy: The Question of Impersonation* (1995), are the ways in which teachers embody and 'impersonate' different selves in the classroom and lecture theatre. 'Impersonation' in this usage has much in common with Butler's ideas of performativity.

Butler is careful to distinguish her concept of the 'performativity' of gender from conventional theatre. In *Bodies That Matter* she directly answers critics of her earlier work who interpreted her as saying that gender is like a costume or role that can be put on and off at will: 'performativity must be understood not as a singular or deliberate "act", but, rather, as the reiterative and citational practice by which discourse produces the effects that it names' (1993: 1). In this use of 'citation', Butler does not imply the existence of an absolute original text like a holy scripture that can be referred to but rather the idea of an imaginary or fantasised origin to which the citation refers and which the citation, in turn, reinforces. Butler draws on the analogy of transvestite 'drag' acts which cite 'the feminine' through a range of signifiers (mascaraed eyelashes, prominent breasts, movements of hips, etc.) that have no point of origin in any female body. For Butler, the everyday performativity of gender resides in similar but unacknowledged, unself-conscious acts of citation which, by repetition, produce the body as *either* feminine *or* masculine as though this were an inevitable product of a particular anatomy. Butler's particular interest in disrupting this appearance of natural continuity is to **queer** the accompanying assumption of heterosexuality. In doing so, she radically disrupts the notion of a sex/gender division which has been one of the mainstays of feminist theory.

'Performativity' and 'impersonation' in Butler's and Gallop's contemporary formulation have links to an early article by Joan Rivière, 'Womanliness as a Masquerade' (1986 [1929]) in which Rivière, working within a Freudian psychoanalytic framework, investigates ways that professional academic women negotiate the apparent contradiction of public, professional (phallic) identity and sexed female body. In the following discussion, some ideas of masquerade, impersonation, performance and discipline will be discussed in relation to the areas of bodybuilding and sport; performance art and other 'staged' performances. Finally, there will be a brief discussion of the 'professional performance' of teachers.

Many of the writers referred to draw heavily on, or work within, theories of psychoanalysis derived from Freud and Lacan. It is not within the scope of this book to be a rough guide to psychoanalysis; however, those interested in pursuing ideas of performance will encounter these theories – particularly in certain areas of film theory – and will find it essential to become familiar with their terms of reference.[4] Absolutely fundamental to the idea of psychoanalysis is the notion of the human unconscious: a domain which functions and has effects beyond the parameters of consciousness and which, therefore, is not accessible to 'commonsense' rational analysis. This marks it as 'uncanny', allied with 'the abject', and it is the association of these terms with the feminine that has lead many contemporary feminist theorists, despite grave reservations about the highly gendered practice and discourses of psychoanalysis, to attempt to appropriate its use for feminism.

Masquerades of femininity

A term that reappears throughout contemporary feminist discussions of performance is 'masquerade'. In its 'dictionary' meaning, masquerading includes within itself the notion of 'mask' with the implied existence of something or somebody beneath a surface appearance which can be revealed if the mask is taken away. It is also linked to a very stylised form of performance in western theatre and to the entertainment of 'fancy dress' or 'masked' ball. In the theorists we are examining here, 'masks' are used rather as a series of embodied presences that call into question the idea of a pre-existing authentic self.

In the Lacanian psychoanalytic context, a 'reality' and presence is assumed for the masculine whereby men can have/own 'the phallus' but women cannot. Thus, as Jane Gallop (1988) explains, 'female' and 'woman' are not so much the binary opposite of 'male' and 'man' as the negation or absence: not $x = y$, but 0 and 1. However, a woman can 'be' the phallus through a form of masquerade whereby she takes on the attributes of male desire. Butler identifies and uses as a springboard for her own discussion, an ambiguity in Lacan's use of 'masquerade': if 'being' the phallus is masquerade then the phallus has no being of its own but is always a mask, a play of surface appearances; at the same time, if women 'masquerade' the phallus, might this imply that there *is* something below the mask, rather than the 'lack' that, for Lacan, constitutes 'woman'? This has clear implications for feminism by releasing women from the permanent deficit model and indicating a lost or masked desire – a body that matters – that, therefore, can be recouped. This implication is taken up in Irigaray's challenge to Lacan when she situates the reasons for the masquerade within the heterosexual economy and positions women as rational subjects: '"the masquerade . . . is what women do . . . in order to participate in man's desire, but at the cost of giving up their own"' (cited in Butler 1990: 47).

Joan Rivière's interpretation of masquerade is that femininity (or 'womanliness') is a mask developed by women who desire to be masculine (to *have* rather than *be* the phallus) but who want to deflect the opposition and resentment this will generate from men.[5] Butler suggests that Rivière, by situating her discussion of masquerade in terms of conflict and aggression, avoids some of the sexual implications of her discussion and remains firmly within the heterosexual economy, retaining a unity 'between gender attributes and a naturalized "orientation"' (1990: 50). It is this assumed unity that Butler herself is interested in exposing as illusory construction rather than natural given.

In Rivière's reading, there is no authentic femininity to be masked since 'femininity' itself is a series of acts and performances. Contemporary film theorists such as Mary Ann Doane (1982) have extrapolated from Rivière a possibility for women's agency: if masquerade produces a distance of the performer from the image she is representing, then the image becomes open to women's manipulation and interpretation – thus allowing a movement beyond the control of the male gaze. However, by situating the significance and production of feminine masquerade in the unconscious, Rivière takes attention away from the material body itself, rendering it as a blank page on which the script is written (like the body of the hysteric) rather than as an active participant in the writing. In this respect, Rivière might be said to prefigure a problem addressed by Vicki Kirby (1997) in regard to contemporary feminist theorists of the body: 'somatophobia' – the paradoxical immateriality of bodies in much of the theorising around the body.

In Butler's reading, which contests 'commonsense' notions of time and space, bodies are not the prepared site or space for a pre-existing performance, nor the raw material over which the mask is hung, but brought into being through the performance itself.[6] This interpretation is crucial to her disruption of that continuity between sexed anatomy, gender, and sexuality which privileges the sexed anatomy as the origin of a, singular, sexual identity:

> Because there is neither an 'essence' that gender expresses or externalizes nor an objective ideal to which gender aspires, and because gender is not a fact, the various acts of gender create the idea of gender, and without those acts, there would be no gender at all. Gender is, thus, a construction that regularly conceals its genesis; the tacit, collective agreement to perform, produce, and sustain discrete and polar genders as cultural fictions is obscured by the credibility of those productions – and the punishments that attend not agreeing to believe in them.
>
> (Butler 1990: 140)

Butler is also concerned with undermining ('queering') the belief that specific anatomical body parts are the origins of sexual desire and of 'natural' gender. She asserts that there is no body that pre-exists discourse and, therefore, no sexuality that is 'natural' to bodies:

> Pleasures are said to reside in the penis, the vagina, and the breasts or to emanate from them, but such descriptions correspond to a body which has already been constructed or naturalized as gender-specific. In other words, some parts of the body become conceivable foci of pleasure precisely because they correspond to a normative ideal of a gender-specific body.
>
> (Butler 1990: 70)

Thus, for Butler, the normalising ways in which we come to be gendered shape our body so that, through a kind of dismembering, only some parts of it are made available for desire. Butler's thesis has excited debate and criticism on the grounds that, while she claims to disrupt the mind/body distinction, the disruption is in the one-sided interest of elevating discourse at the expense of nature. [7]

Vicki Kirby in *Telling Flesh* offers a sustained attempt to rethink the body in ways which bring back the 'oozings and pulsings' to the text and can account not just for the immediately tangible aspects of flesh, of the body that can pinch itself, but 'the peristaltic movements of the viscera, the mitosis of cells, the electrical activity that plays across a synapse, the itinerary of a virus . . .' (Kirby 1997: 76). She points to Butler's avoidance of the term 'substance' as indicative of an evasion of some of these issues: 'To think of substance is to think of the very meat of carnality that is born and buried, the stuff of decay that seems indifferent to semiosis' (p. 125).

In her characteristically trenchant way, Susan Bordo traces the shifts in feminist thinking around the body from a resolute emphasis on discourse and representation (or, in Kirby's terms 'semiosis') to a reappraisal of 'the material'; in doing so, she uses examples from her own academic performance: 'The paper I was presenting was an early version of "Material girl: the effacements of postmodern culture" . . . when the word "material" came out of my mouth it was as though I had farted in public' (Bordo 1998: 88). In the same article Bordo speculates that opposition to engagements with 'material bodies' in philosophy – 'The first time I said the word "thigh" in a talk to (mostly male) philosophers, the gulps were audible' – can be traced to the promises held out by philosophy or 'theory' as a field in which 'the high, heady, and "untouchable" . . . realm of ideas' offers the illusion of mastery: an illusion that can only be maintained by disassociation from those bodies that pull us firmly back to ground (pp. 90–1). Which returns us yet again to questions of the nexus of power relations woven through the body/mind division.

Feminist readings of bodybuilding

Bordo, in her discussion of anorexia, 'Anorexia Nervosa: Psycho-pathology as the Crystallization of Culture', points to some of the continuities between the ways in which anorexia sufferers and body-builders speak of their bodies as recalcitrant material in need of taming by the will (in Bordo 1990: 151). While anorexia and bodybuilding have very different, even opposite, imagined goals in terms of the bodies they aim to produce, each could be said to literalise through the flesh the privileging of mind over matter. Bodybuilding offers a particularly rich site for feminist discussion of 'body matters' since it offers up the female body as spectacle while producing that body in ways that often contradict rather than reiterate the signifiers of femininity. Many feminist commentators on women's bodybuilding have remarked on the ways in which this contradiction is actively addressed in the rules and conventions of competition, and by the women themselves.

The spectacle of women's bodybuilding competitions – until that point of very specialised minority interest – excited a broader atten-tion with the release of the film *Pumping Iron II* (1985). Feminist cultural theorist Annette Kuhn (1997 [1988]) uses the film as a means to explore the film theory question of how women spectators find pleasure in films addressed to 'the male gaze'. At the centre of the film is a challenge to the then-existing bodybuilding conven-tions whereby the criteria for women had been explicitly different from those for men: crucially, women were not required to produce overt muscle. The body of the Australian competitor, Bev Francis, presented a problem because of the extent of her muscular devel-opment. Kuhn points out that the film raises, but never answers, 'the conundrum of the appropriate body for a female bodybuilder' (1997: 197): the spectacle of female bodybuilding contradicts the neatly absolute binary divisions of masculinity and femininity in a very confronting way by calling into question what constitutes a

'naturally feminine' body. Kuhn points out the centrality of performance to bodybuilding and to the conundrum posed by *Pumping
Iron II*:

> If performance proposes fluidity and the body connotes fixity, the
> combination of the two in the instance of bodybuilding confers a
> distinctly contradictory quality on the activity. For bodybuilding
> involves more than placing the body on display, more than simply
> passive exhibition . . . In *Pumping Iron II* . . . innumerable scenes
> emphasize the sheer hard work involved in the production of the
> women's bodies. In bodybuilding – the willed construction of a
> certain physique – nature becomes culture.
>
> (Kuhn 1997: 200)

The demonstration of labour, of the work involved, and the
movement of the body in production, is at the extreme opposite to
the femininity which is based on the denial of effort, the erasure
of labour and thus of history: a femininity which is in fact racially
and socio-economically defined.[8] While the whiteness and class
status of this is most clearly imaged in the Victorian lady reclining
on her couch, it lingers on in new late-twentieth-century formations.
A banal example can be seen in those cosmetic advertisements that
offer promises of a return to nature ('the real you') through an
artifice without effort and which conceals itself.

Elizabeth Grosz (1994) briefly addresses the way in which bodybuilding is manifest work: 'a technique of self-production'. Her
primary interest is in the ways that bodybuilding contradicts the
very notions of a 'natural body' on which it appears to be based.
At the same time as positing an intransigent natural body that must
be whipped into shape, the process of transformation reaffirms
the plasticity of the stuff being worked on (you cannot shape
something which is totally resistant and impermeable). Much
of the literature of bodybuilding suggests there is an unachieved,
authentic, body disguised in the present one: a body which will
emerge through bodybuilding, like Superman emerging from
the body of Clark Kent. Grosz argues, however, that this potential
body is itself a construct: 'there is no "natural" norm; there are
only cultural forms of body, which do or do not conform to social
norms' (Grosz 1994: 143). She points out that Bordo's analysis of
anorexia and bodybuilding as issues of will-power, mind over body,
leaves unexplained the body itself or, rather, leaves it as a kind
of foundation or bedrock, a 'natural' matter that is itself beyond
culture and explanation.

Grosz suggests that the meanings of bodybuilding must be different for men and women because that 'natural matter' is always already cultural and therefore carrying the inscriptions of sex: 'The naked European/American/African/Asian/Australian body . . . is still marked by its disciplinary history, by its habitual patterns of movement, by the corporeal commitments it has undertaken in day-to-day life. It is in no sense a natural body, for it is as culturally, racially, sexually, possibly even as class distinctive, as it would be if it were clothed' (Grosz 1994: 142). The techniques of bodybuilding inscribe the living *male* body as the imaginary phallus, 'hard, impenetrable, pure muscle': a singular and monolithic project. Female bodybuilding, therefore, Grosz conjectures, carries two possible interpretations: as 'an attempt to conform to stereotyped images of femininity, a form of narcissistic investment' or 'an attempt . . . to take on for herself many of the attributes usually granted only to men' (p. 224, fn.7).

Marcia Ian (1991) engages, as a bodybuilder, with the idea of the imaginary phallus as the desired object of bodybuilding. As her title, 'From Abject to Object', suggests, Ian examines the ways in which female bodybuilding challenges the alignment of women with the indeterminate realm of the abject. Bodybuilding has, as one of its objects, the eradication of femininity in its connotations of softness and passivity. Ian's argument is basically in agreement with Grosz's claim that the meaning of bodybuilding is different for men's and women's bodies but she places this firmly within the context of cultural construction, maintaining a belief in a body that is below, or beyond culture, and which has only insignificant sexed differences – specifically in relation to musculature. Her discussion opens with the question, 'Do muscles have gender, or are they, on the contrary, ungendered human meat?'.

Bodybuilding offers rich ground for feminist explorations about gender performance because of the clear play of ambiguities it embodies. It does not clearly fit into traditional categories of sport because the judgements are aesthetic rather than quantifiable. The production of this body as an end in itself – rather than as a more efficient jumper or runner – has aspects more usually identified with the feminine. Similarly, some aspects of the male built body such as enlarged pectoral muscles, and some aesthetic practices of competition such as total body depilation, could be said to feminise the male body. Thus, as Ian observes, some elements of bodybuilding seem to facilitate a collapsing of gender differentiation while others work hard to maintain it. Ian points out that while there is open discussion of the masculinising tendencies of female bodybuilding, and regulated attempts to counter them, there is no equivalent discussion or official monitoring of the feminising aspects of male bodybuilding. Similarly, numerous feminist sports theorists observe that, in the area of competitive sport, it is only women competitors who are subjected to sex-testing to authenticate their sex (see, for example, Hall 1996; Birrell and Cole 1994; Lenskyj 1986).

Feminist discussions of women bodybuilders and other women who have trained their bodies for physical performance draw attention not only to the gendering discourses that attempt to return the muscled female body to femininity, but also to other disciplining discourses, of sexuality, race/ethnicity and class. Laurie Schulze (1990) argues the need for a sophisticated investigation into the different inflections of sexuality and bodybuilding. One of Schulze's lesbian interviewees suggests that female bodybuilders look like 'male female impersonators . . . a transvestite bodybuilder' and compares the female bodybuilder's body 'to a costume that can't be removed' (1990: 77).

Anne Balsamo (1996) focuses on the racial inflections of the film's narrative in *Pumping Iron II*. She points out that the final, compromise victor is the African–American Carla Dunlap whose body, in terms of muscular development, lies between 'masculine' white Bev Francis and 'powder puff' white Rachel McLish. Balsamo suggests that the film naturalises Dunlap's body in a way that is common within white cultural discourses and characterised by the common use of Black models to denote the 'wild' or 'exotic' in advertising, and by references to Black athletes' and entertainers' 'natural' speed and rhythm (see, hooks 1990; 1992; Bordo 1993).

As women bodybuilders produce 'more masculine' muscular development and this is accommodated in competition, a particular form of femininity becomes more prescriptive. When Bev Francis took on the process of becoming 'more feminine' in order to satisfy the judges of competitive bodybuilding:

> Her original 180-lb, bulky size was considerably reduced to the right proportion of muscularity and symmetry, she wore makeup and fluffed her bleached blond hair, she had cosmetic surgery on her nose, and she appeared in nifty, colour-coordinated (usually pink) posing bikinis and Spandex outfits.'
>
> (Hall 1996: 61)

One of Schulze's interviewees comments: '(I)t's overdone, not like high fashion, but like make-up applied in a working-class way, a working-class attempt at glamour. It's like Tammy Wynette with muscles' (1990: 77). The feminist analyses allow us, in Butler's terms, to see the new female bodybuilding body coming into being through the repeated discipline of both a physical-training program and a very specific regime of femininity. As we watch, we see that the new female built body still cites, and thus reinforces, the femininity it, in its muscular development, refutes.

If the site of bodybuilding seems to be perfectly designed to demonstrate some elements of Foucauldian theory it also lends itself to Butler's ideas of performativity and the notion that 'drag' is not an aberration but within the continuum of gender con-struction. As Mansfield and McGinn (1993: 65) point out, the pho-tographer Robert Mapplethorpe's images of the highly muscled arm of Lisa Lyons wearing a lace glove ironically juxtapose mascu-linity and femininity within an erotic framework and thus under-line ironically the performativity of gender. The images, in effect, ask Marcia Ian's question, 'Are muscles gendered?' and resists any absolute answers. This ambiguity contradicts the ideal for the male built body, as made explicit in some of the descriptions by male bodybuilders, of an impermeable, erect and pulsating presence: the body literalising the imaginary phallus.

Histories of healthy bodies

Ann Hall (1996) observes, in one of the most recent surveys of feminist theory in relation to sport, that theorists and practitioners in the fields of sports and physical education have only recently shown any interest in the application of feminist cultural theory. It is relatively rare to find writers who are both feminist aca-demics and active practitioners in a physical arena, like Anne Bolin (anthropologist and bodybuilder) or Philipa Rothfield, who writes as a philosopher and dancer. One might speculate with Bordo that feminist studies, like other areas of the academy and despite its questioning of Cartesian dualisms, still operates as a site privileging mind over matter. Hall's chapter, 'The Significance of the Body', offers a useful and accessible introduction to some of the issues from the perspective of a long-term sports practitioner/academic and feminist.

One prevailing model of femininity that is contradicted by the active training of bodybuilding, athletics or any form of sport emphasises women's lack of strength and fitness. Historically, in many societies, to be feminine has been equated with a delicacy and weakness that shades into an essential deficiency or generic flaw. Helen Lenskyj, one of the few feminist historians of sport, describes the nineteenth-century North American and European ideologies that used medical opinion of the time to bar women from sport on the grounds that it 'wastes vital forces, strains female bodies and fosters traits unbecoming to "true womanhood"' (1986: 18). (Similar arguments were used at the time to bar women from academic study on the grounds that vital forces necessary for reproduction would be re-routed to the brain.) As feminist sports historian, Patricia Vertinsky suggests by her title *The Eternally Wounded Woman* (1994), women's bodies are aligned with the abject through the identification of menstrual bleeding as a permanent 'wound'.

Considerable attention has been given to the history of the 'feminine' body by feminist theorists, often highly influenced by Foucault's suggestion that the **'hysterisation'** of the female body is one of the significant markers in the development of a modern society based on discipline and surveillance. To regard the body historically is a feminist–political act since it returns it from nature into culture. In the last hundred years or so, the west and those countries influenced by western thought have seen, as writers like Lenskyj and Vertinsky demonstrate, a remarkable change in attitudes to the health and bodily discipline of women. This is evident in the state's active intervention in the training of bodies through, for example, the institution of physical education programs in schools. In many ways these moves can be linked to shifts in the state's attitude to reproduction: into the 1930s, the increasing importance of eugenicist theories in which ideas of a fit nation shade into politics of racial supremacy; in more recent times, the ethics of genetic engineering (Cole 1994).

Once again, feminist theorists recognise a cluster of ambiguities, in terms of the positive and negative consequences, surrounding this increased state surveillance of women's bodies. Australian feminist historian, Jill Julius Matthews (1987), for example, has researched the development of the natural health movement in pre-World-War-II years and explored its importance not only in terms of promoting women's physical fitness but as a focus of social interaction among women. However, Matthews also draws attention to the ways in which the public discourses through which the movement evolved initiated also the commodification of fitness which is pervasive in the late twentieth century. Part of that commodification entails the establishment of an ideal 'fit' and youthful body which is not realisable by the majority of women. This analysis of the historical production of a particular body has connections, of course, with cultural practices like cosmetic surgery (as discussed above, Chapter 4).

Disciplining healthy women's bodies in China

Fan Hong (1997) offers a detailed historical survey of ideological definitions and redefinitions of women's bodies in China: *Footbinding, Feminism and Freedom.*
She traces the cultural significance of the mid-nineteenth-century Taiping rebellion, and the place within it of peasant women with unbound feet, the impact of western missionaries on traditional Confucian society, and the marked break between the old and new state literally embodied in the 1902 banning of footbinding. She goes on to offer an account of the parallel but differently motivated policies of both the Nationalist and Communist regimes in the twentieth century regarding the encouragement of women's fitness and participation in competitive sport. Fan Hong contrasts the status of women athletes in the Nationalist area, as exceptional 'emancipationist icons' in an era of neo-Confucianism, with the wholesale espousal of 'the emancipatory ideal of the female liberated body' under Communist rule (p. 155). Both regimes, however, were instrumental in enabling new forms of feminine subjectivity through the state's active regulatory intervention into women's physical movement.

In the western context, some feminist sports theorists, concerned with formally organised sports, have used Foucauldian analyses to explore a dynamics of discipline and resistance in the entry, from the 1920s, of women into various public sporting arenas. Cheryl Cole (1994) argues that the history of women's increased participation in sports, and the potential for this to create new, and more powerful, gender definitions for women, is marked by a gradual reinforcement of conventions of femininity reinforced both by formal sporting regulations and media representation. Parallels can be found with some of the analyses of bodybuilding discussed above. For Cole, the chief actor in this 'makeover' is consumer capitalist culture and the dominance of its 'body-marketing practices'. Other contemporary feminist theorists such as Susan Willis (1990) and Margaret Morse (1988) have, similarly, focused on the consumerism of fitness with special attention to women's aerobics and other fitness programs.

Bodies in space

At the heart of much of the debate about women's participation in organised and competitive sports is a perception of the female body as essentially less than the male body, even when rigorously trained. Over the last 20 years, feminist philosopher, Iris Young has developed an important theorised discussion that informs some of the current debates. She has recently offered a reflection on her earlier article, 'Throwing Like A Girl'. (Both articles can be found in Welton 1988) Young's work is influenced by the French phenomenologist Merleau-Ponty. Young takes Merleau-Ponty's concept of the lived body, explores its potential for gendered analysis of women's bodies, and reads it in conjunction with Simone de Beauvoir's existentialist accounts of femininity.

Young is careful to stress that her discussion is within the context of western society and makes general points which do not pretend to embrace the specific conditions of all women. Starting from the ordinary situation of throwing and catching a ball, Young argues that women's bodies occupy a different relationship to space and action from men's. She characterises this relationship in terms of an ambiguous transcendence; inhibited intentionality; and discontinuity with surroundings. Together, these three terms constitute the limitation of women's bodies in action and a disassociation of the self from action. (This can be linked to ideas that women are outside time/natural, ahistorical, and men within time, historical and cultural.) Young suggests that the projection of the self into and through action is inhibited for women, so that a general understanding that something can be done is separated from the sense that 'I can do it': 'Women in sexist society are physically handicapped' (in Welton: 269).[9] Twenty years on, Young suggests that, despite changes in (some) young women's spatial experience and subjectivity, her argument still has relevance to some of the differences of men and women. Her critique of her former position is that it appears to accept the 'deficit' model of women's movements rather than looking positively at some of the ways women's bodies do occupy and move through space (cf. Aston on gendered acting workshops (Aston 1995: 100–1)).

Philipa Rothfield (1994) seems to take up one of Young's suggestions of exploring dance and other body performance when, also drawing on the work of Merleau-Ponty, she examines some aspects of the corporeality of performance and reinterprets readings of the sexual. Her description of the performance work of Shelly Lasica draws attention to the ways in which the performer's body invites connections with the audience in ways which break with the conventional distance of observer and performer. In this sense, Lasica embodies aspects of Merleau-Ponty's concept of the self making sense of the body in relation to others. Rothfield's analysis offers a description of a female body that has enacted itself beyond all the boundaries defined by Young, extending into space, in what Young might term an *un*inhibited intentionality. For Rothfield, Lasica has successfully negotiated '[a] tension . . . between the social tendency to fix the female body within a taxonomy of (hetero)sexuality and appeal and the body's own movements beyond (or despite) the call of fixity' (Rothfield 1994: 61).

Staged performances

The particular aspects of performance that I now want to draw attention to, take off from Rothfield's identification of a tension between the body's fixture and movement as a primary source of gender ambivalences and, therefore, as a space for both the transgressiveness of active female bodies and for the exercise of limits.

I have chosen three sites: the Japanese popular cultural form, the Takarazuka Revue; circus performance; and contemporary performance art. This section will conclude with a brief return to the ideas of the transgressive female body that inform the chapter as a whole.

Jennifer Robertson describes the process by which a select corps of young women become Takarazuka performers: 'Upon their successful application . . . the student actors are assigned . . . "secondary" genders . . . based on both physical (but not genital) and sociopsychological criteria . . . Ironically . . . gender(ed) differences that are popularly perceived as inherent in male and female bodies are embodied by females alone' (1998: 11–12). In some ways, these female performers of highly formalised male roles seem to exemplify Judith Butler's theory of the performativity of gender. Although Jennifer Robertson's book-length study of Takarazuka deliberately restricts references to contemporary western feminist theory in order to concentrate on addressing the western readership's ignorance of Japanese cultural forms, historical and contemporary, she is clearly familiar with Butler's work and that of western writers on cross-dressing such as Margery Garber. A further and particularly interesting focus of Robertson's work is the integral place played in this gender performance by a kind of *cultural* as well as gendered cross-dressing, since the actors perform a highly stylised music-theatre in which characters and narratives are westernised. Or rather, as Robertson suggests, they represent an *idea* of the west which is both the object of desire and the Other, and which is designed to reinforce 'the real' Japanese culture and identity as incorporated in the 'authentic' Japanese bodies of the performers. Robertson argues that the cross-dressed, and more recently androgynous, bodies of the Takarazuka performers exemplify 'how ambiguity and ambivalence can be used strategically in multiple, intersecting discourses, from the sexual to the colonial, both to contain difference and to reveal the artifice of containment' (Robertson 1998: 215).

The Takarazuka revue, unlike Lasica's performance work, maintains a carefully regulated, distanced relationship between audience and performers. However, its central dislocation of gender from genitals and the absence both of any suggestion of 'passing' on the part of the performers and of any illusion on the part of the audience, can also be interpreted as opening up transgressive performances and desire.

Like Takarazuka in Japan, circuses in the west have occupied a position as popular rather than high culture. Female circus performers on the high wire, and in other physical performances, would seem to incorporate a total antithesis to the idea of the feminine body as being rather than doing. They are however, as part of the circus, framed by the costumes and the surroundings as spectacle – often, in traditional circus, wearing costumes that are glittery, abbreviated versions of a ballet tutu.

Peta Tait (1996) draws on the work of Stallybrass and White (*The Politics and Poetics of Transgression* (1986)) to explore the ways in which the bodies of late-nineteenth-century female aerial acrobats who, unlike the music-hall performers, were in active and continuous movement, provided circus audiences with a transgressive pleasure which was still contained and made safe by the discourses and disciplinary techniques surrounding it. While all 'aerialists helped generate an atmosphere of fantastic glamour, wild daring, and death-defying skill' for the audience, it was the female performers who 'demarcated a site of Imaginary freedoms' (p. 29). Because the feminine body was culturally identified with restraint and passivity, it was the female aerialist who most fulfilled the audience's desires: the extent of her skills was emphasised by the extreme contrast between her use of feminine gestures at the beginning and end of her act, the feminine costume, and the sight of her body in apparent free fall, over which she had sole control. The disciplined site of the circus, therefore, allowed a physical freedom in action to the female body which was denied it outside the circus. Tait suggests the possibility that the female aerialist in some ways offers a figure that escapes momentarily, in the act of flight, from the social classifications that Butler claims are inevitable (Tait 1996: 31).

The collective enterprise, the Melbourne Women's Circus, entails the training to performance level of 'ordinary' women. It originated in the idea of reclaiming, for themselves, the bodies of women who are survivors of incest and other sexual violence. It could be seen as a praxis in which the women bring their bodies into a new relationship with space. Important to the project is the setting of levels of achievement by the individual women themselves. At the same time, performance is one of the collective goals with a conscious commitment to challenging traditional codes. As Alison Richards explains: 'The basic business of the circus in performance is the display of the athletic female body . . . The overall impression is of high theatricality, but the female bodies that produce it are far from passive objects of desire or envy' (Women's Circus 1997: 22). Rather than representing issues of women's lives in a staged performance for an audience, the Women's Circus attempts to embody literally women's lives, negotiating the ambiguities and contradictions of spectacle and gender. In this, the Women's Circus has affinities with some contemporary developments in feminist performance art which also blur the conventional boundaries between 'life' and 'art' and deny those traditions of western realist drama that 'laminate the body to character' (Elin Diamond, cited in Aston 1995: 94).

Transgressive sites for contemporary performing female bodies can be found in performance art and some areas of feminist comedy. Much, though by no means all, feminist performance art and feminist comedy transgresses through the eruption of both body and speech into public space.[10] Judith Butler's most recent work on performativity, *Excitable Speech* (1997), addresses questions of the relationship of the body and speech, in order to further her pursuit of how certain bodies are made 'to matter' more than others. She draws on speech theory to explore the ways in which speech occupies an ambivalent place in relation to the body as both a bodily act and yet different from other bodily acts: 'The (speech) act . . . destroys from its inception the metaphysical dichotomy between the domain of the "mental" and the domain of the "physical', breaks down the opposition between body and spirit, between matter and language' (Shoshana Felman, cited in Butler 1997: 11).

Butler's subsequent discussion of the way that the speech act involves not only the body of the speaker but also that of the 'addressee' would seem a fruitful way of discussing the work of performers like Lasica and also for exploring the range of extreme responses aroused in audiences by many 'transgressive' female performance artists and comic performers (cf. the cosmetic-surgery performance of Orlan (see Chapter 4)).

Feminist performance art, as outlined by Anne Marsh (1993), can be seen as going through several dominant 'waves' from the 1970s to the 1990s. Female artists with a commitment to feminism, experimented with different ways of addressing the issue of the male gaze and its cooption of the public female body as the heterosexual object of desire. Similarly, in feminist theatre, Elaine Aston suggests three main strategies have been deployed: underdisplay, overdisplay and cross-gender display.

Cross-gender might be seen in work that aims at an androgyny or a queering of the female body for serious political ends, and the increasing use in female comedy work of cross-dressing to parody the excesses of the male body and, sometimes, to 'queer' femininity: both forms can be seen in the work of the British actors Dawn French and Jennifer Saunders. The performance work of Australian, Linda Sproul may also be viewed in this category:

> the first sequence depicts the artist's male persona in a transparent business suit with her female body visible beneath. The second segment shows the stereotype of the female body as fantasized by men . . . She performs the body movements of the stripper . . . and then returns to the personal space of the audience and hands out small funeral cards which say: 'words cannot express' and 'ever remembered', suggesting perhaps the death of stereotypes.
>
> (Marsh 1993: 219)

This second segment, in which Sproul wears 'signs of sado–masochism', also falls into the category of over-display. Overdisplay is, perhaps, the most risky of devices since the conscious display of the female body as overdetermined object of the male gaze risks being coopted back into the system it intends to mock.

Some performers such as the, very different, North American Annie Sprinkle and Karen Finley address this problem, or rather try to render it as a non-problem in the extremity of their transgressions which have been seen as highly problematic by some feminists as well as by 'mainstream' critics and, in the United States, censors.

Annie Sprinkle, as described by Linda Williams, performs her body in ways that both refer to pornographic conventions and subvert them. While Linda Sproul performs her fetishised appearance clearly within a feminist–political context that rejects complicity with the erotic signs she wears and enacts, Annie Sprinkle has a more ambivalent relation to them and is in some continuum with the performance rather than detached from it. Williams refers to the 1990 performance *Post-post Porn Modernist* in which Sprinkle offers 'a parodic show-and-tell of her life as a sexual performer' (Williams 1997: 360). Part of Sprinkle's interest for Williams is in the ways she demonstrates, and thus deconstructs, the constructedness of the object of desire, for example in an annotated photograph that juxtaposes the tightly controlled and fetishised body of Sprinkle with handwritten notes such as 'I never wear gloves except in pin-up photos'; 'my feet are killing me'; 'hair dyed to cover some grey' (p. 363). These notations could be seen as a visual, written, equivalent to Butler's ideas of speech as both a bodily act and a site of contradiction to the body.

While Annie Sprinkle still, to some extent, operates, though at an extreme, within the conventions of female body as object of male desire, the work of Karen Finley is more difficult to characterise and much more transgressive. In breaking totally with the idea of a coherent performing persona, Finley disrupts ideas of identity. Her body speaks in a performance where both words and body functions violate taboos (Marsh 1993; Carr 1993). Her use of body exposure, often after her first appearance in what C. Carr describes as 'polyester good-girl getup', combined with a flow of obscene words, many sexually explicit, confronts definitions of the erotic in an extreme transgression: 'A filthy woman (in any sense of the word) has stepped further outside social mores than a man can get' (Carr: 144).

Everyday performances

A woman in free fall or parodying a female stripper in a performance space or inviting an audience to survey her cervix with a torch may seem bizarrely separate from the everyday. In what ways do some feminist theorists make a link from these staged performances to the ordinary? Butler's theories would suggest that the female performers occupying a public, recognised and, therefore, partially licensed, performing space make explicit what women are doing all the time: performing 'Woman'.

The work of Jane Gallop (1995) and other reflexive commentators in the arena of teaching suggest that performativity or 'impersonation' can be usefully applied not only to gender but to other 'social markers' such as race and sexuality to make sense of professional practices and experiences and to form new strategies. Indira Karamcheti (1995) discusses ways in which the visibly different body of the minority-background teacher in a mainstream culture (in her case, the United States) has, before she starts lecturing, already been 'read' in a more personal way than that of a 'mainstream' lecturer: 'the ethnic teacher is involved in a kind of skin-trade, but even more in an impersonation. The ethnic teacher performs a generic ethnicity' (Karamcheti 1995: 145). For Karamcheti it is important that this is acknowledged rather than left as an implicit condition so that different strategies can be developed.

From a different but comparable perspective, British sociologist Felly Nkweto Simmonds (1997) speculates 'How does a Black woman do sociology?' Like Karamcheti, Simmonds comments on the way in which the minority-background body is always more thoroughly identified with its body as the site of an 'authentic identity'. She explores the construction of the female African body in British cultural history: 'Adorned and unadorned I cannot escape the fantasies of the western imagination' (p. 232). She too stresses the importance of a reflexive practice and argues the need for intervention within the theories and disciplines in order to reconstitute the 'body of knowledge'. Simmonds' argument usefully summarises a central direction of feminist theories of the body, identity and knowledge. Since women's bodies, Black women's bodies, a range of Other bodies, are pushed into a limiting category of the natural as the opposite of male, white, Mind, then the knowledge that produces that split must be undermined even though that will be strongly resisted:

> When I teach sociology, as a Black woman in an almost all-white institution, the social reality of academia and of academic discourse is transformed . . . As Black academics (and students), one of our tasks has to be to transform theory itself, if we are not to remain permanent 'curiosities' in academia . . . To have our bodies, ourselves, admitted on our own terms, will be an act of naming ourselves on this journey through the 'heart of whiteness.'
> (Simmonds 1997: 236–7)

At the centre of the issue, for female bodies in general, and for all who are not 'Benchmark Man' (see Chapter 5) is what Simmonds describes as 'theory's insistence that we can articulate truths only through a rational and objective epistemology'; 'Ontological knowledge is suspect and at worst pathologized,' in terms that are reminiscent of the pathologising of the female body itself (Simmonds: 228).

Feminist work on the body in professional areas such as teaching or nursing, is a risky business because it draws attention to the female body in public, and therefore out of place. Just as performance work that overdisplays the female body, even for parody, is easily coopted back into the male gaze, so an attention to the specifics of the female body in the office, courtroom, classroom or hospital ward can incur increased disciplining. Is this, perhaps, one of the reasons why many female academics seem to suffer from 'somatophobia'? Joanna Frueh, whose performances enact what she calls an 'erotic scholarship', aimed at deconstructing the distanced impersonality of the lecturer, offers the following comment, as disruptive as Susan Bordo's metaphorical 'farting':

> After the heat of early '70s feminism . . . (w)e have seen feminists proving they are intellectuals. Perhaps this has been necessary to know, I hope for ourselves, that we are neither simply bodies nor simple bodies. To some degree, however, I see this intellectual production . . . as forced labor. Alice Neel said, 'Women in this culture often become male chauvinists, thinking that if they combine with men, they may be pardoned for being a hole rather than a club'. Fear of the female body separates Logos from Eros. Cunt, and its derisive connotations, scares us. Cunt is dangerous to professional well-being.'
>
> (Frueh 1996: 117)

Summary

- The female performing body exposes the constructedness of femininity

- Theories of 'masquerade', 'impersonation' and 'performativity' undo the clear distinction between staged public performance and everyday maintenance of femininity – they also problematise notions of an authentic single identity and the mind/body division.

- Bodybuilding presents a 'limit case' in its performance of 'mind over matter' and its spectacle of female body: feminist analyses of bodybuilding investigate the class, sexual and racial constructions of femininity embodied in bodybuilding and the ways that female bodybuilders are 'disciplined' back into the femininity which their built bodies would seem to negate.

- Athletic women's bodies also enact an antithesis to many conventions of femininity: feminist historical analyses of mass movements towards 'fitness' for women exemplify the state's disciplining of women's bodies, but also demonstrate sites of women's resistance. A historical perspective returns women's bodies from a timeless 'nature' to culture.

- Feminist appropriations of phenomenology suggest that women's bodies are taught to occupy space in different ways from men.

- Different sites of staged performance all expose the constructedness of gender, often by embodying a contradiction of ambiguity:

  1 Takarazuka Revue in Japan disturbs notions of a sexual-gender-sexed body continuum and exemplifies the tension between discipline and transgression;
  2 circus combines physical expertise, spectacular display and theatricality in ways that, confound notions of 'femininity';
  3 feminist performance artists and comic actors deliberately 'speak the unspeakable' and embody in their performance spaces, experiences and discourses that are kept out of sight, in the male domain, or heavily policed.

- Everyday public life for many professional women also involves performance: the example of teaching/lecturing positions women in a space that demands the erasure of the personal, but then draws attention to the woman's body as different.

Notes

1 It is the irreducibility of the term 'woman' in its implications of an unchanging, ahistorical heterosexual sexed-female body that Denise Riley (1988) challenges in the question that forms her title *Am I That Name?*

[2] A relatively recent phenomenon is the demand on writers to perform in person at festivals, book promotions, etc., a move which immediately re-genders writing and seeks to establish a continuity of body/identity/writing.

[3] Note also that an understanding of these codes, including their class implications, can be understood and used in transgressive ways as detailed in a number of British studies (See for example Angela McRobbie, 1981; Lesko 1988).

[4] For these terms in reference to feminist theory see, for example, the first two chapters of Mitchell and Rose 1982; Grosz 1990.

[5] In classic–Freudian terms, Rivière's interpretation draws on the notion of the Oedipal Complex and castration anxieties: women who compete with men in the public arena arouse castration anxiety in men.

[6] As a corrective to eurocentrism it is worth looking, for example, at Jennifer Robertson's recent detailed exploration of a form of Japanese popular music theatre, Takarazuka Revue. Robertson suggests:

> Although this revelation [of gender as artifice] has come only recently to Euro-American theorists . . . the notion of gender as performance has a centuries-old history in Japan . . . In Kabuki, an actor becomes a type or style of woman or man, as opposed to imitating an actual (feminine) female or (masculine) male . . . Historically, Japanese females have been encouraged to follow the ideal standard of femininity constructed and performed by the Kabuki *onnagata*, or player of women's roles.'
> (Robertson 1998: 38)

See also Chapter 6, p. 126 for further discussion of Takarazuka.

[7] Maxine Sheets-Johnstone (1998), for example, argues the need to return to the body beyond surface anatomy, positioning Butler firmly in the ranks of constructionism for her denial of what Sheets-Johnstone calls 'the evolutionary body'.

[8] The effortless timeless feminine has been exposed as reliant on the historical labour of working-class women and women of colour/Third World women for its maintenance (hooks 1992; Bordo 1993; Ware 1992).

[9] Young's suggestion has resonances for those women formally regarded as 'disabled', suggesting the need for a gendered analysis of disability and a deconstruction of the term itself. Susan Wendell (1996) uses Young's statement as a support for her own call for reassessment of definitions of disability.

[10] For discussions of female/feminist comedy see, for example, Patricia Mellencamp (1992) *High Anxiety: Catastrophe, Scandal, Age and Comedy.* Bloomington: Indiana University Press; Philip Auslander ' "Brought to You by Fem-Rage": Stand-up Comedy and the Politics of Gender.'

In Hart and Phelan 1993. Both Mellencamp and Auslander give considerable attention to the US comedian and actor Roseanne Barr whose body might be said to have moved from transgression into discipline, following her trajectory from the relative openness of live stand-up performance into regular television.

Further reading

Butler, Judith (1998) 'Selections from *Gender Trouble*'; 'Selection from *Bodies That Matter*'. In Donn Welton (ed.) (1998) *Body and Flesh: A Philosophical Reader*. Malolen, Massachusetts and Oxford: Blackwell. (Judith Butler, *Gender Trouble* [first published 1990]; *Bodies That Matter* [first published 1993]).

Gallop, Jane (ed.) (1995) *Pedagogy: The Question of Impersonation.* Bloomington and Indianapolis: Indiana University Press.

Hall, M. Ann (1996) *Feminism and Sporting Bodies: Essays on Theory and Practice.* Champaign, Illinois: Human Kinetics (especially chapter 4, 'The Significance of the Body').

Mansfield, Alan and McGinn, Barbara (1993) 'Pumping Irony: The Muscular and the Feminine'. In Sue Scott and David Morgan (eds) *Body Matters: Essays on the Sociology of the Body.* London and Washington: The Falmer Press.

Simmonds, Felly Nkweto (1997) 'My Body, Myself. How Does a Black Woman Do Sociology?' In Heidi Safia Mirza (ed.) *Black British Feminism.* London and New York: Routledge.

Young, Iris (1998) 'Throwing like a Girl'.; '"Throwing Like a Girl": Twenty Years Later'. In Donn Welton (ed.) *Body and Flesh: A Philosophical Reader.* Malden, Massachusetts and Oxford: Blackwell. ['Throwing Like A Girl' is also in Young, 1990.]

Chapter 7

Virtual bodies

Chapter outline

Feminist explorations of cyberspace: debates about the extent to which the new communication technologies open up different subjectivities for women.

• Feminists in cyberspace	reasons for feminist interest in new technologies.
• Feminist cyborgs	the cyborg hybrid; new 'female' bodies; irony; indeterminacy; prosthesis; cyberspace.
• 'Meat'	release from the body?; new space-old cultural markers.
• Second, third, fourth . . . selves?	identity; subjectivity; real or illusion?
• Feminist revisioning	Jupiter Space; feminist art.
• In conclusion	

Feminists in cyberspace

In this final chapter, we shall look briefly at some recent feminist theorising that engages with the implications of new technologies and, in particular, the technologies of 'cyberspace'. The relevance of these debates for a discussion of the female body lies in the various claims made by some of the more technophile feminists that the new technologies of communication open up possibilities for women – and others identified as Other to 'Benchmark Man' – to develop new and diverse subjectivities that defy the traditional social markers. These claims are disputed by technosceptics – and denied by technophobes – who argue that the novelty of the media of new communications is deceptive: in the new terrain, the same old categories still struggle for dominance. This apparently clear division into opposing camps is resisted by a large number of writers, for example, Donna Haraway and Zoë Sofoulis (Sofia/ Sophia) who suggest a more useful approach to new technologies is a creative ambivalence.

At the centre of the feminist debates around new technologies is the question of the female body: is it potentially liberated by a movement into cyberspace that promises to free women into a new play of unlimited subjectivities? Does this separation from the cultural markers of the 'real-life' (RL) body really disperse 'woman' into a limitless postmodern – or even **posthuman** – set of multiple subjectivities? If so, does this necessarily also disperse the location and subject of feminism? All these questions return us to many of the materialist and radical feminist arguments with postmodernism. While some 'technophiles' seem quite happy to float into cyberspace as 'cyberangels' and attempt to 'leave the meat behind',[1] other feminist theorists like Sofoulis suggest that the relative openness of the new media can enable new *feminist* subjectivities to come into being that still remain embodied: furthermore, these feminist presences are necessitated by the existing, and tenacious, gendered, and other 'marked', paradigms imported into cyberspace. Rather than seeing a necessarily hierarchical opposition whereby the body is relegated to 'meat' as, once again, the Other of a disembodied mind, Sofoulis and others argue for a rethinking of the body within the new technologies and for putting 'the guts' back into the machine.

In a different context, Rosi Braidotti (1996) agrees that there has to be an engagement by feminism with new technologies but not as a route to 'transcendence':

> the last thing we need at this point in Western history is a
> renewal of the old myth of transcendence as flight from the
> body . . . Nowadays, women have to undertake the dance through
> cyberspace, if only to make sure that the joy-sticks of the
> cyberspace cowboys will reproduce univocal phallicity under the
> mask of multiplicity, and also to make sure that the riot girls, in
> their anger and their visionary passion, will not recreate law and
> order under the cover of a triumphant feminine.
>
> (no page number)

The new technologies to be considered here, with some of their feminist interpretations, are: the combination of human with machine: the **cyborg**, related ideas of **prosthesis**, and the repositioning of the 'gaze'. There are of course many other applications and sites within new technologies: some of which have been touched on earlier in the book, for example in the discussions of cosmetic surgery, and reproduction. Here, as elsewhere in feminist theorising, there are heated debates about the extent to which some of the more celebratory feminist writing about 'cyberspace', particularly as it is implicated in the dispersal of identity and the replacement of material body by discourse, is profoundly eurocentric and elitist. Carol Stabile, for example, offers a detailed critique of Donna Haraway, arguing that Haraway's cyborg politics are predicated on a highly literate community with the skills, time and inclination to engage in textual analysis ('Calculating on a Frictionless Plane'. In Stabile 1994).

Feminist cyborgs

'Cyberspace', like many of the terms associated with it, is slippery and multi-faceted. As Zoë Sophia explains it, the term was coined by the novelist William Gibson to describe the imaginary 'visual/ spatial representation of transglobal networks . . . mentally entered by futuristic computer hackers via "trodes" attached to their heads or via other body implants' (Sophia 1992: 22, fn.1). It is now used, however, to designate the existing simulated environments generated by computer programs of various kinds and, more generally, the 'virtual space' of the program or network. In the following discussion, I use this more general definition. Haraway's feminist cyborg is an element within the network, part of the integrated circuit, but one which potentially can break the circuit, rather like a virus infiltrating, and thus changing, the system.

North American Donna Haraway is a central figure in feminist debates about cyberspace and cyborgs. Haraway's curriculum vitae, like that of a number of other writers in the field, combines interests in what are usually thought of as 'arts' subjects to do with textual analysis, and the history and philosophy of science.[2] A highly influential essay by Haraway, 'A Manifesto for Cyborgs', introduces a very controversial figure into feminist thought: the cyborg. This article, which appears in a number of slightly different forms from 1983 onwards, suggests that the cyborg, rather than an irreducibly masculine figure, the stuff of films like *Terminator*, can be appropriated for feminism. Haraway even goes further in suggesting this appropriation may be a necessity for feminism rather than a choice. This claim is one of the central points of contestation for radical feminist commentators such as Renate Klein and Susan Hawthorne (see, for example, Klein 1996).

So what are the particular aspects of the cyborg that incite controversy? Anne Balsamo offers the follow definition:

> Cyborgs are hybrid entities that are neither wholly technological nor completely organic, which means that the cyborg has the potential to disrupt persistent dualisms that set the natural body in opposition to the technologically recrafted body, but also to refashion our thinking about the theoretical construction of the body as both a material entity and a discursive process. These bodies are multiply constituted parts of cybernetic systems – what we now recognize as social and informational networks.
>
> (Balsamo 1996: 11)

Balsamo's definition prioritises the 'hybrid' being of the cyborg: its blending of more than one substance/component into a new entity and its integration into systems of information. This idea of the cyborg is considered to have potential for changing basic patterns of thought in modern western society because it throws into confusion conventional points of reference such as the stable separation of nature and culture, materiality and discourse. And of course, it also challenges the Descartian separation of mind and body, with subsequent implications for the construction of 'woman'.

For Haraway, another important characteristic of the cyborg is its break with history – 'In a sense the cyborg has no origin story in the Western sense' (1991: 150) – and thus also its break from the constraints of psychoanalytic history. Haraway suggests that the cyborg has never been 'innocent'. That is, it is not enmeshed in the oedipal stories that are themselves posited on a version of the myth of the Fall in Judaeo-Christian scriptures and which suggest that human behaviour is always based on a desire to return to a state of innocence and unity with nature/mother: 'The cyborg does not dream of community . . . The cyborg would not recognize the Garden of Eden, it is not made of mud and cannot dream of returning to dust' (151). For Haraway, therefore, the cyborg has the potential to release us from the weight of history, from nostalgia, and from a never-fulfilled desire for transcendence. From a feminist–political standpoint, Haraway argues, this releases woman from the position she has always occupied in those stories, liberates her from the burden of her history. The dissolution of the binary divisions on which western culture has been based is embodied in the cyborg which/who is neither 'natural' body nor 'cultural' machine, neither organic nor inorganic. Kathleen Woodward argues for a reading of 'The Manifesto for Cyborgs' in terms of 'literary science fiction at its best', which uses the imaginary or speculative future as 'a critique of the present, one that is markedly clear in its acknowledgment of the social and historical constitution of gender and race' (1994: 55). But there is a problem, as many materialist and radical feminists have pointed out, in utilising this futuristic figure for political purposes *now*. The feminist–cyborg body of Haraway's desire is a hybrid of integrated, equal components – a speculative fiction – while other forms of boundary crossings between human and non-human, organic and non-organic, take place within RL hierarchical power relations. Living Third World bodies are 'harvested' for organs to transplant into First World bodies and for genetic material to enable science in association with multinational business to provide a definitive map of being human (The Human Genome Project); other forms of technology extend surveillance of human beings into all our activities in what Haraway herself calls, 'an informatics of domination'.

Haraway is, herself, by no means unaware of these issues. In her recent, somewhat cumbersomely titled, *Modest_Witness@Second-Millennium.FemaleMan©_Meets_OncoMouse*™ (1997) Haraway very directly addresses the issue of application of her theories to 'real life', most clearly in a section called 'Pragmatics'. In her discussion of the computer-generated image she calls 'SimEve', she stops in her analysis to say: 'So why do I feel so uncomfortable?' and later, in the same discussion, she voices what sounds like the central concern running through much of her feminist critics: 'It is the resolute absence of history, of the fleshy body that bleeds, that scares me . . . I want something messier, more dangerous' (1997: 263; 264).

Another key element in Haraway's development of a feminist–cyborg politics is the embrace of apparent contradictions and discontinuities within a perspective of irony. Irony, with its implication of detachment, is understood by Haraway to enable a simultaneous creative engagement with new technologies and the critical distance to refuse some aspects of them. The use of 'irony' as a central term, together with her insistence on textual analyses, has led some of Haraway's critics to align her with postmodernist theorists, although she herself resists the identification. As in the debate about the usefulness of speculative fictions for contemporary politics, questions are raised as to whether or not a standpoint in continuous play and ironically aware of contradictions and ambiguities can also be directed to specific issues of material concern and action.[3]

It is the indeterminacy of the cyborg body that holds much of its attraction for many of the writers in this field who associate this aspect of the cyborg with ideas of borderlands and liminality as spaces where movement, challenge and creativity are made possible. As a construction that blurs boundaries between organic and inorganic, and dissolves the boundary of the self into a network or networks of information flows, the cyborg also resembles some of the attributes linked to 'woman'. As Patricia Wise puts it:

> In Western modernity women were always virtually real, 'not quite there' or 'almost absolute'. As the lack against which the male presence was maintained, women's embodied presence was a fact, but it was written over by an absence of autonomy. It did not constitute a presence from which culture or society was spoken about and understood.
>
> (Wise 1996: 1)

This concentration on discursive formations of 'woman' gets short shrift from some radical-feminist critics who point out that, while 'woman' may have been 'not quite there', lots of women were, as feminist–revisionist histories demonstrate (Hawthorne 1996).

Balsamo also seizes on the hybridity and indeterminacy of the cyborg as a key to the way Haraway 'maps the identity of woman onto the image of the cyborg . . . Both Woman and Cyborg are simultaneously symbolically and biologically produced and reproduced through social interactions' (Balsamo 1996: 34). A number of writers also appropriate or refer to some writing on race and 'marginal' cultures as a parallel to the cyborg. Allucquère Roseanne Stone draws on Gloria Anzaldúa's discussion of the 'Mestiza', a figure who is defined by her position on the margins of different cultural groups and inhabits their borderlands, yet who is never totally explained or incorporated. Stone erases the racialised and gendered context of Anzaldúa's analysis to apply it to 'participants in the electronic virtual communities of cyberspace [who] live in the borderlands of both physical and virtual culture, like the Mestiza' (Stone 1991: 20).[4] Susan Hawthorne offers an acerbic comment on the 'whiteness' of technophiles: 'Cyborgs provide a haven for all those dominant-culture theorists who have suddenly been left behind by their own reification of difference. How can you claim difference if you are a white (fe)male heterosexual American? Answer: you claim your cyborg identity' (1996: 6).

Given that the most common representation of the cyborg in popular imagination is the one rampant in films like *Terminator*, the similarities of woman (still less, women) and cyborg can seem more than a little strained. Some critics also question why the similarities of the cyborg, if there are any, to the conventional construction of 'woman' should be of any use to feminism, given that it is a construction of indeterminacy which could also be termed 'lack' or 'deficit': neither term of obvious benefit to those designated by the terms. However, the conventional, *Terminator* image of a hybrid human/robot is only one of the manifestations of the cyborg. For Haraway the category is much wider: '(t)he cyborg is our ontology' (1991: 150). In other words, the cyborg is not simply an imaginary inhabitant of speculative fiction but the pattern for life in contemporary, late-capitalist society.

This extension of the term to describe the unprecedented ways in which contemporary embodiment incorporates technologies, is associated with the idea of prosthesis, a term which features in much of the discussion of cyborgs and cyberspace. A prosthesis is itself an extension, something added on to enable the body to achieve some purpose: a tool. At its most basic, a wooden or plastic leg literally stands in for the limb that is lost or absent. Cosmetic surgery is prosthetic in creating additional or changed body parts for the purpose of constructing a body more in line with cultural norms or perceptions of beauty: for example, a constructed breast supplements an absence for a post-mastectomy patient who no longer feels 'like a real woman'. Post-operative transsexuals could be said to have achieved their reconstructed bodies by prosthetics. Arguably, the extension of the body into cyberspace is a form of prosthesis, whereby the computer technologies enable the body to experience and communicate in ways it could not, unaided. As modern urban society becomes more and more technologically based, the barriers between self and networks of information, body and environment become increasingly blurred.

A further dimension to prosthesis lies in the development of different ways to replace body parts or treat disease: the transplanting of animal organs into humans, the use and manipulation of laboratory-grown genetic material. These and many other emerging technologies challenge boundary definitions of the human and non-human, and put stress on our understanding of what is or is not natural and, through the association of 'woman' with 'nature', on our understanding of 'woman'. A radical-feminist critique, particularly when associated with some ecofeminist agendas, rejects or is deeply suspicious of such blurrings of boundary and surgical interventions dependent as they are on a science perceived as implicitly phallocentric.

Another aspect of prosthesis, and one that seems to excite an enormous amount of interest, involves the prostheses of gender and sexuality. It is possible to argue that many, if not all, accoutrements of gender are a kind of prosthesis aimed at extending a specifically sexed body. This idea has been applied to the copious investigation of sex in cyberspace, or 'teledildonics'. 'Teledildonics' combines the phallic prosthesis ('dildo') with the idea of distance communications ('tele'). For writers, the pleasures of cyberspace as a textual rather than a material space are linked to a possibility of disguising and re-modelling a whole range of material features and attributes, including biological sex and RL sexuality. In this way, its enthusiasts claim, both gender and sexuality can be infinitely 'queered' and shown, in Judith Butler's terms, to be performative.

Shannon McRae (1995) explores some of the ways men and women invent different personae often with different gender and sexual attributes from their real life (RL) selves in the cyberspace environments, MUDs (Multi User Dimensions). MUDs offer a particularly interesting site for looking at the ambiguities of 'body' and 'information system' in cyberspace, because, unlike text-based 'talk', they are located in a 'room' or other space and are brought into being as bodies: you describe your feelings and appearance as well as 'talking'. McRae describes a non-male, non-female gender, 'the Spivak', which is available in some MUDs: 'The Spivak gender . . . has a unique set of pronouns: e, em, eir, eirs, eirself . . . has encouraged some people to invent entirely new bodies and eroticize them in ways that render categories of female or male meaningless' (1995: no page numbers). McRae uses the 'Spivak' to emphasise the way in which cyberspace is discursive: 'The fact that the indeterminacy of the spivak gender allows them to construct their bodies in whatever way they choose foregrounds the fact that netsex is as much an act of writing as it is sex.' Forestalling the objection that this is no different from other forms of erotic writing, McRae points to the interactive nature of netsex and its plasticity: 'In the context of virtuality, gender becomes partly an abstraction – a feature of the particular bodies that are being written rather than an important fact of human identity.' In ways that echo some of Irigaray's descriptions of a multiple, flowing female self/selves, and Cixous' writing the body, McRae suggests that the active writing of 'netsex' language produces a movement into the 'gap between utterance and experience': perhaps, also into the imagined gap between mind and body. McRae points to the paradox that this is enabled by the technology that has often been set up as the opposite of body, pleasure and sensuality.

'Meat'

The expanses of virtual reality and cyberspace may seem to offer new freedoms for 'travellers' who feel frustrated or limited by their RL bodies and the world they inhabit. While not engaging directly with issues of virtual reality, Susan Wendell (1996) offers in her feminist discussion of disability (an area not well represented in feminist debate) a salutary critique of the ways in which feminists assume an 'able' body both in RL and cyberspace. Wendell suggests that both theorists of the body as discourse and those feminists often labelled as 'essentialist' ignore one central reason why some might want to detach mind from body: chronic and persistent pain. Wendell speaks from her own experience of feeling 'taken over and betrayed by a profound bodily vulnerability . . . not the result of any change of cultural "reading" of the body or of technological incursions into the body' (p. 169). She goes on to argue that this gap in the feminist theorising directed at dissolving Descartian binaries leads to an underestimation of 'the subjective appeal of mind–body dualism' and a failure to provide 'an adequate alternative conception of the relationship of consciousness to the body' (p. 169). Wendell might argue that whatever the freedoms opened up to the less able body by the prostheses of communication technologies, the originary body will still feel pain, discomfort and its limitations in RL.

Wendell offers an extreme example of a recurrent theme in all but the most fanatically technophile discussions of current and future technologies: while the 'cyborg' may appear to be 'without innocence' and free of origins in its science fiction manifestations, human bodies and psyches remain the originators of technologies in our contemporary setting and they bring their prejudices and desires with them, along with their mortality. Allucquère Roseanne Stone, an enthusiast for the different potentials of cyberspace, cautions: 'No refigured virtual body, no matter how beautiful, will slow the death of a cyberpunk with AIDS' (1991: 20).

The extreme rejections of 'meat' seem to be universally male, coming from 'cyberspace cowboys'. A number of writers, including Stone, comment that these enthusiasts appear to have a mid- to-late- adolescent western male profile with all the accompanying gender, racial and other markers of world view that this implies. 'Virtual sex' like other forms of 'virtual' activities remains textual and therefore is not risky to the body in the way that sex between bodies in RL can be. Above all, and despite the panic discussions of 'virtual rape' and other forms of violence in cyberspace, there is ultimately the possibility of instant disconnection and removal from 'in there' in a way that is unfortunately not the case 'out here'. The nexus of risk and control that erects a hierarchy of high-value in-control 'virtual self' and low-value, at-risk 'meat' can be all too readily mapped on to the familiar dualism of high-value (male) mind and low-value (female) body – indeed the term 'meat' has resonances from pornography. Far from occupying a place that dissolves the binaries of nature and culture, many SF scenarios, from Gibson's *Neuromancer* to the recent film *Gattaca*, construct class hierarchies whereby a techno-elite has the most privileges, working with the 'clean' mind while the 'natural' is despised and relegated to menial work, and where there seem to be many more men than women. The same discourse that calls the RL body 'meat' refers to the organic brain as 'wetware'. Like some aspects of cosmetic surgery, 'keep young' health regimes, and medical technologies, the desire for the virtual (no)body can be mapped on to dreams of immortality and release from the mortal, wet, swampy, reproductive female body.

For many writers, this flight from the RL body is a product of late-twentieth-century panics about disease, pre-eminently AIDS, as the extreme threat (see Hayles 1993; Penny 1994). Disease reminds the male body, constructed in opposition to the female permeable body, that it too can have its boundaries breached: it too is mortal.[5] In Simon Penny's memorable phrase: 'virtual sex is the ultimate prophylactic' (1994: 240). Thus, it is possible to map a preference for 'virtual sex' on to the fear and distaste of the body and its abjection which, as we have discussed earlier, is primarily associated in the western imaginary with women, homosexual men and/or other 'races': no oozings and exchange of body fluids in cyberspace nor any miscegenation. This is the reverse of visions of multiple fluid subjectivities and a break-down of limiting cultural markers. At the same time, the narrative freedoms of cyberspace allow the discursive construction of engagements with 'bodies' that would be considered too risky and dangerous in RL. As numerous writers have observed, this actually means that the fluid and liberatory potentials of cyberspace as celebrated by McRae and others are far more often inhabited by very familiar misogynist and racist narratives of abuse and domination.

Jodi O'Brien, in her article 'Changing the Subject' (In *Women and Performance*, Issue 17)[6] is sceptical about claims that there are no closets in cyberspace. Exploring how far the medium opens up infinitely queer possibilities for sexuality, she concludes that issues of 'passing' and the desire to know the originary body of the personae encountered in cyberspace still prevail:

> Scholarly explorations of users within and across queer/straight spaces are nearly nonexistent in the academy at this time. Is there considerable cross-over between those in queer and straight spaces, or are the conventional ghettos being reproduced in emerging online communities? This empirical information is pivotal for considerations of the Internet as a realm for changing the subject. I find myself in disagreement with the statement, 'there are no closets online.' In fact, I wonder about which new closets are forming.
>
> (no date; no page numbers)

Stone (1991) offers an interesting psychoanalytic examination of one of the appeals of cyberspace for the young white men (or rather, in Stone's phrase, 'the adolescent male within humans of both sexes) who seem to be its majority population. Stone develops a theory of 'cyborg envy'. The collapse of body boundaries, as one becomes a cyborg, is described in terms that evoke a sense of putting on drag: 'To become the cyborg, to put on the seductive and dangerous cybernetic space like a garment is to physically *put on* the female' (p. 18). It is, in Stone's description, as though the entry into cyberspace might fulfil the impossible desire to return to a unity with the maternal body without losing the control of naming and reading the space: a kind of by-pass of the oedipal dilemma. In some ways this resembles Peta Tait's account of the attractions of the female circus performer in apparent free fall (see Chapter 6). As has been pointed out by Susan Hawthorne (1996), Stone's is a highly gendered reading that might appear to privilege a masculine perspective in ways that the elision of 'adolescent male within both sexes' does not adequately address.

The issue of 'meat' and its relationship to whatever/whoever develops in cyberspace, remains one of the most highly contested areas between feminists as well as between feminists and 'cyberspace cowboys'. Margaret Morse devotes a lengthy article to the issue, evoked neatly in her title 'What Do Cyborgs Eat?' (1994), which critiques the celebration of a machine/human hybridisation. Her complex discussion includes an implied analogy of the contemporary move (of some) to disembodiment in cyberspace with anorexia in terms of a retreat from external and apparently uncontrollable problems, represented by the physical, 'meat' body, into the inner space of the computer. Indeed, one of the female active participants in MUDs interviewed by Sherry Turkle explained that she was anorexic: 'I like making my body disappear'; her virtual persona is 'not someone you want to see sexually . . . "sort of a woman"' (Turkle 1995: 215). For this woman, her persona seems to be a further extension of her anorexic RL body, rather than a substitute for it. Compare Bernadette Flynn's report of ' "sport death", where the hacker pushes himself [sic] beyond the limits of mind and body, not eating or sleeping, for days and nights' (1994: 14).

While a great deal of attention is paid to the relationship of the RL body to the virtual personae in the cyberspace theory, a number of writers point out that the material bodies and lives of those producing the base technologies is often erased totally or glossed over. As material-feminist analysts have researched and recorded, there is an increasing trend towards the feminisation of the production of many primarily First-World consumption goods, including the hard- and software of new technologies. Multinational electronics companies, for example, frequently base their production in Third World countries, using cheap female labour in unregulated or poorly regulated conditions. Allucquere Roseanne Stone observes that Descartes was able 'to forget the body: only

because he had servants to attend to the needs of his' (cited in
Penny 1994: 246). Carol Stabile argues that, despite Haraway's situating of her early 'Manifesto for Cyborgs' in the context of socialist feminism, a celebration of difference and infinite discursive
possibilities 'may well work across the lines of gender, race, and
erotic orientation within an intellectual field' but is not adequate
for 'scaling the increasingly insurmountable walls that divide classes'
(1994: 152) because it pays insufficient attention to the control
and movement of capital.

Second, third, fourth . . . selves?

Sherry Turkle, in a relatively early discussion of new communication technologies, uses psychological perspectives to explore the
idea that the technology enables the development of a 'second self'
(Turkle 1984). Basing her discussion here, as in her later work
(1995; 1996), on extensive interview material, Turkle explores the
ways that users speak about themselves as 'split' or multiple selves
and of the need to develop new discourses for this experience.
New technologies and the spaces they generate, for Turkle, place
a critical stress on grammar, as exemplified in her title, 'Who am
We?' (1996). An enthusiast of the technologies, Turkle's primary
concern is with developing a new discourse and enabling users,
both male and female, to participate without psychological stress.
Her concern with language does not seem to include a strong sense
of its politics: she refers for example to 'sexual tourists' in cyberspace, without any apparent recognition of its RL exploitative connotations; similarly, she enthusiastically endorses the 'return' from
cyberspace as being like 'an anthropologist returning home from
a foreign culture' who 'can return to the real world better equipped
to understand its artifices' (1995: 13; 263). As many feminist
critics have commented, there are too many oppressive resonances
in similar evocations of cyberspace as 'a new frontier' or 'virgin
territory' ready for penetration and colonisation. Lisa Nakamura
observes: 'The political action group devoted to defending the
right to free speech in cyberspace against governmental control
calls itself "The Electronic Frontier"; this is another example of the
metaphorization of cyberspace as a colony to be defended against
hostile takeovers' (Nakamura 1995).

From Sarah Diamond's 'Taylor's Way'

It's simplistic to state that gender conflicts preceded digitization and have carried over into digital space. Still, women appear to be a minority in cyberspace. Work patterns of prior industries are partially embedded in the Net . . . If you doubt this, just flip through the back issues of *Wired* and count the number of women featured on the cover . . . These days the Net spans mass and sub-cultures. The Web is a valued marketing tool for an increasing number of businesses. With advertising and big industry have come unchallenged patriarchal imagery and conservative values. Still, there is the playful and willful [sic] use of new technologies to challenge gender and other oppressively fixed identities by VNS Matrix and other cyber femmes. Not that they ever were safe, but there is increasing trouble in the cyber corridors of power.

The notion that cyberspace is a feminine space of fluidity and undefined identity is utopian . . . There is still a moment of victory when cultural machines take possession of sexual subversion, just ask Mae West.

Source: Terry and Calvert 1997: 82–3.

Compared to the discussion of gender and sexuality there is relatively little theorising of race issues in cyberspace. One exception to this is Nakamura's account of 'identity tourism' and 'racial passing':

> One of the dangers of identity tourism is that it takes this restriction across the axes of race/class in the 'real world' to an even more subtle and complex degree by reducing non-white identity positions to part of a costume or masquerade to be used by curious vacationers in cyberspace. Asianness is co-opted as a 'passing' fancy, an identity-prosthesis which signifies sex, the exotic, passivity when female, and anachronistic dreams of combat in its male manifestation. 'Passing' as a samurai or geisha is diverting, reversible, and a privilege mainly used by white men. The paradigm of Asian passing masquerades on LambdaMOO [one of the best known MUDs] itself works to suppress racial difference by setting the tone of the discourse in racist contours, which inevitably discourage 'real life' Asian men and women from textual performance in that space, effectively driving race underground. As a result, a default 'whiteness' covers the entire social space of LambdaMOO: race is 'whited out' in the name of cybersocial hygiene.
>
> (Nakamura 1995)

Turkle's base in psychology and use of feminist object–relations theory to explore some of the gender facets of her research have incurred criticism. Sophia (1992) suggests that this emphasis leads Turkle into over-valorising cyberspace to the extent that some of the young women in her study who have reservations about the technology are perceived as deficient and in need of 'better' integration: 'Sherry Turkle pathologises young women's attitudes to the computer as "just a tool" . . . Turkle seems to want women to fall for the seductive idealist fantasy wherein a luminous virtual brainchild is an acceptable substitute for a tactile physical body' (1992: 21). Sophia goes on to argue that Turkle's central concept of a technological 'second self' is itself highly gendered: 'need we ask who is the self to whom this brain–world–machine is a second self?' (1992: 20).[7]

One of the potentially stressful areas Turkle explores is gender-swapping: 'Taking a virtual role may involve you in ongoing relationships. You may discover things about yourself that you never knew before' (1996: 9). But who and where is the 'you' that is doing the discovering? Despite the possibilities of disconnecting and returning to what Turkle elsewhere calls the 'parked body', her interviewees indicate a very strong psychological investment in and identification with their virtual personae. This has many implications for debates around the ethics of interactions in cyberspace and the ways in which women may experience it as yet another unsafe place where, for example, 'virtual rape' is possible.

Stone discusses the 'reality' of virtual space for some users and the ways in which a virtual experience of boundaries being crossed can create long-term real-life effects. Stone uses the example of a 1985 computer conference in which the participants discovered that a long-term member, 'Julie', supposedly a disabled older woman, in whom many other people had confided, was in real life a middle-aged male psychiatrist. One female participant apparently said that the discovery felt like rape (1991: 2). Her use of this analogy suggests that a division of virtual space into a kind of mind-game, abstracted from the real-life body, is altogether too neat. The real-life body effects ('it felt like rape') can persist after disconnection. To respond to such accounts as over-reaction or hallucinatory comes close to that earlier 'hysterisation' of women which suggests that women fail to separate mind from body, 'reality' from imagination. Like Turkle's, Stone's position, however, seems to be that these issues are new to the particular media of computer technologies and simply require new vocabularies and explanatory frameworks to respond to the ethical and other problems they raise.

Feminist revisioning of cyberspace

Zoë Sofoulis (Sophia/Sofia) is more pro-active, and explicitly feminist, in her argument for a feminist engagement with the new technologies not only in terms of putting them to feminist use but also
in challenging their conceptual frameworks. Rather than working
within the parameters of the new technologies, which originated
within military and business contexts and exclude the body, she
explores the work of feminist artists aimed at shaping the space
and 'putting the guts back in'. In 'Virtual Corporeality: A Feminist
View' (1992), Sophia introduces an investigation of the myths and
metaphors that circulate in cyberspace: it is an investigation that
she pursues in later work, in particular *Whose Second Self? Gender and
(Ir)rationality in Computer Culture* (1993). The latter is interesting
for its combination of a highly theorised discussion with practical
application to issues of education: the publication is within the
context of an Australian education faculty's research into gender
issues in the classroom.

Sophia appropriates the term 'Jupiter Space' from the film,
2001: A Space Odyssey to designate the discursive systems which constitute our contemporary understanding of science and technology: the belief that everything originates in a masculine, rational
brain. In Jupiter Space the place of the female body, maternity
and feminine-gendered attributes, is minimal – the reproductive
maternal functions are 'displaced on to masculine and corpor-
ate technological fertility' (1992: 15). The omnipresence of this
imagery, with its vocabulary of 'hacking' and 'penetration' has
made it more difficult for women to see the space as in any way
ours: 'Like other kinds of space, cyberspace has been coded as
a feminised terrain to be conquered, invaded, hacked into and
controlled . . . its interior is a matrix . . . The personal computer has
a "mother board" and offers us "access" to its "consoles" ' (1992: 2).
'Dominant culture depicts women as the signs or objects but
not usually the possessors or subjects of knowledges. Here women
and computers are structurally equivalent: friendly to users, not
users themselves' (1992: 16). In this culture, 'users' are implicitly
gendered masculine.

Central to the enterprise of rethinking cyberspace in female-
friendly ways (rather than adjusting women to its masculine norms)
is Donna Haraway's standpoint of irony. Irony, for Sophia, in its
doubling and ambiguity resists the linear, single-goal orientation which characterises what is usually called 'rational thinking'.
Rather than accepting Turkle's definitions of young women who

fear technology as 'irrational', Sophia argues for a rethinking of rationality: perhaps it is more rational to see through some of the seductions of cyberspace as a 'defensive and ultimately misogynistic fantasy of escape from earth, gravity, and maternal/material origins' (Sophia 1992: 21). Wouldn't it be *more* rather than less rational to confront contemporary man-made malaises such as environmental degradation, to 'acknowledge(d) the maternal/planetary axis as origin and (damaged) source' and then 'become more urgently interested in applying technologies to make real rather than virtual reparations?' (1992: 21). Some of Sofia/Sophia's subsequent work, particularly with feminist artists such as the Australian art group VNS Matrix, looks at specific ways of changing metaphors and imagery in order to reconfigure 'Jupiter Space'.[8]

At a very basic level, many critics of the full flight into cyberspace comment on the banality and crudeness (in every sense) of available contemporary graphics. For evidence that programs are necessarily limited by their programmers and just how culturally specific these programmers are, it is hard to go beyond the 'fembots', 'Silver Suzi' and 'Virtual Valerie'.[9] As Virginia Barratt, a former member of VNS Matrix describes, these representations are 'featureless apart from the perfect breasts and curved female form': they are in effect female fetishes devoid of any specifically human referent and enabling 'the narcissistic self reflection of the male viewer' (cited in Flynn, 1994: 15). It is therefore a feminist project to intervene in this construction by 'infecting' the system (Big Daddy Mainframe as 'he' appears in a game created by VNS Matrix) with different metaphors and images.

Barratt and Sofoulis (Sophia/Sofia) have been engaged in an interview-based study of Australian women artists working in digital media (see Barratt and Sofoulis: no date). Sofoulis suggests that many feminist artists, rather than duplicating the discourse of 'taking over' or 'invading' (cyber)space, are looking to create new, different spaces and blurring the distinction of private and public space. She refers to artists like Ruth Luxford who use images of domestic technologies, and Linda Dement who uses 'images of organs and other objects "as paint"': 'Disembodied organs mutate into hybrid objects of beauty and/or horror that are familiar and yet alien . . . She disturbs the immutable cleanliness of the computer, the screen' (Barratt and Sofoulis: 5). By developing a vocabulary of 'infection' and 'slime', these artists are coopting and subverting the idea of woman as 'leaky body', and attempting to restore the (female) body to cyberspace. Linda Dement explains:

'To use technologies which are really intended for a slick clean commercial boy's world to make personal, bodily, feminine work, and to reinsert this work into a mainstream culture, into art discourse and into society, is a political act' (quoted in Barratt and Sofoulis: 6).

A final example of 'putting guts into the machine' is 'Mapping Emotion', an installation piece by Sarah Waterson, which might be compared to Rothfield's discussion of performance artist, Lasica (see Chapter 6):

> It consists of a number of hanging rectangular perspex plates on which are mounted latex casts of different breasts. Wires run between the breasts, which respond to different degrees and speed of visitors' movement in the gallery space by pulsating and erecting their nipples . . . The work is perhaps an example of . . . 'interskin', an alternative to body-switch interfaces mapping bodies into technospace.
>
> (Barratt and Sofoulis, no date: 6)

Bernadette Flynn (1994) also explores some strategies of feminist artists, including VNS Matrix's development of an interactive installation which parodies and subverts the conventions of hierarchical computer games; the installation features a heroine, Gen:

> To win, the players have to bond with her . . . Their enemies . . . are Big Daddy Mainframe . . . and Circuit Boy, a homoerotic bimbo, a gender reversal of the fembots of the boys' game world. One of the weapons of the DNA sluts is hostile ejaculate, and rewards for the user include increased levels of pleasurable G slime.
>
> (Flynn 1994: 17)

These developments could be seen to be subversive proactive uses of the media that still operate from the kind of scepticism and distance that Sherry Turkle would appear to want to remove: without assuming power to change the world, they offer one kind of intervention into dominant paradigms, by asserting female bodies as centres of imaginative and technological power for their own sake, rather than for use as fetishised 'Virtual Valeries'.

In conclusion

This brief excursion into cyberspace is a limited introduction to some ways in which feminist writers are engaging with the new technologies that, for some, open up ways of disrupting the oppressive identification of women with reproductive bodies, and for others open up threats precisely because of that disruption.

Throughout feminist theorising, as it has emerged in the last two hundred years in western thought, there has been a continuous struggle to re-vision ways in which women might be freed from the limitations of a binary identification with a timeless, unthinking nature that our reproductive female flesh is held literally to embody. The most widely circulated of this theorising has been by women whose bodies mark us as relatively privileged in societies that are divided by class and 'race'. More recently, this 'body of theory' has been obliged to reconsider its own privileges and has been challenged to acknowledge, without colonising, different feminisms and their perspectives. A turn to poststructuralist and more recently, postmodernist, theories that insist on the discursive constitution of the world including our bodies, our selves, has been criticised as an elitist retreat from political action. For some, an enthusiastic engagement with cyberspace is the culmination of this retreat from real life and its bodies. This continues to be the source of a central debate between feminisms.

As will be evident from the range of sources briefly touched on, many of these debates have far-reaching implications across both professional and artistic fields, as well as affecting our everyday lives. They are, however, often bracketed off as 'only' feminist and, like other cultural issues, notably 'race', are yet to be integrated as a necessary component of curricula and professional training.

At the centre of most of the diverse feminist theorising about the body in which we engage at the end of the twentieth century, is a concern with what 'identity' might mean as new technologies, new social formations and relationships come into being. For many feminists there is a concern that the relatively secure establishment of some kinds of feminist theory in the academy and in its associated industries, like publishing, forms a kind of domestication of feminism: getting women back off the streets. While many celebrate the new spaces that some women have found to be transgressive, to speak in new and challenging ways, others want to insist that this must not be at the expense of forgetting the women who have little or no freedom. While some of us fly off into cyberspace and the twenty-first century, there are others still well and truly grounded in an everyday inscribed with the old injustices.

Theories of the body may be starting to be yesterday's news in the academy, but the bodies of women and ways of talking and thinking about them, among ourselves, remain central to any feminist agenda.

Summary

- Feminists debate to what extent new communication technologies offer a way out of the traditional impasse of woman's identification with the body and nature.

- Arguments about how far 'cyberspace' constitutes a radically different space have similarities to feminist debates about the usefulness or otherwise of postmodernist theories: in particular, in so far as they enable a play of multiple subjectivities.

- Haraway speculates that the 'feminist cyborg' is a potent metaphor for feminism in its hybridisation of machine and human, and challenge to dualism. The feminist cyborg is a necessary feminist intervention in the 'informatics of domination', whereby surveillance takes on increasingly complex and diverse forms.

- Irony is the stance advocated by Haraway and others who are both critical of, and receptive to the possibilities of 'cyberspace'.

- 'Prosthesis' is another term associated with the cyborg and new technologies: the extension of the human by technology.

- One aspect of the heavily masculine imagination of 'cyberspace' is the rejection of 'meat': the real body. This rejection can be linked to ideas of the female body as abject and leaky.

- Many researchers suggest that the prejudices of real life are transported into cyberspace and reproduce the injustices and biases of real life societies.

- Claims that the new technologies construct second or more selves suggest psychological issues in terms of how these new subjectivities are formed and operate.

- Some feminist artists working in cyberspace try to 'put the guts' back in, by subverting the space to their own purposes. Sofoulis and others argue for the feminising of cyberspace through the construction of new discourses and metaphors.

Notes

[1] 'Meat' is used by 'cyberspace' aficionados to designate the real life (RL) body as opposed to the experience of cyberspace. It was made popular by the SF writer, William Gibson, in the cult novel *Neuromancer* (1984).

[2] Carol Stabile suggests that the influence of Haraway's writing is much greater in arts/humanities theory than in the sciences – although the effectiveness of Haraway's feminist cyber–politics might seem to be crucially linked to its infiltration of the science and technology fields (Stabile 1994: 139).

[3] Useful materialist–feminist discussions of this can be found in Hennessy 1993; Ebert 1996.

[4] Stone comments that the 'Mestiza' analogy was invoked to keep 'the discussion grounded in individual bodies' (1991: 20), but this does not engage with the problematic erasure of the particular 'racialised' bodies of Anzaldùa's analysis. Anzaldùa's article, 'La Conciencia de la Mestiza: Towards a New Consciousness', can be found in Conboy *et al.* (1997).

[5] Cf. Haraway's discussion of contemporary discourses of immunity and immune-deficient disease: 'Immunity and invulnerability are intersecting concepts, a matter of consequence in a nuclear culture unable to accommodate the experience of death and finitude within available liberal discourse on the collective and personal individual. Life is a window of vulnerability. It seems a mistake to close it' ('The Biopolitics of Post-modern Bodies: Constitutions of Self in Immune System Discourse.' In Haraway 1991: 224).

[6] This issue of the online journal is devoted to issues of gender, sexuality and cyberspace. At URL: http://www.echonyc.com/~women/ Issue17.html

[7] For Turkle's further development of gender issues see 'Computational Reticence: Why Women Fear the Intimate Machine.' In Kramarae 1988, pp. 41–61. For the extended critique, see Zoë Sofia 1993.

[8] To see some of VNS Matrix's work visit http://206.251.6.116/ geekgirl/001slick/vns/vns.html

[9] A 'bot' (derived from 'robot') is a rudimentary figure (computer program) created for limited specific purposes and lacking a developed persona.

Further reading

Haraway, Donna (1991) 'A Manifesto for Cyborgs: Science, Technology and Socialist Feminism in the 1980s'. Chapter 8, of *Simians, Cyborg, and Women: The Reinvention of Nature*. New York and London: Routledge.

Klein, Renate (1996) '(Dead) Bodies Floating in Cyberspace: Post-modernism and the Dismemberment of Women'. In Diane Bell and Renate Klein (eds) *Radically Speaking: Feminism Reclaimed*. Melbourne: Spinifex Press.

McRae, Shannon (1995) 'Coming Apart at the Seams: Sex, Text and the Virtual Body'. From URL: at http://dhalgren.english.washington.edu/~shannon/vseams.html [accessed 8/10/98]. Also in Lynn Cherny and Elizabeth Reba Weise (eds) (1996) *Wired Women: Gender and New Realities in Cyberspace*. Washington, Seattle: Seal Press.

Sofia, Zoë (1995) 'Of Spanners and Cyborgs: "De-homogenising" Feminist Thinking on Technology'. In Barbara Caine and Rosemary Pringle (eds) *Transitions: New Australian Feminisms*. St Leonards, NSW: Allen and Unwin.

Stone, Allucquère Roseanne (1991) 'Will the Real Body Please Stand Up'. From URL: http://www.rochester.edu/College/FS/Publications/StoneBody.html [accessed 18/9/98] [first published in Michael Benedikt (ed.) (1991) *Cyberspace: First Steps*. Cambridge, Massachusetts: MIT Press].

For useful search engines on feminist issues try:

FeMiNa at http://femina.cybergrrl.com/

WWWomen at http://www.wwwomen.com/

Gender and Race in Media Indexes and Directories is also useful:

at hhtp://www.uiowa.edu/~commstud/resources/GenderMedia/cybe.html

As all-purpose guide, including glossary and addresses: Senjen and Guthrey 1996.

Glossary

Abjection/the abject: the indeterminate, fluid, borderline area between certainties; an area associated with change and the uncanny, and thus the occasion of fear and revulsion.

Anthropometry: measurement of human physical characteristics to create statistical models; part of the nineteenth-century development of scientific taxonomies.

Binarism (or dualism): the pattern of thinking and conceptualisation that divides everything into opposites; one of the feminist objections to it is that in the set of supposedly equal opposites, one set of terms can clearly be designated as 'feminine' and the other 'masculine', with higher or positive values, on the whole, attached to the latter.

Commonsense: when used in a sociological or philosophical sense, this refers to the shared assumptions of a group or society which go largely unchallenged in everyday conversation. Feminism is a challenge to 'commonsense' statements and beliefs about men and women.

Corporeality: literally 'the being of the body'; when the adjective, 'corporeal' is coupled with 'feminism', it denotes a recently developed theorising that attempts to reorient thinking about the female body and **subjectivity** in ways that challenge the dominant episteme of the mind/body split.

Cyborg: a hybrid of human and high-tech machine.

Decentring of the subject: **postmodernist** deconstruction of a central, unified, self or identity; substitution of **discursive** formations of **subjectivity**.

Discipline: organised management and control; used in **Foucauldian** theory.

Discourse/discursive: The social processes of making and reproducing meanings; not simply language, but meaning systems invested with power that circulate in society and constitute **subjectivities**.

Doxa: the set of holy scriptures that form the basis of a religion and cannot be refuted or changed; so, the way that some pronouncements take on the status of religious truths, and their authors take on the status of priests or even, gods!

Dualism: see **binarism** and **mind/body split**.

Empirical: based on the unmediated experience of 'the real' and associated with positivist science; much feminist attention has been given to reinserting personal experience into research and pointing to the 'situated' and partial ways that knowledge is produced.

Enlightenment project: a term used as shorthand for the dominant directions in western-European thinking from the eighteenth century, including the importance of the individual rational 'subject' within an equitable social structure, and the notion of a progressive improvement of the human condition.

Epistemology: theory of knowledge (hence, 'episteme' as a component of that knowledge, something which is a building block of a particular knowledge system).

Foucauldian: following the theories of French poststructuralist theorist Michel Foucault.

Gender/sex–gender division: 'gender' usually set up as opposition to 'sex', denoting the cultural production of 'femininity' and 'masculinity' and their naturalisation as 'normal' attributes of the sexed (male/female) body. Recently, there has been considerable debate about the usefulness of this distinction, as it can be seen to reproduce the problems of the **mind/body split**.

Genealogy: literally the family history. Its use in contemporary theory indicates an affiliation with **Foucault** who uses the term to denote a practice of constructing the history and development of particular patterns of thought, 'epistemes'.

Heterosexual economy: a system, world view, organised around an assumption of natural and universal heterosexuality.

Hysterisation: the identification of woman with the body; **Foucault** includes this in the four major defining modes of modernity.

Imaginary body: the subjective perception of one's own body.

Inscription: literally, a writing or engraving on or into a surface; in contemporary theory, it signifies the operation of **discourse** whereby something comes into being, or is 'written in'.

Interiorised: taken into the self as part of **subjectivity**; naturalised into the psyche.

Irony: a position or statement deliberately at odds with the speaker's underlying meaning. **Postmodernism** is characterised by irony in its rejection of tradition, authority and fixed meanings.

Liminal: on the threshold, uncanny, associated with the **abject**.

Mind/body split: the concept of the human subject associated with the philosophy of René Descartes and seen as privileging the mind and abstraction (transcendence) over the body and material presence (immanence).

Narcissism: love of one's own appearance to the detriment of relationships with others.

Ontology: the study of being, existing in the world.

Overdetermined: categorised and defined in a single way by multiple determinants. Their number and weight make it hard to resist or transgress against them.

Panoptical: an all-round view; a system of **surveillance** used in nineteenth-century prisons and taken by **Foucault** as paradigmatic of the modern state's surveillance of its citizens.

Pathologising: **overdetermining** something/somebody as inherently diseased.

Performativity: Judith Butler's theory of gender as a continually repeated performance.

Phallocentric: centred around the (imaginary) idea of a single and unified power (the phallus) which, as Jane Gallop has said, can look very much like the not-so-imaginary penis.

Phenomenology: philosophy of the relationships between experiencing subjects and objects in the world.

Plasticity: high degree of flexibility; able to be moulded.

Posthuman: the being produced in postmodernity, after the collapse of the 'human subject'; associated with new communication technologies and the **discursive** construction of **subjectivities**.

Postmodernist/postmodernism: variously used to describe theories and practices concerned with the decentring of contemporary life, the collapse of belief in universal and unified systems, authorities and a 'real' outside **discourse**.

Prosthesis: the artificial extension or replacement of human body parts.

Queer(**ing**): a relatively new theory of sexuality, challenging the idea of sexuality as innate and characterised by the particular object of desire.

Self-identical: completely self-referring and so, outside the system of representation or symbolic order, and inaccessible to meaning.

Social constructionist: favouring a cultural/social explanation of human behaviour as learned rather than innate/biological.

Subjectivity: sense of the self as subject; subject positions produced by particular **discourses** rather than fixed and innate.

Surveillance: overseeing for the purpose of control; associated in **Foucauldian** theory with the panopticon.

Technologies: in **Foucauldian** theory, any organised system designed to control or manipulate the world and others.

Textual: usually the written word, but broadened in contemporary thinking to include any system of signs (Derrida famously asserts that there is nothing outside the text). Texts are never identical with what they appear to represent.

Unconscious: Freud's formulation of a powerful aspect of the mind inaccessible to conscious thought but exerting influence on actions, desires, feelings; manifest through dreams, word slips, art, hysteria.

Bibliography

Abdalla, Raqiha Haji Dwaleh (1982) *Sisters in Affliction: Circumcision and Infibulation of Women in Africa.* London: Zed Books.

Agger, Inge (1994) *The Blue Room: Trauma and Testimony Among Refugee Women: A Psycho-Social Exploration.* London: Zed Books.

Alexander, M. Jacqui (1994) 'Not Just (Any) Body Can Be a Citizen: The Politics of Law, Sexuality and Postcoloniality in Trinidad and Tobago and the Bahamas'. *Feminist Review.* vol. 48 (April): 5–23.

Aston, Elaine (1995) *An Introduction to Feminism and Theatre.* London and New York: Routledge.

Auslander, Philip (1997) 'The Surgical Self: Body Alteration and Identity'. In *From Acting to Performance: Essays in Modernism and Postmodernism.* London and New York: Routledge.

Balsamo, Anne (1996) *Technologies of the Gendered Bodies: Reading Cyborg Women.* Durham and London: Duke University Press.

Barratt, Virginia and Sofoulis, Zoë (no date) 'Women Remapping Technospace'. From URL: http://uiah.fi/bookshop/isea–proc/high&low/j/14.html [accessed 10/10/98].

Behrendt, Larissa (1993) 'Aboriginal Women and the White Lies of the Feminist Movement: Implications for Aboriginal Women in Rights Discourse'. *Australian Feminist Law Journal.* vol. 1: 27.

Bell, Diane and Klein, Renate (eds) (1996) *Radically Speaking: Feminism Reclaimed.* Melbourne: Spinifex Press.

Bell, Susan (1990) 'Sociological Perspectives on the Medicalization of Menopause'. *Social Sciences in Medicine.* vol. 24: 535–42.

Bender, Gretchen and Druckrey, Timothy (eds) (1994) *Culture on the Brink: Ideologies of Technology.* Seattle: Bay Press.

Berger, John (1972) *Ways of Seeing.* Harmondsworth: BBC/Penguin Books.

Bernheimer, Charles and Kahane, Claire (eds) (1985) *In Dora's Case: Freud, Hysteria, Feminism.* London: Virago Press.

Beveridge, Fiona and Mullally, Siobhan (1995) 'International Human Rights and Body Politics'. In Jo Bridgeman and Susan Millns (eds) *Law and Body Politics: Regulating the Female Body.* Aldershot and Brookfield: Dartmouth.

Bibbings, Lois S. (1995) 'Female Circumcision: Mutilation or Modification?' In Jo Bridgeman and Susan Millns (eds) *Law and Body Politics: Regulating the Female Body.* Aldershot and Brookfield: Dartmouth.

Bigwood, Carol (1991) 'Renaturalizing the Body (with the help of Merleau-Ponty)'. *Hypatia.* vol. 6.3 (Fall): 54–73.

Birrell, Susan and Cole, Cheryl L. (eds) (1994) *Women, Sport, and Culture.* Champaign, Illinois: Human Kinetics.

Boling, Patricia (ed.) (1995) *Expecting Trouble: Surrogacy, Fetal Abuse, and New Reproductive Technologies.* Boulder: Westview Press.

Bordo, Susan (1993) *Unbearable Weight: Feminism, Western Culture, and the Body.* Berkeley: University of California Press.

Bordo, Susan (1998) 'Bringing Body to Theory'. In Donn Welton (ed.) *Body and Flesh: A Philosophical Reader.* Malden, Massachusetts and Oxford: Blackwell Publishers.

Braidotti, Rosi (1989) 'Organs Without Bodies'. *differences.* vol. 1.1 (Winter): 147–161.

Braidotti, Rosi (1994) *Nomadic Subjects.* New York: Columbia University Press.

Braidotti, Rosi (1996) 'Cyberfeminism with a Difference'. From URL: at http://www.let.ruu.nl/womens_studies/rosi/cyberfem.htm [accessed 8/10/98]

Braidotti, Rosi (1997) 'Mothers, Monsters, and Machines'. In Katie Conboy, Nadia Medina and Sarah Stanbury (eds) *Writing on the Body: Female Embodiment and Feminist Theory.* New York: Columbia University Press.

Bridgeman, Jo (1995) 'They Gag Women, Don't They?' In Jo Bridgeman and Susan Millns (eds) *Law and Body Politics: Regulating the Female Body.* Aldershot and Brookfield: Dartmouth.

Bridgeman, Jo and Millns, Susan (eds) (1995) *Law and Body Politics: Regulating the Female Body.* Aldershot and Brookfield: Dartmouth.

Bridgeman, Jo and Millns, Susan (1998) *Feminist Perspectives on Law: Law's Engagement with the Female Body.* London: Sweet and Maxwell.

Brook, Barbara (1997) 'Femininity and Culture: Some Notes on the Gendering of Women in Australia'. In Kate Pritchard Hughes (ed.) *Contemporary Australian Feminism 2.* Melbourne: Longman.

Brush, Pippa (1998) 'Metaphors of Inscription: Discipline, Plasticity and the Rhetoric of Choice'. *Feminist Review.* vol. 58 (Spring): 22–43.

Bulbeck, Chilla (1998) *Re-orienting Western Feminisms: Women's Diversity in a Postcolonial World.* Cambridge: Cambridge University Press.

Burroughs, Catherine B. and Ehrenreich, Jeffrey David (eds) (1993) *Reading the Social Body.* Iowa City: University of Iowa Press.

Butler, Judith (1990) *Gender Trouble: Feminism and the Subversion of Identity.* New York and London: Routledge.

Butler, Judith (1993) *Bodies that Matter: on the Discursive Limits of 'Sex'.* New York and London: Routledge.

Butler, Judith (1997) *Excitable Speech: A Politics of the Performative.* New York and London: Routledge.

Butler, Judith and McGrogan, Maureen (eds) (1993) *Erotic Welfare: Sexual Theory and Politics in the Age of Epidemic.* New York: Routledge.

Butler, Judith and Scott, Joan W. (eds) (1992) *Feminists Theorize the Political*. New York and London: Routledge.

Carby, Hazel (1997) 'White Woman Listen! Black Feminism and the Boundaries of Sisterhood'. In Heidi Safia Mirza (ed.) *Black British Feminism*. London and New York: Routledge [first published 1982].

Carr, C. (1993) 'Unspeakable Practices, Unnatural Acts: The Taboo Art of Karen Finley'. In Lynda Hart and Peggy Phelan (eds) *Acting Out: Feminist Performances*. Ann Arbor: University of Michigan Press.

Carrington, Kerry (1998) *Who Killed Leigh Leigh?: A Story of Shame and Mateship in an Australian Town*. Milson's Point, N.S.W.: Random House.

Caskey, Noelle (1985) 'Interpreting Anorexia Nervosa'. In Susan Rubin Suleiman (ed.) *The Female Body in Western Culture: Contemporary Perspectives*. Cambridge, Massachusetts and London: Harvard University Press.

Charlesworth, Hilary (1995) 'Worlds Apart: Public/Private Distinctions in International Law'. In Margaret Thornton (ed.) *Public and Private: Feminist Legal Debates*. Melbourne: Oxford University Press.

Charlesworth, Hilary (1996) 'Women's Human Rights Defined'. In Gillian Moon (ed.) *Making Her Rights a Reality: Women's Human Rights and Development*. Melbourne: Community Aid Abroad/Law Foundation of New South Wales.

Chernin, Kim (1982) *The Obsession: Reflections on the Tyranny of Slenderness*. New York: Harper Colophon Books.

Chernin, Kim (1986) *The Hungry Self: Women, Eating and Identity*. London: Virago.

Cixous, Hélène (1981) 'Sorties'. In Elaine Marks and Isabelle de Courtivron (eds) *New French Feminisms*. Brighton: Harvester Press [first published in 1975].

Cole, Cheryl L. (1994) 'Resisting the Canon: Feminist Cultural Studies, Sport, and Technologies of the Body'. In Susan Birrell and Cheryl L. Cole (eds) *Women, Sport, and Culture*. Champaign, Illinois: Human Kinetics.

Conboy, Katie, Medina, Nadia and Stanbury, Sarah (eds) (1997) *Writing on the Body: Female Embodiment and Feminist Theory*. New York: Columbia University Press.

Coney, Sandra (1994) *The Menopause Industry: A Guide to the 'Discovery' of the Mid-Life Woman*. North Melbourne: Spinifex Press.

Corea, Genea (1985) *The Mother Machine: Reproductive Technologies from Artificial Insemination to Artificial Wombs*. New York: Harper and Row.

Cranny-Francis, Anne (1995) *The Body in the Text*. Carlton: Melbourne University Press.

Creed, Barbara (1993) *The Monstrous-Feminine: Film, Feminism, Psychoanalysis*. London and New York: Routledge.

Crowden, Diane Griffin (1993) 'Lesbians and the (Re/de)construction of the Female Body'. In Catherine B. Burroughs and Jeffrey David Ehrenreich (eds) *Reading the Social Body*. Iowa City: University of Iowa Press.

Cummings, Barbara (1990) *Take This Child . . . From Kahlin Compound to the Retta Dixon Children's Home*. Canberra: Aboriginal Studies Press.

Daly, Mary (1984) *Pure Lust: Elemental Feminist Philosophy.* Boston:
Beacon Press.
Davis, Kathy (1995) *Reshaping the Female Body: The Dilemmas of Cosmetic
Surgery.* New York and London: Routledge.
de Beauvoir, Simone (1953) *The Second Sex.* Trans. H.M. Parshley.
New York: Knopf.
de Beauvoir, Simone (1965) Interview. *Paris Review.* vol. 9.34 (Spring/
Summer): 23–40.
de Lauretis, Teresa (ed.) (1988) *Feminist Studies/Critical Studies.*
Houndmills: Macmillan.
de Ras, Marion E.P. and Grace, Victoria M. (eds) (1997) *Bodily
Boundaries, Sexualised Genders and Medical Discourses.* Palmerston
North: The Dunmore Press.
Diprose, Rosalyn (1994) *The Bodies of Women: Ethics, Embodiment and
Sexual Difference.* London: Routledge.
Doane, Mary Ann (1982) 'Film and Masquerade: Theorizing the
Female Spectator'. *Screen.* vol. 23.3/4: 74–87.
Doane, Mary Ann (1985) 'The Clinical Eye: Medical Discourses in the
"Woman's Film" of the 1940s'. In Susan Rubin Suleiman (ed.) *The
Female Body in Western Culture: Contemporary Perspectives.* Cambridge,
Massachusetts and London: Harvard University Press.
Doane, Mary Ann (1990) 'Technophilia: Technology, Representation,
and the Feminine'. In Mary Jacobus, Evelyn Fox Keller and Sally
Shuttleworth (eds) *Body/Politics: Women and the Discourses of Science.*
New York and London: Routledge.
Donnison, Jean (1977) *Midwives and Medical Men: A History of Inter-
Professional Rivals and Women's Rights.* London: Heinemann.
Douglas, Mary (1966) *Purity and Danger: An Analysis of Pollution and
Taboo.* London: Routledge and Kegan Paul.
Douglas, Mary (1975) *Implicit Meanings: Essays in Anthropology.*
London: Routledge and Kegan Paul.
Duden, Barbara (1993) *Disembodying Women: Perspectives on Pregnancy
and the Unborn.* Trans. Lee Hoinacki. Cambridge, Massachusetts and
London: Harvard University Press.
Ebert, Teresa (1996) *Ludic Feminism and After: Postmodernism, Desire and
Labor in Late Capitalism.* Ann Arbor: University of Michigan Press.
Ehrenreich, Barbara and English, Deirdre (1973) *Witches, Nurses and
Midwives: A History of Women Healers.* Old Westbury, New York:
The Feminist Press.
Eisenstein, Zillah R. (1988) *The Female Body and the Law.* Berkeley:
University of California Press.
Ellsworth, Elizabeth (1982) 'Woman as Body: Ancient and
Contemporary Views'. *Feminist Studies.* vol. 8.1 (Spring): 109–131.
Fausto-Sterling, Anne (1985) *Myths of Gender: Biological Theories about
Women and Men.* New York: Basic Books.
Firestone, Shulamith (1970) *The Dialectic of Sex: The Case for a Feminist
Revolution.* New York: William Morrow.
Flynn, Bernadette (1994) 'Woman/Machine Relationships: Investigating
the Body Within Cyberculture'. *Media Information Australia.* vol. 72
(May): 11–19.

Foucault, Michel (1977) *Discipline and Punish: The Birth of the Prison.* Trans. A. Sheridan. London: Allen Lane.

Fox, Marie (1995) 'Legal Responses to Battered Women Who Kill'. In Jo Bridgeman and Susan Millns (eds) *Law and Body Politics: Regulating the Female Body.* Aldershot and Brookfield: Dartmouth.

Frank, Arthur W. (1990) 'Bringing Bodies Back In: A Decade Review'. *Theory, Culture and Society.* vol. 7.1 (February): 131–162.

Frueh, Joanna (1996) *Erotic Faculties.* Berkeley: University of California Press.

Fuss, Diana (1989) *Essentially Speaking: Feminism, Nature and Difference.* New York and London: Routledge.

Gallop, Jane (1988) *Thinking Through the Body.* New York: Columbia University Press.

Gallop, Jane (ed.) (1995) *Pedagogy: The Question of Impersonation.* Bloomington and Indianapolis: Indiana University Press.

Garrett, Catherine (1998) *Beyond Anorexia: Narrative, Spirituality and Recovery.* Cambridge: Cambridge University Press.

Gatens, Moira (1990) 'Corporeal Representations in/and the Body Politic'. In R. Diprose and R. Ferrall (eds) *Cartographies.* St Leonards: Allen and Unwin.

Gatens, Moira (1996) *Imaginary Bodies.* London and New York: Routledge.

Gatens, Moira (1998) 'Institutions, Embodiment and Sexual Difference'. In Moira Gatens and Alison Mackinnon (eds) *Gender and Institutions: Welfare, Work and Citizenship.* Cambridge: Cambridge University Press.

Gatens, Moira and Mackinnon, Alison (eds) (1998) *Gender and Institutions: Welfare, Work and Citizenship.* Cambridge: Cambridge University Press.

Gerson, Deborah (1989) 'Infertility and the Construction of the Desperate'. *Socialist Review.* vol. 19.3 (July–September): 45–64.

Gibson, William (1984) *Neuromancer.* New York: Ace.

Gilman, Sandor (1985) 'Black Bodies, White Bodies: Toward an Iconography of Female Sexuality in Late Nineteenth-Century Art, Medicine, and Literature'. In Henry Louis Gates (ed.) *'Race', Writing, and Difference.* Chicago: University of Chicago Press.

Graycar, Regina (1995) 'The Gender of Judgements: An Introduction'. In Margaret Thornton (ed.) *Public and Private: Feminist Legal Debates.* Melbourne: Oxford University Press.

Greer, Germaine (1991) *The Change: Women, Aging, and the Menopause.* London: Hamish Hamilton.

Griffin, Susan (1978) *Women and Nature: The Roaring Inside Her.* New York: Harper and Row.

Grinham, Timmee (1998) 'Substantial Matters'. (Review of Vicki Kirby, *Telling Flesh) Australian Women's Book Review.* vol. 10: 18–19.

Grosz, Elizabeth (1990) *Jacques Lacan: A Feminist Introduction.* London: Routledge.

Grosz, Elizabeth (1994) *Volatile Bodies: Toward a Corporeal Feminism.* St Leonards: Allen and Unwin.

Grosz, Elizabeth and Probyn, Elspeth (eds) (1995) *Sexy Bodies: The Strange Carnalities of Feminism.* London and New York: Routledge.

Gunning, Isabelle R. (1992) 'Female Genital Surgeries'. *Columbia Human Rights Law Review.* vol. 23(2): 189–248.

Hall, M. Ann (1996) *Feminism and Sporting Bodies: Essays on Theory and Practice.* Champaign, Illinois: Human Kinetics.

Haraway, Donna (1991) *Simians, Cyborgs and Women: The Reinvention of Nature.* New York and London: Routledge.

Haraway, Donna (1997) *Modest_Witness@Second_Millenium.FemaleMan©_Meets_OncoMouse™.* New York and London: Routledge.

Harris, Melissa (ed.) (1990) *The Body in Question.* New York: Aperture.

Hart, Lynda and Phelan, Peggy (eds) (1993) *Acting Out: Feminist Performances.* Ann Arbor: University of Michigan Press.

Hartmann, Barbara (1987) *Reproductive Rights and Wrongs: The Global Politics of Population Control and Contraceptive Choice.* New York: Harper and Row.

Hartouni, Valerie (1997) *Cultural Conceptions: On Reproductive Technologies and the Remaking of Life.* Minneapolis: University of Minnesota Press.

Hartsock, Nancy (1990) 'Foucault on Power: A Theory for Women?' In Nicholson, Linda J. (ed.) *Feminism/Postmodernism.* New York and London: Routledge.

Hawkridge, Caroline (1996) *Living with Endometriosis.* London: Macdonald Optima.

Hawthorne, Susan (1996) 'Organic Bodies, Cyborgs and Virtual Bodies: Theoretical Feminist Responses'. Paper presented at the Sixth International Interdisciplinary Congress on Women, Adelaide: 23/4/96.

Hayles, N. Katherine (1993) 'The Seductions of Cyberspace'. In Verena Andermatt Conley (ed.) *Rethinking Technologies.* Minneapolis: University of Minnesota Press.

Hennessy, Rosemary (1993) *Materialist Feminism and the Politics of Discourse.* New York: Routledge.

Heywood, Leslie (1996) *Dedication to Hunger: The Anorexic Aesthetic in Modern Culture.* Berkeley: University of California Press.

Holland, Janet, Ramazanoglu, Caroline, Sharpe, Sue and Thomson, Rachel (1998) *The Male in the Head: Young People, Heterosexuality and Power.* London: The Tufnell Press.

Hong, Fan (1997) *Footbinding, Feminism and Freedom: The Liberation of Women's Bodies in Modern China.* London and Portland, Oregon: Frank Cass.

hooks, bell (1990) *Yearning: Race, Gender and Cultural Politics.* Boston: South End Press.

hooks, bell (1992) *Black Looks: Race and Representation.* Boston: South End Press.

Huggins, Jackie (1994) 'A Contemporary View of Aboriginal Women's Relationship to the White Women's Movement'. In Norma Grieve and Ailsa Burns (eds) *Australian Women: Contemporary Feminist Thought.* Melbourne: Oxford University Press.

Ian, Marcia (1991) 'From Abject to Object: Women's Bodybuilding'. *Postmodern Culture.* vol. 1.3 (May). From URL: http://jefferson.village.virginia.edu/pmc/txt–only/issue.591/pop.cult.591 [accessed 10/9/98]

Irigaray, Luce (1985a) *This Sex Which Is Not One.* Trans. Catherine Porter. Ithaca, New York: Cornell University Press [first published 1977].

Irigaray, Luce (1985b) *Speculum of the Other Woman*. Trans. G.C. Gill. Ithaca, New York: Cornell University Press.

Jacobus, Mary (1990) 'In Parenthesis: Immaculate Conception and Feminine Desire'. In Mary Jacobus, Evelyn Fox Keller and Sally Shuttleworth (eds) *Body/Politics: Women and the Discourses of Science*. New York and London: Routledge.

Jacobus, Mary, Fox Keller, Evelyn and Shuttleworth, Sally (eds) (1990) *Body/Politics: Women and the Discourses of Science*. New York and London: Routledge.

Jaggar, Alison and Bordo, Susan (eds) (1989) *Gender/Body/Knowledge*. New Brunswick, New Jersey: Rutgers University Press.

Jolly, Margaret (1998) 'Introduction'. In Kalpana Ram and Margaret Jolly (eds) *Maternities and Modernities: Colonial and Postcolonial Experiences in Asia and the Pacific*. Cambridge: Cambridge University Press.

Jordanova, Ludmilla (1989) *Sexual Visions: Images of Gender in Science and Medicine Between the Eighteenth and Twentieth Centuries*. New York and London: Harvester Wheatsheaf.

Kabeer, Naila (1991) 'The Quest for National Identity: Women, Islam and the State in Bangladesh'. *Feminist Review*. vol. 37: 38–58.

Karamcheti, Indira (1995) 'Caliban in the Classroom'. In Jane Gallop (ed.) *Pedagogy: The Question of Impersonation*. Bloomington and Indianopolis: Indiana University Press.

Keefe, Terry (1990) 'Women's *Mauvaise foi* in Simone de Beauvoir's *The Second Sex*'. In Helen Wilcox, Keith McWatters, Ann Thompson and Linda R. Williams (eds) *The Body and the Text: Hélène Cixous, Reading and Teaching*. New York: Harvester Wheatsheaf.

Keywood, Kirsty (1995) 'Sterilising the Woman with Learning Difficulties – In Her Best Interests?' In Jo Bridgeman and Susan Millns (eds) *Law and Body Politics: Regulating the Female Body*. Aldershot and Brookfield: Dartmouth.

Kirby, Vicki (1997) *Telling Flesh: The Substance of the Corporeal*. New York and London: Routledge.

Klein, Renate (1996) '(Dead) Bodies Floating in Cyberspace: Post-modernism and the Dismemberment of Women'. In Diane Bell and Renate Klein (eds) *Radically Speaking: Feminism Reclaimed*. Melbourne: Spinifex Press.

Klinge, Ineke (1996) 'Female Bodies and Brittle Bones'. *The European Journal of Women's Studies*. vol. 3: 269–283.

Komesaroff, Paul, Rothfield, Philipa and Daly, Jeanne (eds) (1997) *Reinterpreting Menopause: Cultural and Philosophical Issues*. New York and London: Routledge.

Kramarae, Cheris (ed.) (1988) *Technology and Women's Voices: Keeping in Touch*. London: Routledge and Kegan Paul.

Kristeva, Julia (1982) *Powers of Horror: An Essay on Abjection*. Trans. Leon S. Roudiez. New York: Columbia University Press.

Kristeva, Julia (1985) 'Stabat Mater'. In Susan Rubin Suleiman (ed.) *The Female Body in Western Culture: Contemporary Perspectives*. Cambridge, Massachusetts and London: Harvard University Press [first published in French, 1977].

Kuhn, Annette (1997) 'The Body and Cinema: Some Problems for Feminism'. In Katie Conboy, Nadia Medina and Sarah Stanbury (eds) *Writing on the Body: Female Embodiment and Feminist Theory*. New York: Columbia University Press [first published 1988].

Kwok, Wei Leng (1995) 'New Australian Feminism: Towards a Discursive Politics of Australian Feminist Thought'. *Antithesis*. vol. 7.1: 47–63.

Laqueur, Thomas (1987) 'Orgasm, Generation, and the Politics of Reproductive Biology'. In Catherine Gallagher and Thomas Laqueur (eds) *The Making of the Modern Body: Sexuality and Society in the Nineteenth Century*. Berkeley: University of California Press.

Laqueur, Thomas (1990) *Making Sex: Body and Gender from the Greeks to Freud*. Cambridge, Massachusetts: Harvard University Press.

Lawler, Jocalyn (ed.) (1997) *The Body in Nursing*. South Melbourne: Churchill Livingstone.

Lawrence, Marilyn (1988) *The Anorexic Experience*. London: The Women's Press.

Laws, Sophie (1990) *Issues of Blood: The Politics of Menstruation*. Houndmills: Macmillan.

Lennon, Kathleen and Whitford, Margaret (eds) (1994) *Knowing the Difference: Feminist Perspectives in Epistemology*. London: Sage.

Lenskyj, Helen (1986) *Out of Bounds: Women, Sport, and Sexuality*. Toronto: The Women's Press.

Lesko, Nancy (1988) 'The Curriculum of the Body: Lessons from a Catholic High School'. In Leslie G. Roman, Linda Christian-Smith, with Elizabeth Ellsworth (eds) (1988) *Becoming Feminine: The Politics of Popular Culture*. London: The Falmer Press.

Lewis, Jane (1980) *The Politics of Motherhood: Child and Maternal Welfare in England, 1900–1939*. London: Croom Helm.

Leysen, Bettina (1996) 'Medicalization of Menopause: From "Feminine Forever" to "Healthy Forever"'. In Nina Lykke and Rosi Braidotti (eds) *Between Monsters, Goddesses and Cyborgs: Feminist Confrontations with Science, Medicine and Cyberspace*. London and New Jersey: Zed Books.

Lloyd, Genevieve (1984) *The Man of Reason: 'Male' and 'Female' in Western Philosophy*. London: Methuen.

Lorde, Audre (1981) 'The Master's Tools Will Never Dismantle the Master's House'. In Cherrie Moraga and Gloria Anzaldúa (eds) *This Bridge Called My Back: Writings by Radical Women of Color*. New York: Kitchen Table Press.

Lovering, Kathryn (1995) 'The Bleeding Body: Adolescents Talk About Menstruation'. In Sue Wilkinson and Celia Kitzinger (eds) *Feminism and Discourse*. London: Sage.

Lovering, Kathryn (1997) 'Listening to Girls' "Voice" and Silence: The Problematics of the Menarcheal Body'. In Marion E.P. de Ras and Victoria M. Grace (eds) *Bodily Boundaries, Sexualised Genders and Medical Discourses*. Palmerston North: The Dunmore Press.

Lucashenko, Melissa (1994) 'No Other Truth?: Aboriginal Women and Australian Feminism'. *Social Alternatives*. vol. 14(1): 19–22.

Lumby, Judy (1997) 'The Feminised Body in Illness'. In Jocalyn Lawler (ed.) *The Body in Nursing*. South Melbourne: Churchill Livingstone.

Lykke, Nikki and Braidotti, Rosi (eds) (1996) *Between Monsters, Goddesses and Cyborgs: Feminist Confrontations with Science, Medicine and Cyberspace.* London and New Jersey: Zed Books.

Lynch, Lee and Woods, Akia (eds) (1996) *Off the Rag: Lesbians Writing on Menopause.* Norwich, Vermont: New Victoria Publishers.

Mackie, Fiona (1997) 'The Left Hand of the Goddess: The Silencing of Menopause as a Bodily Experience of Transition'. In Paul Komesaroff, Philipa Rothfield and Jeanne Daly (eds) *Reinterpreting Menopause: Cultural and Philosophical Issues.* New York and London: Routledge.

MacKinnon, Catharine A. (1997) 'Rape: On Coercion and Consent'. In Katie Conboy, Nadia Medina and Sarah Stanbury (eds) *Writing on the Body: Female Embodiment and Feminist Theory.* New York: Columbia University Press [first published 1989].

MacSween, Morag (1993) *Anorexic Bodies: A Feminist and Sociological Perspective on Anorexia Nervosa.* London and New York: Routledge.

Mansfield, Alan and McGinn, Barbara (1993) 'Pumping Irony: The Muscular and the Feminine'. In Sue Scott and David Morgan (eds) *Body Matters: Essays on the Sociology of the Body.* London and Washington: The Falmer Press.

Marcus, Sharon (1992) 'Fighting Bodies, Fighting Words: A Theory and Politics of Rape Prevention'. In Judith Butler and Joan W. Scott (eds) *Feminists Theorize the Political.* New York and London: Routledge.

Marks, Elaine and de Courtivron, Isabelle (eds) (1981) *New French Feminisms.* Brighton: Harvester Press.

Marsh, Anne (1993) *Body and Self: Performance Art in Australia 1969–1992.* Oxford: Oxford University Press.

Martin, Emily (1987) *The Woman in the Body: A Cultural Analysis of Reproduction.* Boston: Beacon Press.

Martin, Emily (1997) 'The New Culture of Health: Gender and the Immune System in America'. In Marion E.P. de Ras and Victoria M. Grace (eds) *Bodily Boundaries, Sexualised Genders and Medical Discourses.* Palmerston North: The Dunmore Press.

Mason, Gail (1995) '(Out)laws: Acts of Proscription in the Sexual Order'. In Margaret Thornton (ed.) *Public and Private: Feminist Legal Debates.* Melbourne: Oxford University Press.

Matthews, Jill Julius (1984) *Good and Mad Women: The Historical Construction of Femininity in Twentieth-Century Australia.* St Leonards, NSW: Allen and Unwin.

Matthews, Jill Julius (1987) 'Building the Body Beautiful'. *Australian Feminist Studies.* vol. 5 (Summer): 17–34.

Matuschka (1996) 'Barbie Gets Breast Cancer'. In Nan Bauer Maglin and Donna Perry (eds) *Bad Girls, Good Girls: Women, Sex and Power in the Nineties.* New Brunswick, New Jersey: Rutgers University Press.

McCrea, F. (1983) 'The Politics of Menopause: The "Discovery" of a Deficiency Disease'. *Social Problems.* vol. 13: 11–23.

McDowell, Linda and Sharp, Joanne P. (eds) (1997) *Space, Gender, Knowledge: Feminist Readings.* London and New York: Arnold.

McMillan, Carol (1982) *Women, Reason and Nature: Some Philosophical Problems with Feminism.* Oxford: Basil Blackwell.

McNay, Lois (1991) 'The Foucauldian Body and the Exclusion of Experience'. *Hypatia.* vol. 6.3 (Fall): 125–139.

McRae, Shannon (1995) 'Coming Apart at the Seams: Sex, Text and the Virtual Body'. From URL: at http:// dhalgren.english.washington.edu/~shannon/vseams.html [accessed 8/10/98]. Also in Lynn Cherny and Elizabeth Reba Weise (eds) *Wired Women: Gender and New Realities in Cyberspace.* Washington, Seattle: Seal Press.

McRobbie, Angela (1981) 'Working Class Girls and the Culture of Femininity'. In Women's Study Group (ed.) *Women Take Issue.* London: Hutchinson.

Mellencamp, Patricia (1992) *High Anxiety: Catastrophe, Scandal, Age and Comedy.* Bloomington: Indiana University Press.

Mernissi, Fatima (1987) *Beyond the Veil: Male-Female Dynamics in Modern Muslim Society.* Bloomington: Indiana University Press.

Mernissi, Fatima (1991) *Women and Islam: An Historical and Theological Enquiry.* Trans. Mary Jo Lakeland. Cambridge: Polity Press.

Mirza, Heidi Safia (ed.) (1997) *Black British Feminism: A Reader.* London and New York: Routledge.

Mitchell, Juliet and Rose, Jacqueline (eds) (1982) *Feminine Sexuality: Jacques Lacan and the École Freudienne.* London: Macmillan.

Mohanty, Chandra Talpade (1991) 'Under Western Eyes: Feminist Scholarship and Colonial Discourses'. In Chandra Talpade Mohanty, Ann Russo and Lourdes Torres (eds) *Third World Women and the Politics of Feminism.* Indianapolis: Indiana University Press.

Mohanty, Chandra Talpade, Russo, Ann and Torres, Lourdes (eds) *Third World Women and the Politics of Feminism.* Indianapolis: Indiana University Press.

Morgan, D.H.J. and Scott, Sue (1993) 'Bodies in a Social Landscape'. In Sue Scott and David Morgan (eds) *Body Matters: Essays on the Sociology of the Body.* London and Washington: The Falmer Press.

Morgan, Kathryn Pauly (1991) 'Women and the Knife: Cosmetic Surgery and the Colonization of Women's Bodies'. *Hypatia.* vol. 6.3 (Fall): 25–53.

Morris, Anne and Nott, Susan (1995) 'The Law's Engagement with Pregnancy'. In Jo Bridgeman and Susan Millns (eds) *Law and Body Politics: Regulating the Female Body.* Aldershot and Brookfield: Dartmouth.

Morse, Margaret (1988) 'Artemis Aging: Exercise and the Female Body on Video'. *Discourse.* vol. 10: 20–54.

Morse, Margaret (1994) 'What Do Cyborgs Eat? Oral Logic in an Information Society'. In Gretchen Bender and Timothy Druckrey (eds) *Culture on the Brink: Ideologies of Technology.* Seattle: Bay Press.

Mulvey, Laura (1975) 'Visual Pleasure and Narrative Cinema'. *Screen.* vol. 16.3 (Autumn): 6–18.

Naffine, Ngaire (1995) 'Sexing the Subject (of Law)'. In Margaret Thornton (ed.) *Public and Private: Feminist Legal Debates.* Melbourne: Oxford University Press.

Nakamura, Lisa (1995) 'Race In/For Cyberspace: Identity Tourism and Racial Passing on the Internet' in 'CyberSpaces: Pedagogy and Performance on the Electronic Frontier', *Works and Days 25/26.*

vol. 13. Nos 1 & 2. At URL: http://acorn.grove.iup. edu/en/
workdays/nakamura.html [accessed 12/10/98]

Nenadic, Natalie (1996) 'Femicide: A Framework for Understanding
Genocide'. In Diane Bell and Renate Klein (eds) *Radically Speaking:
Feminism Reclaimed.* Melbourne: Spinifex Press.

New South Wales Anti-Discrimination Board (1993) 'Why Don't You
Ever See a Pregnant Waitress?' Redfern, New South Wales:
New South Wales Anti-Discrimination Board.

Nicholson, Linda J. (ed.) (1990) *Feminism/Postmodernism.* New York and
London: Routledge.

Oakley, Ann (1979) *Becoming a Mother.* Oxford: Martin Robertson.
(Reprinted with additional introduction, as *From Here to Maternity*
(1986).)

Oakley, Ann (1980) *Women Confined: Towards a Sociology of Childbirth.*
Oxford: Martin Robertson.

Oakley, Ann (1984) *The Captured Womb: A History of the Medical Care of
Pregnant Women.* Oxford: Basil Blackwell.

O'Brien, Jodi (no date) 'Changing the Subject'. *Women and Performance,*
Issue 17. At URL: http://www.echonyc.com/~women/Issue7/
art_obrien.html [accessed 3/10/98]

O'Brien, Mary (1981) *The Politics of Reproduction.* Boston, London and
Henley: Routledge & Kegan Paul.

Omolade, Barbara (1983) 'Hearts of Darkness'. In Ann Snitow,
Christine Stansell and Sharon Thompson (eds) *Powers of Desire:
The Politics of Sexuality.* New York: The Monthly Review Press.

O'Sullivan, Sue (ed.) (1987) *Women's Health: A Spare Rib Reader.* London
and New York: Pandora Press.

Parashar, Archana (1995) 'Reconceptualisations of Civil Society: Third
World and Ethnic Women'. In Margaret Thornton (ed.) *Public and
Private: Feminist Legal Debates.* Melbourne: Oxford University Press.

Parker, Judith (1997) 'The Body as Text and the Body as Living Flesh:
Metaphors of the Body and Nursing in Post Modernity'. In Jocalyn
Lawler (ed.) *The Body in Nursing.* South Melbourne:
Churchill Livingstone.

Pateman, Carole (1988) *The Sexual Contract.* Cambridge: Polity Press.

Penny, Simon (1994) 'Virtual Reality as the Completion of the
Enlightenment Project'. In Gretchen Bender and Timothy Druckrey
(eds) *Culture on the Brink: Ideologies of Technology.* Seattle: Bay Press.

Petchesky, Rosalind Pollack (1987) 'Fetal Images: The Power of Visual
Culture in the Politics of Reproduction'. *Feminist Studies.* vol. 13.2:
263–92.

Pettman, Jan Jindy (1996) *Worlding Women: A Feminist International
Politics.* St Leonards, NSW: Allen and Unwin.

Phoenix, Ann (1997) 'Theories of Gender and Black Families'. In
Heidi Safia Mirza (ed.) *Black British Feminism.* London and New York:
Routledge [first published 1987].

Purdy, Laura M. (1996) *Reproducing Persons: Issues in Feminist Bioethics.*
Ithaca, New York: Cornell University Press.

Ram, Kalpana (1993) 'Too "Traditional" Once Again: Some
Poststructuralists on the Aspirations of the Immigrant/Third World
Female Subject'. *Australian Feminist Studies.* vol. 17: 5–28.

Ram, Kalpana (1998a) 'Epilogue: Maternal Experience and Feminist Body Politics: Asian and Pacific Perspectives'. In Kalpana Ram and Margaret Jolly (eds) *Maternities and Modernities: Colonial and Postcolonial Experiences in Asia and the Pacific.* Cambridge: Cambridge University Press.

Ram, Kalpana (1998b) 'Maternity and the Story of Enlightenment in the Colonies: Tamil Coastal Women, South India'. In Kalpana Ram and Margaret Jolly (eds) *Maternities and Modernities: Colonial and Postcolonial Experiences in Asia and the Pacific.* Cambridge: Cambridge University Press.

Ram, Kalpana and Jolly, Margaret (eds) (1998) *Maternities and Modernities: Colonial and Postcolonial Experiences in Asia and the Pacific.* Cambridge: Cambridge University Press.

Ramazanoglu, Caroline (ed.) (1993) *Up Against Foucault: Explorations of Some Tensions between Foucault and Feminism.* London and New York: Routledge.

Raymond, Janice G. (1994) *Women as Wombs: Reproductive Technologies and the Battle over Women's Freedom.* Melbourne: Spinifex Press.

Reiger, Kerreen M. (1985) *The Disenchantment of the Home: Modernizing the Australian Family 1880–1940.* Melbourne: Oxford University Press.

Rich, Adrienne (1976) *Of Woman Born: Motherhood as Experience and Institution.* London: Virago.

Rich, Adrienne (1980) 'Compulsory Heterosexuality and Lesbian Existence'. *Signs.* vol. 5 (4): 631–60.

Riley, Denise (1988) *Am I That Name?: Feminism and the Category of 'Women' in History.* London: Macmillan Press.

Rivière, Joan (1986) 'Womanliness as a Masquerade'. In Victor Burgin, James Donald and Cora Kaplan (eds) *Formations of Fantasy.* London: Methuen [first published 1929].

Robertson, Jennifer (1998) *Takarazuka: Sexual Politics and Popular Culture in Modern Japan.* Berkeley: University of California Press.

Robertson, Matra (1992) *Starving in the Silences: An Exploration of Anorexia Nervosa.* North Sydney: Allen and Unwin.

Rogers, Wendy (1997) 'Sources of Abjection in Western Responses to Menopause'. In Paul Komesaroff, Philipa Rothfield and Jeanne Daly (eds) *Reinterpreting Menopause: Cultural and Philosophical Issues.* New York and London: Routledge.

Roman, Leslie G., Christian-Smith, Linda K., with Ellsworth, Elizabeth (eds) (1988) *Becoming Feminine: The Politics of Popular Culture.* London: The Falmer Press.

Rothfield, Philipa (1994) 'Performing Sexuality: The Scintillations of Movement'. In Michelle Boulous Walker (ed.) *Performing Sexualities.* Brisbane: Institute of Modern Art.

Rothman, Barbara Katz (1986) *The Tentative Pregnancy: Prenatal Diagnosis and the Future of Motherhood.* New York: Viking.

Rowland, Robyn (1992) *Living Laboratories: Women in Reproductive Technologies.* Bloomington: Indiana University Press.

Rowland, Robyn and Klein, Renate (1996) 'Radical Feminism: History, Politics, Action'. In Diane Bell and Renate Klein (eds) *Radically Speaking: Feminism Reclaimed.* Melbourne: Spinifex Press.

Russo, Mary J. (1995) *The Female Grotesque: Risk, Excess and Modernity*.
   New York and London: Routledge.
Saghal, Gita and Yuval-Davis, Nira (eds) (1992) *Refusing Holy Orders:
   Women and Fundamentalism*. London: Virago.
Sandoz, Joli (ed.) (1997) *A Whole Other Ball Game: Women's Literature on
   Women's Sport*. New York: Noonday Press.
Sartre, Jean–Paul (1992) *Being and Nothingness: A Phenomenological Essay
   on Ontology*. Trans. Hazel E. Barnes. New York: Washington Square
   Press [first published 1956].
Sbisà, M. (1996) 'The Feminine Subject and the Female Body in
   Discourse about Childbirth'. *The European Journal of Women's Studies*.
   vol. 3: 363–376.
Schiebinger, Londa (1993) *Nature's Body: Sexual Politics and the Making of
   Modern Science*. Boston: Beacon Press.
Schultz, Vicki (1992) 'Women "Before" the Law'. In Judith Butler and
   Joan W. Scott (eds) *Feminists Theorize the Political*. New York and
   London: Routledge.
Schulze, Laurie (1990) 'On the Muscle'. In Jane M. Gaines and
   Charlotte Herzog (eds) *Fabrications: Costume and the Female Body*.
   New York and London: Routledge.
Schwichtenberg, Cathy (ed.) (1993) *The Madonna Connection:
   Representational Politics, Subcultural Identities, and Cultural Theory*.
   St Leonards, NSW: Allen and Unwin.
Scott, Sue and Morgan, David (eds) (1993) *Body Matters: Essays on the
   Sociology of the Body*. London and Washington: The Falmer Press.
Senjen, Rye and Guthrey, Jane (1996) *The Internet for Women*.
   Melbourne: Spinifex Press.
Sheets-Johnstone, Maxine (1998) 'Corporeal Archetypes and Power:
   Preliminary Clarifications and Considerations of Sex'. In Donn
   Welton (ed.) *Body and Flesh: A Philosophical Reader*. Malden,
   Massachusetts and Oxford: Blackwell Publishers
   [first published 1992].
Shildrick, Margrit (1997) *Leaky Bodies and Boundaries: Feminism,
   Postmodernism and (Bio)Ethics*. London and New York: Routledge.
Shilling, Chris (1993) *The Body and Social Theory*. London: Sage.
Shuttle, Penelope and Redgrove, Peter (1978) *The Wise Wound:
   Eve's Curse and Everywoman*. New York: Richard Marek.
Simmonds, Felly Nkweto (1997) 'My Body, Myself. How Does a Black
   Woman Do Sociology?'. In Heidi Safia Mirza (ed.) *Black British
   Feminism*. London and New York: Routledge.
Singer, Linda (1998) 'Bodies–Pleasures–Powers'. *differences*. vol. 1.1
   (Winter): 45–65.
Smart, Carol (1989) *Feminism and the Power of the Law*. London: Routledge.
Sofoulis, Zoë (1995) 'Cyberfeminism: The World, the Flesh, and the
   Woman-Machine Relationship'. From URL: http://www.woodvale.wa.
   edu.au/acec95_papers/volume1/sofouli.html [accessed 6/10/98]
Sophia, Zoë (1992) 'Virtual Corporeality: A Feminist View'. *Australian
   Feminist Studies*. vol. 15 (Autumn): 11–24.
Sofia, Zoë (1993) *Whose Second Self? Gender and (Ir)rationality in Computer
   Culture*. Geelong: Deakin University Press.

Sofia, Zoë (1995) 'Of Spanners and Cyborgs: "De-homogenising" Feminist Thinking in Technology'. In Barbara Caine and Rosemary Pringle (eds) *Transitions: New Australian Feminisms*. St Leonards, NSW: Allen and Unwin.

Sourbut, Elizabeth (1996) 'Gynogenesis: A Lesbian Appropriation of Reproductive Technologies'. In Nikki Lykke and Rosi Braidotti (eds) *Between Monsters, Goddesses and Cyborgs: Feminist Confrontations with Science, Medicine and Cyberspace*. London and New Jersey: Zed Books.

Spelman, Elizabeth (1982) 'Woman as Body: Ancient and Contemporary Views'. *Feminist Studies*. vol. 8.1 (Spring): 109–131.

Squier, Susan M. (1995) 'Reproducing the Posthuman Body: Ectogenetic Fetus, Surrogate Mother, Pregnant Man'. In Judith Halberstam and Ira Livingstone (eds) *Posthuman Bodies*. Bloomington and Indianopolis: Indiana University Press.

Stallybrass, Peter and White, Allon (1986) *The Politics and Poetics of Transgression*. London: Methuen.

Stabile, Carol A. (1994) *Feminism and the Technological Fix*. Manchester: Manchester University Press.

Steinem, Gloria (1984) 'If Men Could Menstruate'. *In Outrageous Acts and Everyday Realities*. New York: Flamingo.

Stiglmayer, Alexandra (1994) 'The Rapes in Bosnia–Herzogovina'. In Alexandra Stiglmayer (ed.) *Mass Rape: The War Against Women in Bosnia-Herzogovina*. Lincoln and London: University of Nebraska Press.

Stone, Allucquère Roseanne (1991) 'Will the Real Body Please Stand Up'. From URL: http://www.rochester.edu/College/FS/Publications/StoneBody.html [accessed 18/9/98] [first published in Michael Benedikt (ed.) (1991) *Cyberspace: First Steps*. Cambridge, Massachusetts: MIT Press].

Suleiman, Susan Rubin (ed.) (1985) *The Female Body in Western Culture: Contemporary Perspectives*. Cambridge, Massachusetts and London: Harvard University Press.

Summers, Anne (1994) *Damned Whores and God's Police: The Colonisation of Women in Australia*, Ringwood: Penguin [first published 1975].

Sykes, Roberta (1984) 'Roberta Sykes'. In Robyn Rowland (ed.) *Women Who Do and Women Who Don't Join the Women's Movement*. London: Routledge Kegan and Paul.

Tait, Peta (1996) 'Feminine Free Fall: A Fantasy of Freedom'. *Theatre Journal*. vol. 8.1: 27–34. From URL: http://direct press.jhu.edu/demo/theatre_journal/48.1tait.html [accessed 18/9/98]

Terry, Jennifer and Calvert, Melodie (eds) (1997) *Processed Lives: Gender and Technology in Everyday Life*. London: Sage.

Terry, Jennifer and Urla, Jacqueline (eds) (1995) *Deviant Bodies: Critical Perspectives on Difference in Science and Popular Culture*. Bloomington: Indiana University Press.

Thornton, Margaret (1995a) 'The Cartography of Public and Private'. In Margaret Thornton (ed.) *Public and Private: Feminist Legal Debates*. Melbourne: Oxford University Press.

Thornton, Margaret (ed.) (1995b) *Public and Private: Feminist Legal Debates*. Melbourne: Oxford University Press.

Tompkins, Jane (1990) 'The Pedagogy of the Distressed'. *College English.* vol. 52: 653–660.

Treichler, Paula A. (1990) 'Feminism, Medicine, and the Meaning of Childbirth'. In Mary Jacobus, Evelyn Fox Keller and Sally Shuttleworth (eds) *Body/Politics: Women and the Discourses of Science.* New York and London: Routledge.

Turkle, Sherry (1984) *The Second Self: Computers and the Human Spirit.* New York: Simon and Schuster.

Turkle, Sherry (1995) *Life on the Screen: Identity in the Age of the Internet.* New York: Simon and Schuster.

Turkle, Sherry (1996) 'Who Am We?' *Wired.* vol. 4.1 (January). From URL: http://www.wired.com/wired/4.01/index.html [accessed 6/10/98]

Turner, Bryan S. (1991) 'Recent Development in the Theory of the Body'. In M. Featherstone, M. Hepworth and B.S. Turner (eds) *The Body: Social Process and Cultural Theory.* London: Sage.

Urla, Jacqueline and Swedlund, Alan C. (1995) 'The Anthropometry of Barbie: Unsettling Ideals of the Feminine Body in Popular Culture'. In Jennifer Terry and Jacqueline Urla (eds) *Deviant Bodies: Critical Perspectives on Difference in Science and Popular Culture.* Bloomington: Indiana University Press.

van Wingerden, Ineke (1996) 'Postmodern Visions of the Postmenopausal Body: The Apparatus of Bodily Production and the Case of Brittle Bones'. In Nina Lykke and Rosi Braidotti (eds) *Between Monsters, Goddesses and Cyborgs: Feminist Confrontations with Science, Medicine and Cyberspace.* London and New Jersey: Zed Books.

Vertinsky, Patricia (1994) *The Eternally Wounded Woman: Women, Doctors and Exercise in the Late Nineteenth Century.* Manchester: Manchester University Press.

Ware, Vron (1992) *Beyond the Pale: White Women, Racism, and History.* London: Verso.

Weare, Tessa (1987) 'Round in a Flat World'. In Sue O'Sullivan (ed.) *Women's Health: A Spare Rib Reader.* London and New York: Pandora Press [first published in 1979].

Weekes, Debbie (1997) 'Shades of Blackness: Young Black Female Constructions of Beauty'. In Heidi Safia Mirza(ed.) *Black British Feminism: A Reader.* London and New York: Routledge.

Welton, Donn (ed.) (1998) *Body and Flesh: A Philosophical Reader.* Malden, Massachusetts and Oxford: Blackwell.

Wendell, Susan (1996) *The Rejected Body: Feminist Philosophical Reflections on Disability.* New York and London: Routledge.

Whitford, Margaret (1991) 'Irigaray's Body Symbolic'. *Hypatia.* vol. 6.3 (Fall): 97–110.

Wilcox, Helen, McWatters, Keith, Thompson, Ann and Williams, Linda R. (eds) (1990) *The Body and the Text: Hélène Cixous, Reading and Teaching.* New York: Harvester Wheatsheaf.

Williams, Caroline (1994) 'Feminism, Subjectivity and Psychoanalysis: Towards a (Corpo)real Knowledge'. In Kathleen Lennon and Margaret Whitford (eds) *Knowing the Difference: Feminist Perspectives in Epistemology.* London: Sage.

Williams, Linda (1997) 'A Provoking Agent: The Pornography and
    Performance Art of Annie Sprinkle'. In Katie Conboy, Nadia Medina
    and Sarah Stanbury (eds) *Writing on the Body: Female Embodiment and
    Feminist Theory*. New York: Columbia University Press.
Willis, Susan (1990) 'Work(ing) Out'. *Cultural Studies*. vol. 4.1: 1–18.
Wise, Patricia (1996) 'The Virtual Subject and Cyber-Politics'. From
    URL: http://www.gu.edu.au/gwis/akccmp/papers/Wise.html
    [accessed 5/10/98]
Wittig, Monique (1992) *The Straight Mind and Other Essays*. Boston:
    Beacon Press.
Wittig, Monique (1996) 'One is Not Born a Woman'. In Katie Conboy,
    Nadia Medina and Sarah Stanbury (eds) *Writing on the Body: Female
    Embodiment and Feminist Theory*. New York: Columbia University Press
    [first published 1981].
Wolff, Janet (1990) 'Reinstating Corporeality: Feminism and Body
    Politics'. *Feminine Sentences: Essays on Women and Culture*. Berkeley:
    University of California Press.
Women's Circus (1997) *Women's Circus: Leaping off the Edge*. North
    Melbourne: Spinifex Press.
Wollstonecraft, Mary (1975) *A Vindication of the Rights of Women*.
    Harmandsworth: Penguin [first published 1792].
Woodward, Kathleen (1994) 'From Virtual Cyborgs to Biological Time
    Bombs: Technocriticism and the Material Body'. In Gretchen Bender
    and Timothy Druckrey (eds) *Culture on the Brink: Ideologies of Technology*.
    Seattle: Bay Press.
Young, Iris Marion (1990) *Throwing Like a Girl and Other Essays in
    Feminist Philosophy and Social Theory*. Bloomington and Indianapolis:
    Indiana University Press.
Young, Iris (1998) 'Throwing Like a Girl'; ' "Throwing Like a Girl":
    Twenty Years Later'. In Donn Welton (ed.) *Body and Flesh:
    A Philosophical Reader*. Malden, Massachusetts and Oxford: Blackwell.
    ('Throwing Like a Girl' is also in Young 1990)

Index

Abdalla, Raqiha 109–10 *n 9*
abject(ion) 5, 14–15, 17, 44–6,
　50, 114, 120, 123, 152–3
abortion 7, 25, 91, 95, 109 *nn 4, 5*
agency 83, 85, 112
　see also speaking selves *and*
　violence against women,
　survivors of
Agger, Inge 101
AIDS
　and cyberspace 145
　pathologising of 66, 156 *n 5*
　and risky sexual practices 66
Alexander, Jacqui 109 *n 2*
anorexia 68, 69–76, 87 *n 1*
　and bodybuilding 118
　and cyberspace 147
　discourses of 74–5
　as medical construction 74–5
　narratives of 76
　and racial stereotyping 76
antenatal care, as state
　surveillance 29–30
anthropology, critiques of 50–1
anthropometry 80–1
Anzaldúa, Gloria 141–2, 156 *n 4*
art, feminist 51
　and cyberspace 152–3, 156 *n 8*

Balsamo, Anne 8, 80–2, 121, 139,
　141
Barbie dolls 80

Barratt, Virginia 152, 153
Bartky, Sandra 67, 83, 84
battered women 99, 109 *n 3*
Bell, Susan 64 *n 4*
Benchmark Man 97–8, 103
Berger, John 35
Bibbings, Lois 106
binarism 8, 15–16, 18, 72, 122,
　131, 139, 144, 154
Black British Feminism 9
Black women
　and the academy 131
　and 'beauty' 79–81
　and bodybuilding 121
　and eating disorders 76, 87 *n 6*
　and feminism 105
　and identity politics 9
Bodies that Matter 14, 113
body
　as communication system 5
　and eating disorders 69–73
　of hysteric 12
　sociology of 20
　as *tabula rasa* 11, 13
　see also woman's body
the body politic 89–90
bodybuilding 118–22
Bordo, Susan 71–3, 75, 76,
　78–9, 81, 87 *nn 5–6*, 117,
　119
Braidotti, Rosi 5, 45, 61, 137
Brush, Pippa 81, 84

Bulbeck, Chilla 42 *n 3*, 101–2, 106, 109 *n 8*
Butler, Judith 5, 13, 14–15, 61, 113–14, 116–17, 126, 128–9

The Captured Womb 29
Carby, Hazel 105
Carrington, Kerry 67, 87 *n 3*
Caskey, Noelle 70
The Change 60
Charlesworth, Hilary 100–1
childbirth
  as abjection 45
  cross-cultural issues of 33
  pathologised 27–31, 33
  politics of 24–7
  representations of 31, 51
circus 127–8
Cixous, Hélène x, 13, 15, 18, 144
class differences 13, 40, 81–2, 119–20, 121–2, 134 *n 8*, 145, 147–8
Cole, Cheryl 124
colonialism, and the law 92, 105
  and slavery 96
comedy 134–5 *n 10*
'commonsense'
  gender divisions 14
  ideas of time and space 116
  ideas of 'woman' 4, 6
  and language x
Coney, Sandra 60, 61
corporeal feminism 3, 61
  critiques of 4, 38, 53
corporeality 2, 125
cosmetic surgery 77–85
  and cultural norms 79–81
  as performance art 84–5
Creed, Barbara 45, 51
cross dressing – *see* drag
cultural relativism 107
Cummings, Barbara 63–4 *n 1*
cyberspace 136–8, 151–2
  as colony 148–9
  feminist revisioning of 151–3
cyborg 138–42, 147

Davis, Kathy, 78, 82–4, 107
de Beauvoir, Simone 6, 11, 15, 20 *n 2*, 23, 24, 26, 42 *n 1*, 46, 47
Descartes, René 18, 147
  see also binarism
disability 98, 134 *n 9*, 144
Discipline and Punish 65
Doane, Mary Ann 116
Donnison, Jean 27, 29
Douglas, Mary 5, 14, 15, 50, 73
drag 109 *n 7*, 114, 122, 126, 129, 146
dualism – *see* binarism
Duden, Barbara 34, 39, 40, 41

eating disorders – *see* anorexia
Ebert, Teresa 78, 81
eco-feminism 7
Ehrenreich, Barbara 27
Eisenstein, Zillah 98, 100
Ellis, Havelock 55
Ellsworth, Elizabeth 72
endometriosis 62
essentialism 6–8, 9
eugenics 123
eurocentrism – *see* racism

female pollution, as western concept 50
femininity, as discourse 13
  as regime 122
  as western construct 134 *n 8*
feminist theatre 129
fetal photography 37
  politics of 40–1, 42 *n 4*
film theory 51, 116, 118, 121
Finley, Karen 129–30
Firestone, Shulamith 6–7, 23, 47
Flynn, Bernadette 153
Foucauldian theories 14, 65, 70, 72, 74, 87 *n 1*, 122, 124
Foucault, Michel 3, 5, 10, 28, 65, 71, 73, 80, 123
Fox, Marie 99
Freud, Sigmund 26, 42 *n 1*, 114

Freudian psychoanalysis 114, 134
  n 5
  and eating disorders 75
  and hysteria 20 *n 3*
Frueh, Joanna 132

Gallop, Jane 113, 114, 115, 131
Garrett, Catherine 76, 84
Gatens, Moira 2, 13, 16, 90–1, 98, 103
gender, as performance – *see* performance; performativity
gender theory
  and heterosexism 5
  and racism 5, 12
Gender Trouble 14
genital mutilation 106–7
Gerson, Deborah 48–9
Gibson, William 138, 145, 156 *n 1*
Graycar, Regina 97–8, 104–5
Greer, Germaine 58, 60
Griffin, Susan 7
Grosz, Elizabeth 3, 11, 13, 16, 53, 57, 60, 68, 84, 100, 119–20
Gunning, Isabelle 106–7
gynogenesis 47–8

Hall, Ann 122
Haraway, Donna xii, 4, 5, 39, 42 *n 4*, 61, 137, 138–41, 142, 148, 151, 156 *nn 2, 5*
Hartsock, Nancy 8, 9
Hawkridge, Caroline 64
Hawthorne, Susan 139, 142, 147
health care, politics of 59, 82, 123
heterosexism 5
  and compulsory heterosexuality 14, 52, 67, 85
  in cyberspace 146
  of medical models 62
  and menopause 59
heterosexual economy 66–9
  and cosmetic surgery 81
Hong, Fan

hooks, bell 8, 9, 69, 79
hormone replacement therapy (HRT) 57–8, 70, 82
human rights, discourses of 93, 99–103
hysteria 20 *n 3*, 103
hysterical body 12, 18

Ian, Marcia 120–1
identity politics 9–10
imaginary body 68
  and anorexia 68, 84
Indigenous issues 4, 15
  and definitions of 'mother' 63–4 *n 1*
  and 'mainstream' culture 79–80
  of reproduction 25
infertility, discourses of 48–9
Internet 149
  childbirth on 51
  and gender issues 143–4
  and sex 143–4, 146, 149, 150
Irigaray, Luce 5, 13, 16–17, 18, 35, 90, 91, 109 *n 1*, 115, 144
irony, as feminist strategy 55, 140–1, 151
Islam 96, 109–10 *n 9*, 112

Jacobus, Mary 36
Jolly, Margaret 33, 50
Jupiter Space 151, 152

Karamcheti, Indira 131
Keywood, Kirsty 96
Kirby, Vicki 13, 61, 116, 117
Klein, Renate 4, 139
Kristeva, Julia 15, 32, 34, 36, 38, 45, 50, 64 *n 2*
Kuhn Annette 118–19

Lacan, Jacques 5, 114
Lacanian psychoanalysis 115
Lasica, Shelly 125–6, 129
Laws, Sophie 52, 62
Lenskyj, Helen 123

lesbian, existence 13
  and menopause 53
  responses to bodybuilding
    121
  as subject of law 94, 109 *n 2*
Lewis, Jane 29
Leysen, Bettina 58, 59, 60
Lloyd, Genevieve 97
Lorde, Audre 3
Lovering, Kathryn 52–3

Macdonald, Judith 64 *n 3*
Mackie, Fiona 60
MacKinnon, Catherine 103
MacMillan, Carol 7
MacSween, Morag 71
the male gaze 35, 57, 66–7, 112,
    116, 129, 138
The Male in the Head 66–8
male pregnancy 46
'A Manifesto for Cyborgs' 138,
    140, 148
Marcus, Sharon 102
Marsh, Anne 129
Martin, Emily 23, 31–2, 34, 54,
    55–6, 59, 61, 68, 73
Marx, Karl 26
Mason, Gail 94
masquerade 114–18
Matthews, Jill Julius 29, 123
McRae, Sharon 143, 146
medical discourses, of women's
    bodies 5, 27–9, 31, 33, 46, 49,
    55, 56, 74–5, 77
menopause 56–62
  and consumerism 58
  feminist revisionings of 60
  problems in defining 68
  see also hormone replacement
    therapy
menstruation 45, 50–7
  and abjection 50–1, 53, 123
  discourses of 55–6
Merleau-Ponty, Maurice 3, 32,
    125, 126
Mernissi, Fatima 110 *n 9*, 112

mind/body split 8, 15, 99, 122,
    feminist revisioning of 3, 131
Mirza, Heidi Safia 9
Mohanty, Chandra Talpade 107
Morgan, David 2, 20 *n 1*
Morgan, Kathryn Pauly 82, 83
Morris, Meaghan x
Morse, Margaret 147
MUDS 143–4
Mulvey, Laura 35

Naffine, Ngaire 93, 103
Nakamura, Lisa 148–9
narrative, as feminist research tool
    76, 83–4
natural health movement 123–4
Nietzsche, Friedrich 3

Oakley, Ann 29–30
O'Brien, Jodi 146
O'Brien, Mary 23, 26–7
obstetrics – *see* childbirth,
    pathologised
Off the Rag 53, 60
Omolade, Barbara 79
Orbach, Susie 73, 75
Orlan 84, 129
osteoporosis 60–1

pain 144
Penny, Simon 145–6
performance 111
  art 129–30
  staged 126
performativity 14, 113–14, 122, 143
  and race 131
Pettman, Jan Jindy 107
phallocentrism x, 15, 18
phenomenology 32, 125
Phoenix, Ann 12
physical education and the state
    123
  in China 124
postmodernist theory 80, 141, 154
  and the body 5
  and feminism 8, 78, 81

pregnant body 27, 30–3, 35
  discourses of 38–41
  feminist rethinking of 32–3
  and the law 95, 98
  representations of 34–8
  in workplace 15, 98
Profet, Margie 55–6
prosthesis 138, 142–3, 144
Pumping Iron II 118–19, 121
Purity and Danger 50
psychoanalytic theory
  and fear of pregnancy 49
  and menstruation 52
  see also Freudian theory

queer theory 14, 114, 117, 143,
  146

racism 63 *n 1*
  and contraception 42 *n 3*
  in cyberspace 146, 149
  and eating disorders 76
  and femininity 13, 37, 76,
    79–81
  and gender theory 12
  and identity politics 9
  and modern science 140, 141–2
  and teaching 131
  and western feminism 4, 20 *n 4,*
    25, 27, 105
  and women's rights 106–7
radical feminist critiques 4, 23, 47,
  143
Ram, Kalpana 50–1, 53, 64 *n 2,*
  107
Ramazanoglu, Caroline 87 *n 1*
rape 67, 87 *n 3*, 91, 104
  culture 102; *see also* Carrington
  in cyberspace 150
  marital 94
  in war 102
Reiger, Kerreen 29
reproductive technologies 23,
  46–8
Rich, Adrienne 6–7, 14, 32
Richards, Alison 128

Rivière, Joan 114, 115–16, 134
  n 5
Robertson, Jennifer 126–7, 134
  n 6
Robertson, Matra 74–5
Rogers, Wendy 58
Rothfield, Philipa 122, 125–6

Sartre, Jean-Paul 42 *n 1*, 46
Schilder, Paul 68
Schultz, Vicki 98
Schulze, Laurie 121–2
Scott, Sue 2, 20 *n 1*
The Second Sex 11
the sex–gender division 10–13
sex role theory 11–12
The Sexual Contract 94
Shildrick, Margrit 77, 92
slavery 13, 63 *n 1*, 79, 96
Smart, Carol 90
Smith, Dorothy 83
social constructionism 8, 10,
  11–12
  critiques of 14
social contract 95–6
Sofia (Sophia) *see* Sofoulis
Sofoulis, Zoë 137, 138, 150, 151
Sourbut, Elizabeth 48
Speculum of the Other Woman 35
'speaking selves'
  absence of 60
  as feminist research strategy
    60–1, 82–5
  see also agency *and* narrative
spirituality 76, 87 *n 7*
sport, and bodies 122, 124–5
Sprinkle, Annie 129–30
Sproul, Linda 129
Stabile, Carol 7, 36–7, 39, 42 *n 4,*
  95, 138, 148, 156
Steinem, Gloria 55
sterilisation, and the law 96–7
Stone, Allucquère Roseanne 141,
  145, 146–7, 156 *n 4*
'The Straight Mind' 67; *see also*
  heterosexism

subjectivity 3, 5
  and body 9–10
  and narcissism 68
  and pregnancy 32
Summers, Anne 20 *n 4*
Sykes, Roberta 25

Tait, Peta 127–8, 147
Takarazuka Revue 126–7, 134
  n 6
teachers x, 113, 131, 132
teledildonics 143
Telling Flesh xiii, 117
the 'Third World' xi, 24, 25, 96,
  140, 147
This Sex Which Is Not One 16–17
Thornton, Margaret 92, 93, 94,
  95, 97, 104
torture 101
transgression, female 112, 126,
  127, 128, 129–30, 135 *n 10*
transsexuals 8, 46, 54, 142
Treichler, Paula 28–9, 31, 34
Turkle, Sherry 147, 148, 150, 153,
  156 *n 7*

Unbearable Weight 71, 72, 79, 87 *n
  4*
uncanny 114
  see also abject
United Nations 100–2, 109 *n 8*

van Wingerden, Ineke 60, 61
Vertinsky, Patricia 123

violence against women 101–2,
  109 *n 3*
  survivors of, 128
  see also rape, battered women,
    genital mutilation
virtual sex 142, 143, 145, 146
VNS Matrix – *see* art, and
  cyberspace

Weare, Tessa 30–1, 35
Weekes, Debbie 87 *n 6*, 125
Wendell, Susan 61, 144–5
Williams, Linda 130
Williams, Patricia J. 63 *n 1*
Wise, Patricia 141
Wittig, Monique 13, 14, 20 *n 4*, 67
Wolfe, Susan J. 57, 58
Wollstonecraft, Mary 24, 42 *n 2*
The Woman in the Body 31
woman's body
  as abject 46
  as hysteric 12
  as nature 31
Women Confined 30
women, over-determined as
  reproductive 23
women's agency *see* agency
Women's Circus 128
Woodward, Kathleen 140
workplace, women's body in 15,
  98, 112–13, 114, 132
'world-travelling' 106–7
Young, Iris Marion 32–3, 39, 40,
  83, 84